My Life in Fragments

My Life in Fragments

Zygmunt Bauman

Edited by Izabela Wagner

With translations by Katarzyna Bartoszyńska

polity

First published in 2023 by Polity Press

Polity Press
65 Bridge Street
Cambridge CB2 1UR, UK

Polity Press
111 River Street
Hoboken, NJ 07030, USA

ISBN-13: 978-1-5095-5130-9 (hardback)

A catalogue record for this book is available from the British Library.

Library of Congress Control Number: 2023934250

Typeset in 11 on 14pt Warnock Pro
by Cheshire Typesetting Ltd, Cuddington, Cheshire
Printed and bound in Great Britain by CPI Group (UK) Ltd, Croydon

The publisher has used its best endeavours to ensure that the URLs for external websites referred to in this book are correct and active at the time of going to press. However, the publisher has no responsibility for the websites and can make no guarantee that a site will remain live or that the content is or will remain appropriate.

Every effort has been made to trace all copyright holders, but if any have been overlooked the publisher will be pleased to include any necessary credits in any subsequent reprint or edition.

For further information on Polity, visit our website:
politybooks.com

Contents

Introduction

Izabela Wagner

My Life in Fragments is a book that was created as a patchwork – from very different pieces. Not only, as the title suggests, because Zygmunt Bauman is telling stories about his life in a nonlinear way. This is not his autobiography, even if some chapters are autobiographical. This volume is composed of different texts written by Zygmunt Bauman across a span of thirty years. The lengthy diary entries and stories were written in Polish and English – two languages that Bauman mastered and used in both his work and his private life. The status of these pieces also varies. While one part, devoted to his childhood and teenage years, is private, written for his daughters and grandchildren, another part is public. Some pages were never published, while other pages were published in Polish as chapters in a book or press articles several years ago.[1] Constructing a book from such varied writings was highly challenging.

The core of the book is Bauman's typescript dated 1987, which contains fifty-four pages, with the first title page as follows:

The Poles, The Jews, and I
An Investigation into Whatever Made Me
What I am

The Memory of My father
Entrusted to the Memory
of My Children –

sixty two years and three months
after my birth.

'Feb. 1987' was added in pencil by a family member and was the result of an arithmetic calculation carried out much later: 19 November 1925 (the date of Bauman's birth) plus 62 years and 3 months. Except that the author of the note erred in the calculation, and the year in which the text was being composed was in fact 1988. This text was written for the family. There are no references; it contains private family secrets and has never before been published in its entirety. Now, his family has decided to share with his readers this unique piece of Bauman scholarship. I read it for the first time in mid-December 2017, when, almost a year after Zygmunt Bauman passed away, the family sent me the text as a PDF file, along with the permission for quotations to be used in *Bauman: A Biography* – the book I was then working on, published over two years later. I am grateful to Bauman's family for their trust, and I am relieved now – thanks to their decision – that this precious text is available to all English-speaking readers. I confess that it was challenging to choose which parts of the manuscript to quote in my book, since the entire account is fascinating.

Not only was the story captivating, but it was the first time that Bauman wrote about his life and focused on it. In these pages, it is not an intellectual speaking about the world, but a person making a confession in a way typical for people in the later stages of their lives. People tell their life stories to preserve them from oblivion. The purpose here is intergenerational transmission within a family, and the preservation of family history. I felt privileged, and tried to include in my book *Bauman: A Biography* as many quotations as possible. In the biography, Bauman's voice was intertwined with analysis of the historical and political contexts, which helped with understanding his situation and life choices. In this volume, his account is not cut but completed by his other writings, which focus on his life experiences. 'The Poles, The Jews, and I' is the only material published in this book written in English. This may be surprising if we consider that all these souvenirs concern childhood, youth and family history, and that his childhood and youth were spent in contexts where Polish was spoken. Then Bauman reflects on his identity (ethnic identity), asking himself the question: why write in English? And he responds convincingly – indeed, this is the main topic of his reflection.

The second part of the material included in this book is from twenty-four pages written in 1997, entitled 'Historia jeszcze jednego życia?' ('The story of just another life?'), and is in the form of a diary. Thanks to the dates clearly stated each time Bauman started a new note, we can conclude that keeping a journal was not his daily habit or routine. As his daughters remember, it was a typical New Year's resolution, which was abandoned after a couple of weeks. This diary started probably on 1 or 2 January,[2] and ended on 7 February in the same year.

The third, lengthiest part of the text was edited at the end of his life and contained 136 pages, starting with a chapter entitled 'Dlaczego nie powinienem tego pisać' ('Why I should not write this'). This text, written in Polish, has the form of a manuscript almost ready for the process of publication. The same family stories were told in the English typescript; however, the text contains some changes, mainly developments of the same topics. Bauman here provides more details in

order better to explain events that are described in a different way in the other available sources.[3] We should remember
that Bauman was a scapegoat for Polish extreme-right and
nationalist movements. He was accused of being an active sup-
porter of communism, which is virtually a sin in contemporary
Poland. It was often mentioned that Bauman never 'explained
himself' about his participation in the construction of communism. It was expected that he would present an apology for
what he supposedly did (he was never charged with any crime).
He was the target of a 'witch hunt', an extreme example of the
treatment left-leaning individuals with a communist past could
experience in Poland after 1989. This Polish text is partially a
response to these attacks, and Bauman devotes ample space
to his political engagements and the recent political situation
in Poland. The text from the English manuscript in chapters 2
and 3 is written in a different style. Another type of narrative
appears when Bauman is speaking about his identity – the
core question of his reflection being 'Who am I?' In English,
Bauman is more direct, using the form 'I' when speaking about
being a Jew – 'I am a Polish Jew.' In Polish, he is more distanced
and becomes part of a collective – he is a part of a group. The
English text is more private, which is only to be expected as his
audience was his family; but also, in English, he seems to feel
safe, as though the Polish language cannot provide the same
security when confronting antisemitism.

     The three sources that make up this book were written over
the span of thirty years. It is not surprising that Bauman started
writing about his parents and childhood in 1987. A couple of
months before he wrote the first pages of his memoirs, his wife
Janina Bauman published her autobiographical book *Winter
in the Morning*, which became a significant turning point in
his life.[4] That book – partially based on Janina's diary, which
was miraculously preserved during and after World War II –
recalls the life of a young teenage girl in the Warsaw Ghetto.
Janina Bauman is telling her story, a story of a Holocaust

survivor. From this substantial testimony for Holocaust studies, Bauman's family learned about Janina's tragic past. Zygmunt's reaction to that painful and astonishing history, of which he was previously unaware, was to write. He did it in two ways: academically – he published in 1989 his groundbreaking book *Modernity and the Holocaust*; and privately. All of that deeply personal writing appears in this volume.[5]

While the long Polish text contains similar material to that in the English manuscript, the latter took priority in assembling this text. Because of the style of writing (direct and personal, which is unusual in Bauman's work) and the fact that it was the original,[6] it seemed more appropriate to keep this English version and complete it, if needed, with fragments of text translated from the Polish. However, the composition of the successive chapters, their titles and structure mainly follow Bauman's organization, which can be seen in the third text (the long Polish manuscript). While this book is made up of different texts that were written at different times in both Polish and English, and that overlap in various ways, the material has been integrated here into a single coherent text of seven chapters, following the logic that was evident in the material itself.

The book starts with a general reflection on autobiographical writing. Here, Bauman's readers will be at home, finding an unpublished text written in a typical Bauman style and discussing with writers and intellectuals the subjectivity of memory and the influence of time on the content of stored memories. Bauman is guiding his readers through the fascinating labyrinth of the mystery of human memory, the interpretation of facts, and the complexity of a life recalled later – all this contributing to the construction of the author's persona. After this sketch of the theoretical frame, we jump into Bauman's life – his family history, interwar Poland and, despite antisemitic discrimination, quite a happy childhood. The third chapter is the story of the war years – Bauman is a teenage refugee, then a soldier liberating his homeland from the Nazi occupation.

These prewar and wartime chapters are full of personal details
and almost without references to other authors. It is Bauman's
life, as he remembers it now (in 1987). The chapter entitled
'Maturation' is different, as the author focuses on the beginning
of his leftist engagement and discusses the post-war period
as an intellectual. The voice of a former refugee and soldier
is replaced by the voice of the sociologist Zygmunt Bauman,
who, with mastery, is conversing about human choices with
many authors – historians, sociologists, writers and poets. This
is a very important chapter that directly responds to the claims
of Bauman's opponents in Poland, who complained about
his silence regarding his political engagement and post-war
experiences.

The following chapter is devoted to a reflection on
Bauman's ethnic identity. It is an important piece that may
join today's other classical reflections on Polish-Jewish and/or
Jewish-Polish identities. His non-contested Jewishness meets
contested Polishness. Bauman refuses a simple categorization
(into 'tribes') and the imposition of choice, claiming the rights
of each individual to choose their way of belonging and living
on our planet. This powerful chapter will surely be discussed
mainly in light of current political changes and the revival
of nationalistic, simplistic, black-and-white perceptions of
the world. After this personal reflection, in the sixth chapter,
Bauman returns to his role as a public intellectual.

Focusing on Polish political changes, this chapter was written in Polish for a Polish audience; however, thanks to the
notes, the text is accessible to readers unfamiliar with Polish
politics. Despite being closely connected to current affairs (the
first decade of the twenty-first century), this chapter contains
a precious reflection on authoritarianism and dictatorships.
These phenomena destroy fragile democracy not only in
Poland but also elsewhere in the world. Unfortunately, this
topic, so dramatically experienced and deeply researched by
Bauman, is becoming more and more part of life because of

the developments that we are witnessing now. The last chapter concludes the book beautifully with Bauman's acceptance of his life's experiences. Bauman is making peace with his past and a difficult history (not particularly because of his individual experiences, but because of history itself) and takes full responsibility for his choices. This is the last message in this posthumous book, which, I hope, will be no different from the one that Zygmunt Bauman would have published.

Zygmunt Bauman's Polish texts are incredibly challenging, even though his erudition and language skills are outstanding. He was the best student at the best school in Poznań, and also in other schools that he attended. A voracious and 'addicted' reader throughout his life, he had an extraordinary memory with the capacity to incorporate into his writing many different vocabularies (specific terms from medicine, chemistry, biology and physics), along with classical – but also unusual – references to poetry, movies, theatre and literature, not only from the world of Polish culture but also from other languages and cultures. He added to this treasure many current, popular expressions, or even the occasional vernacular or slang term – not always from the present day, sometimes from the nineteenth century. This is why translation and incorporation into English and Western culture were very challenging – an impossible task for one person, so successive collaboration was needed. The collective effort started with Katarzyna Bartoszyńska, who did the first translation, including of citations from Polish, derived from books which were not published in English. Then, Paulina Bożek helped me to preserve Bauman's wealth of language. In the final stage, Leigh Mueller brought the translated text as close as possible to the English style of Bauman's writing. Then, the last significant corrections were made by Anna Sfard. We focused on preserving Bauman's extremely erudite way of expressing himself, with some elements of humour and hidden and double meanings. It was a long process in which it felt like I was discussing and discovering Bauman all over again. After many years of study devoted to his life's trajectory, I was back into a direct conversation, which invited me one more time to reflect on our human condition today.

The personal character of the writings was also the source of additional work, which was needed to locate missing references. Bauman included some notes, but not many, and these are preceded below by his initials, 'ZB'. This is also the case for notes added by Katarzyna, the translator (preceded by 'TN'). The notes without attribution are mine. In this challenging task (for example, citing poems published in a Polish journal seventy years ago, by an excellent poet who, unfortunately, is not widely known), I was helped by my friends and colleagues, for whose contribution I am most grateful. I wish to thank, for their invaluable responses: Natalia Aleksiun, Alicja Badowska-Wójcik, Izabela Barry, Michael Barry, Agnieszka Bielska, Dariusz Brzeziński, Beata Chmiel, Mariusz Finkielsztein, Andrzej Franaszek, Jan Tomasz Gross, Irena Grudzińska-Gross, Roma Kolarzowa, Adam Kopciowski, Katarzyna Kwiatkowska-Moskalewicz, Joanna Beata Michlic, Jack Palmer, Krzysztof Persak, Adam Puławski, Michał Rusinek, Leszek Szaruga and Natalia Woroszylska.

Last, but not least, I would like to express my gratitude again to the Bauman family for their willingness to allow publication of the private manuscript and for giving me the chance to work on this exceptional book. I also wish to thank John Thompson, who not only supported me in this process, but took an active part in the organization and design of the book as well. Thanks to everyone who collaborated on this project; I hope we can meet the challenge. I am convinced this volume will contribute to the re-reading and better understanding of Bauman's work. It is one more step, after *Bauman: A Biography*, that will bring Bauman closer to his readers. They have a chance to do what was only partly possible until now: to enter his private life, and share his most personal memories and reflections.

Enjoy this fascinating journey!

1

The Story of Just Another Life?

Who needs it? And what for? One life is like another, one life is not like another . . .

You look at someone else's life – at the *story* of someone else's life – as you do into a mirror, but only in order to confirm that your pimples are on a different side of the nose from theirs; that there are more, or fewer, wrinkles under your eyes; that the eyebrows are thicker, and the nostrils hairier . . . In order to uncover, in the clutter of the features, the logic of the face. Or also perhaps the comfort – if, in those features as in your own, no order is to be found. Is this what the stories of a life are needed for?

To narrate a life; to turn a life into a story; to become convinced that it is possible to do this, and therefore to calm fears all the more terrible because they are so rarely spoken – that your life cannot be told, because there is no main thread, even if there are many twists. What can be told 'has a point'. As much of a point as plots do. Stringing the beads onto a necklace, making coloured shards into a mosaic; the necklace is the point of the beads, the mosaic the point of the shards. This point is a supplement, an addition – that 'something more' that the beads acquire when you string them all together. But, first, they are smooth balls and uneven blocks, fragments large and small, unwieldy, strangely shaped. Necklaces and mosaics come later. We live twice. Once, breaking and flattening; the second time, gathering the pieces and arranging them in patterns. First, living; second, narrating the experience. This second life, for whatever reason, seems more important than the first. It's only in the second one that the 'point'[1] appears.

The first is only the preface to the second, the transportation of bricks to the construction site. It is a strange construction – life. First you bring the bricks and gather them into a pile; only later, when you've run out of bricks, when the kilns have gone dark and the brickmakers are approaching bankruptcy, do you sit down at the drawing board to sketch out an architectural plan. The promotion from builder to architect comes after you have finished construction – but, in distinction from the law, *retro agit . . .* Is it for this promotion that you tell your life story?

The first life passes. The second – the narrated one – lasts; and that existence is a ticket to eternity. In the first one, you can't redo anything; in the second – everything. Eternity is an extension of existence (this is why it is easier to imagine eternity than nothingness; one doesn't have the experience that could serve as the point of departure, to say about nothingness: 'the same, only more'). In every experience, there is *something*: the subject experiencing. Nothingness would have to be the absence of the subject. Non-existence carries the stigma of absurdity; there is nothing absurd in eternity – eternal being has a whiff of the empirical. And in eternity, anything can happen, everything can happen an infinite number of times – everything can be experienced many times and in infinitely many ways. In eternity, nothing ever ends, and certainly nothing ever ends irrevocably. In eternity, there are no foolproof locks, and you can enter every river twice. This is probably why we long for existence. Existence as the one more chance, the chance to reclaim lost chances. A repeated experience – this time knowing how it will turn out. A happy ending instead of a tragedy. Prudence instead of naivety, wisdom instead of stupidity. 'This or that could have turned out entirely different, if only . . .' But that which could have been only becomes apparent when it is no longer possible. Possibilities that are still open give you a headache; those that are foreclosed – a guilty conscience.

Narrating life as a compensation for the life you lived. This is probably what leads to the dream of immortality. Immortality tempts you with the opportunity to tell everything *anew* – telling it anew *again*, as many times as needed, until nothing has to be compensated for. Immortality allows you to redeem *everything* that needs redemption (this cannot be done in a less-than-infinite time). Is it in hopes of a second chance that you tell your life story?

Kundera wrote of exile that it is a state of alienation. Not from the country you have arrived in – that country, on the contrary, you tame by being tamed by it: what is distant today becomes close tomorrow; the foreign, domestic. In exile, you are alienated from the country that you have abandoned: 'That, which was familiar, by degrees becomes strange.' 'Only returning to the native land after a long absence can reveal the substantial strangeness of the world and of existence.'[2] But all of life is an exile: exile out of every present moment, from every 'now', from every 'here'. Life is a journey from the familiar to the strange. Its 'substantial strangeness' is revealed by the world in every passing moment, immediately after the movement which cannot be retreated from, and the moves in the game of life cannot be taken back. The futile hope for the persistence of familiarity is sparked by the past imperfect – but, after a second, the past moment mercilessly unmasks the 'substantial strangeness' of existence. It is hard not to notice this strange, stubborn, unfavourable, hostile inertia of the world. With the passing of time, you speak ever more in the past tense, ever less in the past imperfect, and the future imperfect disappears practically without a trace. Is it possible to restore that which has been alienated, to make it familiar? You can try – by telling your life story . . .

The subject of the story is not the old, once free but now ossified, movements – but the memories of them. In this second remembered life of theirs, one can mark out a boundary line that separates possibility from being; can restore, in this way, the present of those moments of 'now' ('now' is characterized by the fact that in it the boundary between what could be and what irreversibly is cannot be seen – the first time because you do not notice it, and the second because you eliminate it). In the first life, you trespassed this boundary line unknowingly, and in the second, you can cross back and forth repeatedly. It is like throwing hardened events into a crucible, where they become soft again, susceptible to moulding, obedient to a newly wise wisdom. Narrating one's life is the same as going to war with alienation, as boldly proclaiming that exile never happened. It is the same as seeking the recovery of time. Is that why you tell your life story? And is it a confirmation of the delusion that the goal we seek can be reached in stories of other people's lives?

3 January 1997

This was an introduction to something I wasn't sure would ever exist. Even a few days ago, I did not know that this introduction would come into being. Even today, I have no idea what will come after, as, against my habits as a writer, this time I am starting without the slightest idea of what to do next. I have no plan beyond the desire to sit, day by day, in my usual habit from 6 a.m. to noon, in front of the keyboard and screen of an obsolete – by today's standard – Amstrad,[3] counting on each new sentence to summon forth another one . . .

It is all because of the New Year . . . I am a superstitious person – that is, I have my favourite superstitions, matters in which I like to be superstitious; superstition is the best way I know of to have some ersatz control over one's own fate, so it is worthwhile playing Blindman's Bluff with it: so I try to organize the New Year period in accordance with the shape that I hope that the coming year will take, and then treat the results of my efforts as an omen. Thus, it was necessary to take as an omen the fact that, this time, my plans came to nothing, and instead I found myself confronted with 'the thing itself' – that is, fate. A blizzard prevented friends from dropping in for a glass of champagne on their way to a New Year's party; the snowdrifts it left behind made impossible the arrival of a few kind hearts – those friends helpless now, and doomed to loneliness and no New Year's chat; a final phone call before midnight brought news of which it can only be said that it was a bolt out of a blue sky or a downpour on a sunny day. New Year's Day was thus preceded and followed in the same style, passed in the company of two ladies, by all measures worthy of respect and kindness, but of the category of those who ask questions only to have the opportunity to provide the most lengthy answer to them; ladies who, for reasons entirely understandable and not at all exclusive to them (a lack of regular listeners), did not even trouble themselves this time to ask questions. It is hard to be surprised that the New Year did not leave me feeling optimistic. Instead of the annual 'May it continue this way!', it informed me that 'Things cannot go on like this.' Something must be done. Something must change. It must be otherwise – but how?

The New Year period, for both rational reasons and the superstitious ones that sprout from them, and the predictions one seeks in them, is also an occasion for summarizing and planning. At such a time, one does not make discoveries and rarely has new ideas. It is, rather, the thoughts that have long been tumbling around in one's mind – or in that secret, no more clearly defined seat of the subconscious – that drift to the surface decked out in words, and take on clear contours. That is certainly what happened this New Year. Except that, at the surface, two thoughts collided – both long present, but so far repressed; and their meeting led to something like a chemical reaction, as if two gaseous substances, colourless and volatile, merged into a solid body, hard, with loud colours, but undissolvable . . .

4 January

This first thought is about death. Not so much about it being close (though it came closer by a ferocious leap in the moment when I outlived my father: he died on the day of his seventieth birthday), as about how to behave in regard to it, and how to arrange things, so as to act in the way that was decided upon. I know that I am not lying to myself when I tell myself that what is important is not how long one lives, but, rather, to live out the time one has in a dignified and meaningful way. The nightmare is not so much death, as the kind of meaningless vegetation that modern medicine inserts between the moment when a person was supposed to die and the moment when doctors decide that they are allowed to die – between human death and clinical death. With such a set of options, a sensible person should choose to 'leave at their own demand'. The catch is that, alongside good sense, one also needs a stroke of luck. I love life: the people among whom that life is spent, and that which my – conscious, active – presence contributes or can contribute; I do not want to leave life *prematurely*. But how to grasp that moment in which 'prematurely' is transformed into 'too late'? And, once grasped, how to admit to oneself that it has been grasped, or even to enter into the Pascalian wager with oneself and stick to it? Koestler succeeded in doing it, Kotarbiński did not.[4] So the best solution is not one that can really be counted on. There remains the second: not to cooperate with doctors, and, especially, not to help them – and certainly not to invite them – to demonstrate the artistry that they strive to perfect: cultivating cabbages. When a so-called 'fatal illness' arrives (the very concept is already the exanthema of medical technology: the point is mainly to conceal the fact that the only truly fatal, incurable illness is life), not to oppose it – if anything, to give it a leg up. For a long time now, I have had various disorders, some of which, according to textbooks, testify to something 'serious' – but as long as they do not disturb my work or interrupt my everyday routine, it is better not to confess to doctors about them.

But, if so, then it is necessary to reckon with the finitude of time, which we have known about since birth but which, for the longest part of our life, we do not have to consider, because the tasks we set ourselves are cut to such a measure as to fit comfortably within a 'foreseeable phase of life'. Nothing in a life so organized will prepare us for turning the abstraction that is human mortality into a practical problem – we learn to select among matters to be dealt with, but this selection is free from the pungent sense of an ultimate decision: it is not so much that we resign, as that we delay. If not today, tomorrow . . . Tomorrow seems like an eternity, because every task that demands our efforts can be fitted into some number of tomorrows and day-after-tomorrows. But what happens when we start to see the bottom of the bag of tomorrows? Then it is an entirely different kind of 'selection', and there was no time to learn that other kind. When the doctors told Stanisław Ossowski[5] that he had a few months left to live, this worldly man, whose gaze could penetrate to the depths of fate and bravely face his opponents, confessed to a hitherto unknown feeling of loss and powerlessness. 'I had always considered which issues to take up first, which later, what to write first, what later, which books to read right away, which to set aside for later . . . And now suddenly there is no more later, instead of "later" there is never.'[6] The experience of even the most reasoned choices between 'now' and 'later' does not produce any lessons in how to choose between 'now' and 'never'.

But at some age – such as mine – a thinking person should not wait for a reminder from doctors to begin to live *as if* confronted by the choice between 'now' and 'never'. It is necessary to get rid of the comforting belief that what is put off will not escape, and if life without it seems like a nightmare, at least break the nightmare's fangs and clip its claws by striving to arrange your days so that 'delaying' weighs as little on your conscience as possible: in other words, only do things that are important, the most important.

At this point, the first thought has ripened enough to encounter the second thought . . .

I read yesterday in the third volume of Maria Dąbrowska's diaries a sentence that glimmers in its sagacity, and faced with which the fat volumes on the topic by respected sociologists are dwarfed, seem worthy of laughter and a contemptuous shrug of the shoulders. (Did she just blurt it out? Did she realize the power of it?) On the occasion of a visit to Nieborów in the company of intellectuals 'of a Jewish origin'[7] in a hot, pre-October period,[8] Dąbrowska notes that 'justice demands that we acknowledge, that if there is any sort of free and creative thought circulating, it is among them. In this moment they are the bravest "destroyers of police-enforced order". Even in social conversations they are more interesting than native-born Poles . . . Personally, as a writer, I must say, qu'ils ne m'embêtent jamais comme nos gens[9].'[10] And just after comes this major sentence: 'With all of this, it irritates people; as if someone, who is not entirely us, wanted in all ways to live our lives instead of us.'[11] Yes, that is what it is all about, here is the point – the rest is ideological beautification/justification. Not to be entirely one of us is not, in and of itself, a sin; wanting to live instead of us – also isn't. The combination creates a combustible mixture.

Dąbrowska was better 'positioned' than many others to perceive this. Her allosemitism,[12] typical of the gentry,[13] granted Jews a prominent and uncontested place: Jewish tailors, peddlers, tenant farmers. In the context of such otherness, Jews were like everyone else. You can be an excellent tenant farmer just like you can be an excellent overseer or gardener; and you can be a good person even as a tenant farmer, and a forester – everyone in their own way. It is the Jew who deviates from their role who causes concern and outrage: not wanting to 'live for himself', at the same time he wants to 'live instead of us' – a life that is reserved *for us*. And what if he also succeeds in these ignoble efforts? If he is 'excellent' in the role that we are meant to play, but that we somehow are not eager for? Rubbing salt into the open wounds of the conscience . . .

The cursed vicious circle: that 'our people' cannot not feel as they feel, and 'ethnics' cannot not behave as they behave. On the one hand: to the same degree that the social position of Dąbrowska sharpened her gaze, the social position of 'ethnics' makes them natural 'destroyers of order', because it is to them that the now poisonous fumes of the rot reach, when others are still breathing an air that is admittedly stale, but still breathable. And, on the other hand: their room for manoeuvre is smaller than that of others. If they refuse to do what the nation in a state of war with the unwanted order considers proper, they will be accused of their foreignness or natural tendency to treachery; if they do the thing, they will have to try harder than others, because what is acceptable for a voivode . . .[14] And if they succeed and are worthy of reward – it will be said that it was stolen.

And the second feeling, which it became increasingly harder for me to silence, and which it was increasingly harder for me to live with, was a feeling of disillusionment and discouragement, towards that 'academic discipline' which, for a great majority of my life – with enthusiasm or gritted teeth, but always as much as I was able to honestly afford – I served.

5 January

Sociology; 'social science'; when did the hope that was its mid-wife transform into deceit? Did it become a deceit that was consciously practised, and if so, when?

A promise of certainty is deceit. A promise never fulfilled and with no chance of being fulfilled, but an ever-renewing, gal-vanizing illusion, which hinders humans from looking into the eyes of that which is the most human in their fates. The promise of exorcizing magic forces from human life, as was done for the revolutions of heavenly spheres or the transformations of matter. The promise of getting rid of, once and for all, secrets, doubts, 'fear and trembling'. The promise of creating a world in which the path from action to consequences will be always and everywhere equally short and simple, as the one from pressing a button to lighting up a TV screen – a world without accidents and surprises, without disappointments and tragedies, but with a handyman available on call, ready to fix a loose button and exchange a telescopic lamp. A promise of transforming human life into a collection of problems to be solved. A promise of recipes, tools, specifications to solve every problem.

I am too much of a sociologist to accuse sociology of *causing* the 'technological bias' that deprives life of its human charm, along with its human, oh-so-human, torment and suffering. Accusing it of that is the same as directly or indirectly granting credence to its pretensions and mending the sagging pedestal on which it has placed itself (on which it has been placed?). Sociology is only a modest, secondary participant in the technological conspiracy – a messenger, an errand-boy, occa-sionally a minute-taker, sometimes an author of propaganda leaflets. But it *is* a participant in this conspiracy – even when it enters into conflict with other participants, in the name of better, more effective methods of collective action.

The history of my discouragement is lengthy and comprises many chapters. In the years of my Marxist youth, I could not digest the idea of 'scientific ideology'; I think that this was the reason I broke out of the obediently lined-up ranks, from an idea of straightening the winding routes of history; and using unambiguous rules for doing so had a stench of corpses about it. But a rebellious nature did not allow me to seek shelter in the opposite camp; both camps pitched their tents in the graveyard of human freedom. Learned Marxist critics accused it of not being scientific *enough* – that its predictions did not come true; that, despite the predictions, it did not guarantee control over human actions; that the bridle which it placed on the bucking bronco of history was frayed and did not restrict the horse's movements enough. Some wanted to 'scientize' Marxism; others, doubting the possibilities for success in this approach, to reject it – not because of the idea of scientific ideology, but for an insufficient, or even an entirely invented, scientificity of the ideology. From my conflicts with the Marxism of the barracks, the road led not to another camp, but to a desert, to a hermitage. Gramsci, who had dug the tunnel that I escaped through, would lead the escape committee in every one of the sociological camps of that time.

And today? I am where I began. My critics say: people need hard, strong principles – and you undermine them. People want certainty, and you sow doubt. They are right. 'Hard, strong principles' – coming from the revelation, or the interpretation of the secrets of history, or from a private audience in the court of Reason – are to me, in the best case, lies, and in the worst, another version of, and a functional equivalent to, Auschwitz's 'Arbeit macht frei.' I repeat this as a profession of faith with a maniacal stubbornness, year after year, book after book. In various ways, expressed with various words.

I am tired. I have ridden my Rocinante almost to death; but my peregrinations were not especially picturesque. They were rather too monotonous to merit a Cervantesque smile, though they were just as successful as Don Quixote's mission.

I cannot find the energy within myself to seek out yet another way, to find new words. And what's worse, there is the nagging suspicion that the owners of windmills need Don Quixotes to confirm the windmill-ness of windmills and thereby to handily get rid of the unfaithful. Again, a vicious circle: using the academic mode of duelling, one can only join the academic duel, and by playing the academic game you guarantee its rules. '[I]t makes no sense to transgress a game's rules', warns Baudrillard, 'within a cycle's recurrence, there is no line one can jump (instead, one simply leaves the game).'[15] A paradox: this is why they are merely conventions, they are 'only' provisional – outside of the game taking place they have no other premises, the rules of the game are invincible as long as the game continues. Those who play are players only thanks to the rules; those who refuse to play do not count. Do you want to change the rules? First you must play the game. But as soon as you join the game, you endorse the rules . . . The choice is between contributing to the galvanization of illusion, or silence.

Each of my successive books was – it couldn't not be – a recreation of the academic ritual; and a protest against the ritual can be understood in the temple where the ritual takes place only as a deviation from the liturgy – and the notion of 'deviation' upholds the ritual in the same way as the notion of an 'exception' proves the rule. Just as a protest against ritual must take place in accordance with the liturgical codex. A protest against the insane grievances of the humanities regarding 'scientificity' must take the form dictated by academic canons and decked in all of the caricatures of academic argument required of the adepts of 'academic humanities'.

If the knot cannot be untangled, it must be cut. That is how scissors think. At least those that, supposedly, Alexander the Great armed himself with. But knots, at least the Gordian ones, are an impossibility for scissors – just as, according to Kafka, heaven is an impossibility for crows.

Kundera – wise after reading Nietzsche, but also after his own losses and those of his countrymen – writes:

> a person who thinks should not try to persuade others of his belief; that is what puts him on the road to a system; on the lamentable road of the 'man of conviction'; politicians like to call themselves that; but what is a conviction? It is a thought that has come to a stop, that has congealed, and the 'man of conviction' is a man restricted; experimental thought seeks not to persuade but to inspire; to inspire another thought, to set thought moving.

Kundera calls for 'systematically desystematiz[ing] [. . .] thought, kick[ing] at the barricade'.[16] This call, nothing strange, is directed to *novelists*. Whoever answers this call can only be a 'novelist'. A teller of tales. With a wink, half-serious, half-joking. Mocking seriousness, and serious in mockery. A poet, Szymborska:

> but what is poetry anyway?
> More than one rickety answer
> has tumbled since that question first was raised.
> But I just keep on not knowing and I cling to that
> like a redemptive handrail.[17]

Cling to it! So that Maria Dąbrowska's terrible prophecy is not fulfilled: 'The present is like a complicated piece played on a piano with many mute, silent keys. And there will be ever more mute keys, and no one will know what piece history is playing, though there will be many words, but it will be a false tongue, like the ears of the deafmutes.'[18]

A paradox. A pun. A figurative expression – absorbent and porous. Self-contradiction. A substance containing its opposite, gathering and dissolving it. Such elements would comprise the logic of the humanities, cut to the size of its own subject. Or a net, which could contain the experience of being human. Other logics are simpler and more harmonious; other nets are thicker and have more tightly tied knots. So what – if those other logics fall apart when used, and those other nets return from fishing half empty?

This logic and this net can be tested on an individual life . . . But why mine? Because I know it better than others. Which doesn't mean that I know it. And certainly doesn't mean that I know it *well*. The point of the effort is, among other things, to find out whether I know – and how.

This is really the only argument in favour of choice. Little else speaks in its favour, and there is much to suggest that the choice is an unfortunate one.

6 January

The choice is not the most fortuitous, because it was a life at the margins. At the sidelines of great events and far from the great figures that are the salt and pepper of 'interesting stories'. As if an amoeba were describing a storm at sea, or a fencepost a giant flood . . . a fencepost which, among other posts, is not distinguished by anything in particular, and is not a particularly brilliant storyteller (half a century of sociological grooming has not gone by without a trace: the world of the sociologist is composed of 'variables', 'factors' and 'indicators', and the language of the sociologist serves to describe the interactions into which they enter). The world of a sociologist is deceptively similar to the world of Kafka's *Trial*, which Kundera calls 'extremely non-poetic' – or one in which 'there is no longer a place for individual freedom, for the uniqueness of the individual, where man is only the instrument of extrahuman forces: of bureaucracy, technology, History'.[19] But, precisely to reveal how 'extremely non-poetic' the world is, Kafka created a language that is actually 'extremely poetic'. In the process, he hoped to allow the windows covered with blinds to return to their original role – the role of windows.

9 January

Lévi-Strauss wrote about the dramas of the anthropologist: when there is someone to ask, they don't yet know what to ask; once they know the question, there is no one left to answer. As an anthropologist of my family past – that past which was the present of my family – I am experiencing this drama on my own skin. When my parents were alive, I did not ask. When my head is full of questions – there is no one to ask.

When my mother or father would reminisce about their youth (and this happened rarely), I listened with one ear, or didn't listen at all, already bored by stories of a world that decidedly was not my world, into which I did not know how to enter and that I had no desire to enter into. Maybe in order to save my own children from the sense of powerless misery that consumed me after my father's passing, and, along with him, the last chance to look behind that door that was irreversibly slammed shut – maybe for that reason, I sat down exactly nine years ago to write (in three copies, one for each of my daughters) a handful of information about the world that was mine but not theirs. I wrote, at the time, this introduction addressed to them: 'Why have I decided to write down my life story? I guess I have reached the age when life stories are written. I am already in this world longer than my mother ever was. Not much is left to level up with my father, who died at seventy. If there ever is a right time to sum up and give an account – it is now.'[20]

Or so people seem to feel, which amounts to the same. Living towards death makes life absurd. I suppose writing memoirs is an act of desperation. As a story, life makes sense; if the story is good, it may even show some logic.

Or perhaps I have decided to write for some other reason. Or perhaps there is no reason, only a need and a push. Frankly, I do not know. I do not think I care either.[21]

Clearly, the 'proper time' has passed, because today I did not perceive within myself any overwhelming need or internal pressure. Then, I carried my task out to its completion – I passed on to my daughters what I remembered of the world that existed before they appeared and made it their world, weaving its image, each of them in her own way, from the threads of her own experiences and hopes. Maybe someday they will take a look at these notes – when they reach that moment in which I mourned the lack of notes that I could look at. My purpose is fulfilled, so why am I telling this tale anew? In the name of what? To whom – and what do I have to offer, telling it? I do not know how to answer this question, and, this time, the lack of an answer worries me. Or, rather, it depresses me and deprives me of energy – and courage!

The issue is not that I 'don't see the addressee' though – regardless of what I write, I write having a 'reader' in mind, a reader-interlocutor, a co-author of the meanings that I laboriously, sentence by sentence, assemble; I try to share with the reader the dilemmas that I cannot untangle, the puzzles I cannot penetrate, the doubts that I live with even though (or perhaps because) I cannot manage them myself. This reader-interlocutor of mine is not quite like Umberto Eco's 'model reader': he is not my own mirror reflection, myself in a different garb, me looking over my own shoulder as I write, me listening respectfully as I speak about how to understand me the writer. Actually, he doesn't remind me of anyone. Among those who wander bookstores and libraries, everyone chooses their kin (kin by choice: a bad translation of *Wahlverwandtschaft*,[22] and this phrase is badly pleonastic – one always enters into kinship by choice; the paradoxical discovery is chosen blood-ties). My writing is 'for being chosen'. All of it is a meditation on the experience of life, and it will be of interest to those who experienced the world in a similar way, and who, turning the pages, will encounter experiences similar to their own. It is the one who is choosing who decides whether a blood-tie exists and is strong enough to spend more time with the book. It is such a reader who is always before my eyes. If he ever existed, he exists now. If he was ever to be found, then he will not be lacking now. Except that I have less and less to say to him. I have already shared with him my thoughts about what, in my experiences, could have grabbed him with its resonance or as a counter-point, similarity or difference. We used to walk side by side, we dealt with the same obstacles. Today, he has gone farther. I got stuck. My legs do not carry me, or do I not want to go? I am going deaf, or am I covering my ears? Either way – the world that he is living in now, I probably won't enter, at this point. So, neither harmony, nor counter-point. One by one, the bridges are crumbling, the clearings where we met become overgrown with weeds. We wander different paths; or rather, he wanders along paths that I have never walked. If lions could speak, as Wittgenstein accurately observed, we would not understand them. I do not know who is the lion here, but I anticipate problems with translation.

11 January

Roland Barthes once distinguished between *l'écrivain* and *l'écrivant* – the 'writer' and the 'author'.[23] Generally, the writer writes to write, the author for something else – for example, to raise spirits or elevate the soul, but most often with the aim of transforming the world for the better. Barthes divided people aspiring to be writers on the basis of their authorial inten-tions. It is not at all clear how the divisions made from this perspective will square with those of other perspectives – the type of written product or the attitudes of the reader, and the 'tangible effects' of the existence of the work, immediate or long-term. Rorty does not ponder Conrad's motives when he debates the ways of reading *Heart of Darkness*; it is, rather, the approach of the reader that 'makes a difference'. You can read like a butcher, quartering a hog's carcass, or like a bureaucrat, sorting files into folders. Or you can read in such a way as to – communing with Kurtz – 'change your life'.[24] But the question is, does every book lend itself to both interpretations? And, especially – can you intend to be a 'writer', without turning out, upon interpretation, to be an 'author'? And do the motives of the 'author' have any chance of being accomplished, if the author is not simultaneously – initially, from the first – a 'writer'? To be a 'writer' – that seems to be the same as being open to the kind of interpretation that would allow the reader to 'change their life' (being open to it as well in the kind of moments and circumstances that the author cannot predict and which cannot be part of their motivations; this discrepancy between timescales makes it difficult, or even impossible, to compare the categorizations, conducted from different perspectives). The work that lends itself to such interpretations turns the creator into a 'writer'. The practical effect is that only a 'writer' can be an 'author'.

Ortega y Gasset pointed out that, in the problem of generations, the important thing is not that each of them carries the burden of different experiences and therefore thinks and behaves differently from other generations, but the fact that, at every moment, there live alongside each other – with each other – several generations. This is the good fortune of culture – but also the vexation of its creators and bearers. Culture gains, because every attempt to disambiguate what is multiple, to close what is open, to nail what is volatile (and such efforts culture, which is precisely culture – that is, an office of standards and norms – cannot renounce) is condemned from the start to failure. What culture masks, the multiplicity of generations reveals. The failures of culture are not symptoms of crisis – or, speaking more precisely, 'crisis' is the normal state of culture and a symptom of its health. Culture must strive towards a multiplicity of meaning, but it is not allowed, under threat of atrophy and death, to attain it. What is redemption for bureaucracy – is a torment for bureaucrats. What for the office (and its client!) is a gain, for the crew and staff is a loss. Laws and statutes age as soon as they are amended. The paragraphs argue with each other and start new disputes as soon as they are reconciled. The rules are all the more toothless, the more precise they are . . . What the bureaucrats were promised (or dreamed of) – a state of harmony and good spirits in which it will not occur to anyone to contradict the content of a command or ban – turns out to be a horizon that gets farther away the faster you run towards it.

It is good when those in conflict know what to fight against. It is better if they know what they are fighting for. In hopes of such knowledge, round tables were invented, commissions and conferences, and some philosophers have even created a canon of perfect discourse. But knowledge still only comes rarely; and if it does, it is seldom in the issues of the greatest import. And if such knowledge is lacking, the difference cannot turn into a dispute. Standing at one edge of the precipice, we cannot see the other side – so not only can we not build a bridge, we cannot even design one. From whichever side you look, on the other shore there are only lions.

I am standing at the brink of such a precipice. Lacking a bridge, I tried to build a spyglass (telescope?); some even elevated me to the ranks of a master of lenses – but what of it, when the view through the spyglass cannot be seen without it, and, seeing them in a photograph, one will not recognize the hills and valleys that have been trampled along and across by feet; that is how much a picture has in common with the coastline photographed: as much as the glimmerings awaiting

Plato outside the cave have with the wisdom of its permanent residents – and Plato was concerned, not without reason, that the residents of the cave might see Plato's visions as fraud or the sign of a weakening mind.

It came to pass recently that a certain elderly sociologist became interested in the sex lives of the generation of students of his grandchildren's age; to learn about their exotic-to-him customs, he could not, however, ask questions any different from the ones that he asked their fathers, and, even earlier, himself, when he was their age. So he learned, then, how different the sexual mores of today's students are from those of their fathers and grandfathers. But on the topic of what sex is in their lives, how they see it and how they experience it – he did not learn anything. These lions can speak – but he does not understand them. And he, of course, has his own lion's language – but will they be able to grasp it?

The same can be said about what happened to me, when I wanted to describe and understand the world that to me is virgin territory, and that for those whose experiences I would like to understand is home. I called this world 'postmodern': that is, a world that came after the world – or, rather, that *replaced the world* – that was my home.

12 January

So, for me, postmodernity is primarily *post*-modernity – or, rather, post-*modernity*. But for them? It is not 'post' anything: we could just as well (or just as ineptly) call it the post-Alexandrian or post-Napoleonic epoch. That dusk, when my owl spread its wings, they did not experience, because they did not experience the day that preceded that dusk. For me, their world is, above all, what it is not: it is not all those things that constituted my world (their world thus cannot be for them what it is for me: for them, it simply is, full stop). What to me is

clashing colours, to them is grey on grey. They did not experience that last desperate effort to put a collar on the world,
the war that was to be the last one, times of boastfulness and
madness, blindness taken as visionary, a cult of humanity and
a contempt for the person; times where one totalitarianism
impressed on another, and only one totalitarianism could crush
another one; nothing strange that they cannot take such times
seriously, and, even more, that they take them as a canvas, on
which the contours of their own world ought to be drawn, in
order to correctly (by contrast, singularly) assess it. They know
better than (differently from) me what their world is; they
know not as well (differently), what it is not. But to describe *to
them* their world by referencing the past which *I* experienced is
like explaining to them what water is, by hammering into their
heads that it is not a hard substance.

Well – and the most important thing – they don't have
burnt fingers; and if they do have some blisters, it is not from
those fires; if they lick their wounds, they are those produced
by other blades. The old nightmares are today's adventure; the
old wisdom, naivety; and the old naivety is a sin. It is hard for
them to believe in the blaze of those fires, the sharpness of
those knives. How can they grasp those hopes, those dilemmas,
those disappointments? We cannot fault them for it. But how
are we to talk with them?!

And sometimes I think to myself: is it *necessary* to talk (make
people aware, forestall, warn)? Isn't it true that ignorance is a
privilege? That the fullness of knowledge entails a fully para-
lysed will? Isn't forgetting more creative than memory?

And sometimes I think to myself: will my wisdom, if they
accept it, add wisdom for them? Maybe the opposite – it
will mislead, turn their attention from matters that are more
important in their world, will direct them to blow on already
cooled ovens and ignore the ones that are burning white-hot
around them? Maybe it is better not to know the past, so as
not to acquire an arrogance that could be suicidal, a sense that

one knows how things go, what needs to be done and what to avoid – that it is not necessary to be on one's guard against the future, that it is already in one's pocket?

Je n'écris plus, je m'occupe – wrote Martin du Gard near the decline of his life.[25] Maybe this doleful judgement had a similar motivation. Or maybe the point was something else, more personal: the withering of the senses with which one perceives the world and the atrophying of the tools that transform those sensory impressions into thoughts. In brief: old age, when those ripples on the water become threatening billows, gentle hills grow to mountains of exorbitant heights, and scattered copses thicken into unconquerable woods.

Maybe the point was something else still. Should one give birth to children in an overpopulated world, should one add more words to a world drowning in an excess of them? In this world, texts die sooner than their authors; when it comes to texts, the progress of civilization is measured by the unhampered growth of infant mortality and the violent shortening of a predictable life.[26] The path of life is strewn with the graves of books; most of them do not receive tombstones – one slogs through thoughts, treading over the corpses of anonymous texts; every step of the intellectual path is layered with the rotting bones of thoughts that were thought by someone, sometime, busily, laboriously, with a singular focus on writing. Texts are born in the graveyard and rarely leave it before their own death. It is hard to believe that what once motivated writers was a desire to conquer death . . . That the word seemed like a pass to eternity.

Je n'écris plus, je m'occupe. I do not know how to live without thinking; I do not know how to think without writing. I have condemned myself to write; now I serve out my endless sentence in front of the screen of a word-processor. Less and less do I live to write, more and more do I write to live: so that, after today, there will be a tomorrow; to fall asleep with the hope of waking, and in waking to joyfully set my mouth watering with the thought of the flavours of the dawning day.

Je n'écris plus, je m'occupe.

16 January

Yesterday at ICA:[27] I went, in spite of my principles, because it was hard to turn down a personal request from Giddens. I knew very well what was awaiting me, so I can only fault my own weakness of will. An overwhelming feeling of strangeness. What do I have to do with this vanity fair? With this gang of people in love with themselves, gazing at their own navels and convinced of their intellectual superiority, telling the world and the little people inhabiting it how to live in order to avoid their reprimand? Or with that rabble of paid clackers, who have arrived in multitudes, as they always do on such occasions, in the hopes that they will be able to nibble a bit on someone else's fame, to stay closer to the candle – and perhaps a few drops of wax will fall and cling to their skin?

I hate herds. And mutual adoration societies. And stardom. And the exchange-market of publicity. And popularity contests. There at the top the air is too rarefied for me, or overly perfumed, to breathe. I was not born at the top, and I have not acquired a taste for climbing. The climb is always crowded, and I can't stand crowds. It always pushes me in the direction opposite to the one that the crowd moves in. I seek those hallways that are not noisy, but empty. I think to myself that this is why I have never settled in any of the 'one hand washes another' cliques, in any of the silk-lined academic nests of patented wisdom; I fled from those places as far as possible. Which has, after all, its good sides. The grumblings and mockery that make their way to me from the centre of the nests – it sails past my ears; the buckets of dishwater are like water off a duck's back. Any young whipper-snapper, when supported by a crowd, has enough courage to give me a kick; there is no danger to him. But there is no danger to me either! I have nothing to lose, other than my self-respect.

The 'event' at the ICA was one more illustration of the deterioration of today's thoughtfulness, reflection, argumentation, the arduous effort to understand the essence of things – all that which formerly comprised the phenomenon of 'debate' or 'discussion'. The programme was overloaded, but with thoughts only of packing in as many important names as possible, and so that none of those possessing such an important name would be offended. For a calm and sensible exposition of the issue, none of the speakers had the time – but also, probably no one was expecting it of them. The only thing that mattered was 'soundbites' and witty 'one-liners'. As for the audience, the bursting-at-the-seams programme made sure that they would not depart from their role: as listeners only. The 'event' was just one more ceremony, ritually recreating the division into those who speak and those who listen – those who were heard, and those who were mute. (The presence of sound is obnoxious; one cannot 'avert one's ears', they cannot even be properly plugged. The presence of beings who do not make noise can be cancelled simply by averting one's gaze.)

28 January

At the Tate Gallery: a painting by Constantin A. Nieuwenhuys. Full of Hieronymus Bosch-esque predatory and blood-thirsty little monsters, except that, as appropriate for a modern age, they were crammed into an incredibly tight crowd; there is no green space, like Bosch has, in which the little monsters roam; in Nieuwenhuys, the world is full of monsters to the brim: they are the world itself. The canvas, by decision of its author, bore various names at various times. In 1920, the painter gave it the title *To Us, Liberty!* In 1950, he changed the title: *After Us,*

Liberty![28] Thirty years is a lot. It's far more than the life-span of hope. Hope wanders to that eternity that awaits us after death, before us. We trail behind it.

I accidentally happened across an article by Romana Kolarzowa[29] (I learned from Anka[30] that she is a Ph.D. student at Poznań), and, in it, these wise words – it's a wonder that they could come from such a young pen:

> Shamefully rarely does it cross our minds that deriding some kind of intellectual position with the assertion that 'hardly anyone shares it' should actually be understood as recognizing a strength; proclaiming beliefs that almost everyone shares is not any kind of intellectual effort, but a recitation of banalities. The courage of beliefs, subdued by the intention of not offending anyone with their contents . . . is reminiscent of an exercise in bowing without ever turning your back on anyone.

And more: 'given that conformism is the most ardently desired state, it is hard not to have a crisis of values: conformism is practically taught, it doesn't matter how. Just not to stand out – so there is no point in having one's own passions and attachments, nor faith, nor even an opinion.'[31]

Hola – the words came from me, 'it's a wonder that they should come from such a young pen'. But how is it really? For whom is it easier to be a nonconformist? Who can more readily rage against conformism? Common wisdom whispers that it's the young: young people don't know yet what the risks are (like that snotty jeweller's apprentice Shlomo, who, without a moment of doubt and without a tremor in his hand, drilled a hole in the rare pearl that the masters of the craft did not want to touch, because, unlike Shlomo, they knew its worth); and they have less to lose – no family to support, no mortgages to pay, no career to save. But does such a wisdom err? One could make a few arguments against it.

The first is that young people break rules almost by discouragement: probably they don't know yet what they are – and this lack of knowledge explains more about their behaviour than an ignorance of the punishment awaiting those who break the rules or an insouciance with regard to the harm that they wreak. When older people complain about the nonconformism of youth, it's usually about run-of-the-mill ignorance and a sluggishness in learning. We wrongly take as a sign of 'nonconformism of youth' the dissonance emerging not so much from a lack of desire to sing with the choir, as from the un-set voices.[32] Falling out of the choir is not enough to make you a soloist.

The second, moreover, is that you will not encounter among the youth a disinterest in singing in the choir. Quite the opposite, it is only in a choir – and one crowded full of people – that they find their voice. And nothing strange in that: a frail voice will not carry far on its own; one needs a quantity of throats to make up for the weakness of vocal chords. And in a choir, it is jollier, and louder, and more momentous; a false note will melt away and vanish in the general noise, and a sickly voice will be backed up, bursting the eardrums with its echo. Both in cases where, from a mixture of disgust and fear, they cross the street at the sight of masquerading youth, and when they peep round the curtains of their living rooms at the screaming and rock-throwing at those in power (this power, other powers – but always the ones guilty today of being those in power here and now) and youth militias, 'grown-ups' wrongly accuse the youth of lacking respect for values, and of breaking the rules; they are looking on at the successive lessons of the most important of all schools of conformism.

Third, it is one thing to rebel against what is, here and now, conformism, but something entirely different to be against conformism as such: against the *principle* of obedience, closing ranks and disciplined lines. It is one thing not to accept the wisdom of the herd, and another to deny the herd wisdom. One thing to revolt against the room being stifling, and another to protest against the ban on sticking your neck out . . . We are mistakenly conflating these two attitudes when we give them both the same name. Tearing off an excessively tight collar is different from despising a uniform. It might be appropriate to distinguish between a nonconformism that is instrumental and one that is autotelic. Kolarzowa stood up for the second. It's a wonder that this should come from such a young pen . . .

Well, and finally: to be a nonconformist, and persist in nonconformism . . . it is fiendishly simple to fall into noncon- formism through insouciance or inattention – this happens to many people, pleasantly warming themselves in the mass of nonconformism, and many are drawn to its heat. But it is harder to persist in nonconformism when the masses gallop under a different banner, or when one has experienced the costs of nonconformism – when the body is covered in scars and still nursing unhealed wounds. This difficulty, from its very nature, swells with age. The more wounds, the more they give pain. Or maybe it is the other way around? Maybe one can become accustomed to pain? I, for example, have become accustomed. Or maybe I just think so?

30 January

Dąbrowska's spiritual torments are fascinating. Maybe they weren't experienced by her as torments, because references to them, or rather sentences that testify to them, appear without any clear linkages, strewn throughout a multi-volume work, separated from each other by many months, and sometimes even years. The anxiety: that the most important – the most joyful, the most exciting – is already behind her. The more they carried her in their arms yesterday, the more excitedly the eyes of boys and girls lit up when seeing her, the louder the applause in full-to-the-brim rooms for her readings, the more her needs grew, the higher the expectations were raised, the more brightly the eyes need to shine today and the more sonorously the applause to sound, for her to notice. Fame is a narcotic, one needs ever larger doses. And these doses bring less and less joy – there is a mere glimmer of comfort that this is not yet the end, that one can still experience ecstasy, that the game continues and there is still something to be won . . . Or the memories of those former times, when the drug had stronger effects, because there was not so much of it yet in the past and every dose was like the first – every one was a revelation.

It would seem that, as a stimulus, fame ought to run its course quickly; the more of it there is, the less it entertains. The colours fade; the high is shorter, shallower, sometimes it doesn't come at all. And a gradual bitterness gains the upper hand over delight; a bitterness that there is less of it than formerly – even if this 'less' was a delusion, even if it was about a slightly smaller increase, another example of the law of diminishing soil productivity? A gigantic effort is needed to produce the effect that once was achieved (or so it seemed) without even trying! But it is only the surfeit that is growing, not the effort . . .

So Dąbrowska – revered, cherished, covered in honours and drowning in human gratitude – complains every few pages that she is no longer able to do anything, that her writing is not going well, that she can no longer muster anything from herself. The complaints are sincere, the worry real – though only she can attest to its truth. Readers will not understand her pains. Each of her words that is directed to them carries the memories of all the previous ones said and written, each successive word is more capacious and ample than the previous one, until finally the words glimmer brightly before they are written, they sound out clearly before they are spoken: each of them is the word of *that Dąbrowska*, who herself, from her own words, from one word to the next, becomes more powerful, gigantic – who for years has already been this medium that itself is a message stronger than all other messages.

A writer – a mighty person?

31 January

I am pondering, what is the authority of the writer. In the grand scheme of things, it is a fiction. The writer has authority in a certain milieu only if he[33] accepts a priori all opinions of that milieu. If he differs in his opinions, he loses his authority in that milieu and gains it in the opposing group. It probably never happened that a writer who counted as an authority in a certain milieu changed an opinion of that milieu. He could only reinforce this opinion, support it with arguments. And here lies the powerlessness of the individual in the face of 'social bonds'. The only unquestionable source of authority is the so-called cleanliness of hands – individual honesty, both artistic and intellectual. But today, even this trait is not appreciated too highly.[34]

So a writer is not a mighty person,[35] but a bard, a courtier, a chronicler of ambiances? The soloist in a choral lilt? The producer of imaginative mirrors in which their face – but not quite their face, because free of pimples and blackheads and softer on the eye – will be present for readers, tender and grateful, to admire?

The idea of a writer's power emerges when other people – with clucks of approval and humble adulation – repeat the author's words. But they only repeat the words that they had already been seeking, so that their still naked and not-ready-to-be-revealed-on-the-streets feelings can be dressed in the robes sewn to size by the author. Without a tailor, not a chance – who would deny that the tailor is useful . . .? But the tailor only has as much renown as is provided by grateful clients. The tailor sews to measure, to measure! Or closes up shop.

You, tailor, can also stop bothering yourself with clients, measuring waists and hips. You can get yourself a fiddle, set up on a roof, grab the bow and drill the ears of passers-by – what good will it do them to avert their gaze? Romana Kolarzowa asks: 'What is an intellectual for?' And answers: 'Nothing, of course. Thinking is a great luxury, and thus a "superfluous" good, and, what is more, frequently utterly unnecessary.'[36] But how many tailors will feel comfortable on the roof? How many will agree to bear the discomfort? And those who agree – how long will they last, in the wind and the rain? To allow themselves such luxuries, first they need to earn enough to satisfy their basic needs, and they can only do that through their work as tailors. From screeches on the roof, one cannot live; from authority – and how!

At the bottom of all this lurks a banality: people hear what they want to. They yearn for confirmation, not conversion. They wander to an unfamiliar book with hopes similar to those that the British have when they set out for a vacation on the Costa Brava: that the waiter babbling in a foreign language will serve them familiar-smelling English sausages and a pint of English beer. This human quality explains why the idea of McDonald's turned out to be a golden goose. McDonald's is not selling hamburgers, but being at home, a good that is more expensive than all others, because it is desired more than any other. Satisfy that desire, and the customers will be hammering at the doors and windows. Assuring themselves that in every location the McDonald's sign is nearby, they gain the courage for travels to unknown countries. And when they travel, they will seek out the sign all the more readily. Every year multi-lingual crowds swap territories, each seeking McDonald's in the homeland of other crowds. Acknowledging authority confirms the fulfilment of hopes. It is not a particularly honourable order. But, admittedly, of a high exchange value: it brings increased print runs and tax breaks.

Dąbrowska knows about this.

But Dąbrowska suffers. And many like her, along with her.

Don't lie, and say that you're not suffering because you've understood. Saying so, even you are lying – you writers, who care about something more than print runs.

And so I have seen in Dąbrowska what I wanted to see.

7 February

I dive into the language, plunging, tumbling.[37]

2

Where I Came From

Of my family past, I know little. So little as to be ashamed, in our age of root-digging. Too little to extract from oblivion what had been forgotten, or never known. As for family documents, there are none left, because they were lost in successive exiles, and no trace of them remains. I need not spell out what I won't do with them. And so there will be no discoveries which came too late to matter or change anything. In the chains of kinship, many links melted and vanished, the distant rings which survived are scattered all over the globe – indifferent, untraceable, alien. For a Polish Jew like me, the family tree is redolent with odours of wood dust and burning, not life.

My knowledge about my parents is full of holes, and a skilled archivist would doubtless disqualify it. But that which invalidates knowledge does not discredit memory. Memory is always full and unbroken. My memory has no holes and no blank spots; neither does yours. It is only when we confront our memories that they seem incomplete. This would matter if I wished to retrace your life. It does not here, as the life I am about to retrace is mine. In this life of mine, I am the only resident. Only I can give an insider report. My memory of life had no holes. If there were any, they would not belong to my life anyway.

And so, I won't waste the time of the Missing Persons Bureaus. I won't hire private detectives. I won't hunt down the relatives I never met and never heard about, to rummage through their memories for the gems missing from my own collections. I won't hunt down actual or ostensible witnesses whose existence I was not aware of, counting on the possibility that, by consulting their memories, I would happen upon something that was lacking in my own – and that in such a way I could learn how things *really* happened; and this is because such a method of supplementing and correcting would lessen the force of the reckoning of *my* life: what I have *lived through*.[1] It would not tell the story of *my* life. If your memory has retained something that my memory sidestepped, this is part of your life, not mine.[2]

Why have I decided to write down my life story? I guess I have reached the age when life stories are written. I am already in this world longer than my mother ever was. Not much is left to level up with my father, who died at seventy. If there ever is a right time to sum up and give an account – it is now.

Or so people seem to feel, which amounts to the same. Living towards death makes life absurd. I suppose writing memoirs is an act of desperation. As a story, life makes sense; if the story is good, it may even show some logic.

Or perhaps I have decided to write for some other reason. Or perhaps there is no reason, only a need and a push. Frankly, I do not know. I do not think I care either.

How did my parents meet?

They never told me. And I did not ask . . . as far as I was concerned, they had been together forever, *since always.* And what was there before this always began for me? A triple Nobel Prize awaits the wise person who explains what caused the Big Bang, the prototype of any and all beginnings of eternity. I am not surprised that my father did not confide in me. He was a self-effacing, humourless, taciturn man. He never boasted and never complained. I suppose he did not respect himself enough to believe that his life was worth a story. He did not believe either that anything that happened to him could be interesting, even to his children – myself and my sister, seven years older than me. I do not remember my father ever reminiscing about his childhood or youth – well, I do not remember him reporting his feelings, joys or sorrows. I think his vocabulary lacked the words which other people use to share their emotions. I suppose his silence had one more, perhaps deeper, reason: dignity. My father thought that he got what he deserved, that he did not deserve anything else, and that to wish for something one did not deserve was undignified, if not blasphemous. And so he did not fret or grumble. Silence helped him to retain his dignity: life cannot humiliate a man who does not complain. Nothing is humiliating unless made into a grievance. For the record, my father did complain – once. During the last weeks of his life, I sat at his bedside in an Israeli kibbutz, where he settled after his wife died. One day, in no connection with anything we talked about before or anything which was to be said later, my father said: 'When I was in *kheder*,[3] I often cried. Our *melamed*[4] kept us in the school all day with a brief interruption for lunch. All the children brought their lunches with them. Other boys had their bread and dripping; but my father allowed me only dry bread. I cried with envy.' On his pale face, perhaps for the last time, a flush began to spread – and, if my memory is to be trusted, it was also for the first time. I cannot say whether it was my father's complaint about the cruelty of fate, or an acknowledgement, before death, of an ignoble sin.

My mother's silence about their first meeting did not conform with her character. She was everything my father was not: vivacious, exuberant, unable to contain the energy which kept spilling over in bouts of inexplicable gaiety and equally abstruse anger. Unlike my father, she felt life had hit her hard.

Her childhood dreams, which she was given to believe were legitimate expectations, failed to come true. Life proved to be anything but the cloudless, worry-free existence she grew up to expect as hers of right.

And the life she did have was filled with the endless misery of making ends meet and working to scrimp and scrape for shoes and decent clothing for the children. A daily struggle to make ends meet; days which did not differ from the days before and which she gradually stopped hoping would be different from the days to come; the dreary, monotonous rhythm of daily routine leaving no room for the unexpected, the unusual, the out-of-the-ordinary – nothing in her childhood prepared her for this kind of life. So she suffered, yet unlike father she suffered loudly and defiantly, all too often venting her grief on her husband (he worshipped her, seeing her as a magnificent – and in no way earned by his own virtues – gift from God, whose right to a fate better than his own he never doubted), which made him recoil still further into the protective fortress of silence. She did not surrender though; she refused to give up her faith that life could be different, if only . . . She kept re-stating her demands – claims without address, just colourful pictures of what life could be like were it not what it was. In her fantasy, she lived another, parallel life, immune to trials and hence uncontaminated by daily reality. This imaginary life was pithy, picturesque, romantic. Above all, it was open-ended, full of promise, pointing towards a tomorrow different from today. From the un-enticing life, her husband retreated into silence, she into day-dreaming. I suppose she would have mulled over a romantic adventure. So I gather that meeting her future hus-band was not one of those. I suspect it was not romantic, and it promised no adventure. She was 24 when she married; she must have felt slightly spinsterish at the time and so in a hurry to fulfil what others told her was her life's duty. In brief, she did not talk about her past, because what was there to remember? And why – to pick open an unhealed wound?

And so I do not know how my parents met. I regret now that I did not insist on an answer. Their meeting each other was, by all standards, a highly improbable event. I suspect the finger of a match-maker. Without an outside intervention, they would remain what they were: thoroughly un-matched.

My father's family lived in the part of Poland which, during the Partitions, went to Prussia, to be later inherited by the united Germany. My mother's family lived in the part of Poland appropriated by Russia. As World War I broke out, the advancing German troops shifted the boundary far to the east, thereby bringing the two homesteads under one state administration. What they did not do is to level up the social, the cultural and many other differences which kept the two families apart.

My father's father was a village shopkeeper – a smaller off-shoot of a family stem which on its other branches (so I heard) carried also some learned rabbis and renowned *zaddiks*.[5] He started his business in the small village of Zagórów, moving later to the minor regional centre of Słupca.[6] As far as I know, my father's father had no education apart from that provided by the *kheder*. When his wife died in the early 1930s, he wound up whatever remained of his business and came to spend the last years of his life with us in Poznań. I remember him as a tall man with a long beard, which would have been white if not for the yellowish stains of tobacco. He hardly spoke any Polish – or any other language for that matter, except Yiddish. Our communication was therefore limited. He insisted on teaching me the Bible, of which I had the vaguest of ideas. As I could neither read nor understand Hebrew, nor Aramaic, and his knowledge of Polish was confined to the few words one needs in a life spent mostly at a shop counter, the Bible remained a total mystery to me long after grandfather's religious instruction. I was afraid to open it – I associated it with the terrors of the *kheder* that my grandfather improvised for one dimwitted student in apartment 5 at 17 Prus Street. He refused to recognize the difference between Poznań and the *shtetl*[7] in which he spent his life. Every day, weather permitting, he strolled a few hundred yards to a small public garden next to Asnyk Plaza, where, sitting on a bench, smoking cigarette after cigarette (it was my daily task to roll 'medium' tobacco into cigarettes for him and my father), he surveyed the passers-by and children in the sandpit. The local antisemites were too shocked by the sight of a Jew in a *bekishe*[8] (a sight that the young people of Poznań knew only from newspaper cartoons, and the older people had aged sufficiently to forget) to remember their duty to jeer. In the practically Judenrein city[9] (in our neighbourhood, in Jeżyce, we were the only Jewish family), the fortress of violently antisemitic National Democracy,[10] which fought the demon of clandestine Jewish conspiracy, an old man blatantly putting his untidy, provincial Jewishness on display simply did not fit the picture of the enemy. And so my grandfather made his daily strolls undisturbed – which was much more than I was able to do.

Grudgingly, grandfather agreed to support secular education – but only of his youngest son. My father was not the youngest, and so, like most of his brothers, he had the village *melamed* for his only teacher. Yet all the sons – except for the eldest, who stayed with the father in his shop – rebelled and left home, one by one. One emigrated to America; another to Germany; the favoured youngest son – appropriately named Benjamin – to Palestine. My father's rebellion took another form and did not include changing places. He knew Polish quite well. Learning languages was his passion – as well as reading books, into which he sank at every free moment, and which he devoured without hoping to satisfy the hunger that grew with each subsequent reading. The combination of the two passions produced a curious knowledge of languages: in writing, but not spoken (partly influenced by my father's innate reticence and his reserved character, as well as the fact that he worked his way through all the languages on his own, substituting dictionaries for teachers). He mastered German and was fluent in Russian. He was quite competent in French and English (I repeat: he understood the texts he read; but at speaking, he was decidedly worse). He perfected his knowledge of Hebrew, though in its mothball-covered, biblical form.

Mastering Hebrew was an uncommon feat at a time when the language of the Bible was confined to religious ritual and, by most of the Yiddish speakers, seen as arcane magical incantation, the meaning of which one should not explore (Gershom Scholem, later to become the greatest Judaist scholar of the century, learned Hebrew at approximately the same time;[11] his friends, much more enlightened and open-minded than my father's company, considered that to be another manifestation of Sholem's arrogance). My father read avidly in all of these languages, but he fell in love with Judaism, once he discovered that there was more to it than the drab and uninspiring routine of perfunctory daily prayers and dietary rules.

Shortly before leaving Poland in 1957, my father worked for a few months for the Jewish Historical Institute in Warsaw as – what else? – an accountant. He hardly had time for his proper job, as the seasoned, learned scholars of the Institute pestered him with requests for his hermeneutical expertise. Later, in the kibbutz Givat Brenner, he delighted the local librarians with his Hebrew style – like him, they were living relics of the Diaspora dream of Hebrew renaissance. It was for him that, for the first time, they pulled down from the shelves volumes of poetry by Jehuda Halevi or Agnon, brushing off the dust of many years.[12] He also attempted to address his grandchildren. Bewildered and dumbfounded, they listened to the fluent flow of beautiful sounds and the harmonious melody of the grammar; they complained to their mother that 'grandad speaks like the Prophets' – the nightmares from their childhoods, whose prophecies they would struggle in vain to understand during their lessons from the Pentateuch.[13] They themselves had at their disposal only the few hundred words of the modern Sabra[14] with which to respond.

I think my father's Zionism – heartfelt, life-long and central to his world-vision – was part of his rebellion; it *was* his rebellion. I cannot be sure, but I imagine that his luminous, fragrant vision of Zion had been built of absences alone, such as the antithesis of the world into which he was thrown and which he experienced daily – and it remained so, in the final reckoning, to the very end. Zion was something which had no room for the drabness and filth of the *shtetl*, for greed and callousness, for penny-pinching or people made into treadmill horses. It meant some sort of a brotherhood and universal goodness, I presume, where working, creating and engaging in philosophical debates were the only joys people cared about. He did not find his Zion in Israel when he finally settled there. And this was the greatest, final failure in a life full of calamities.

My mother's father was an educated, worldly man with wide cultural interests. A builder by profession, he developed a prosperous building materials business in Włocławek, a middle-sized town well to the west of Warsaw. There were towns like this scattered over the huge territory of pre-Partition Poland: suspended over a vast peasant sea, isolated from other similar towns by dozens of miles of often impassable roads, and thus left most of the time to stew in their own juice. For the neighbouring villages and manor-houses, they practically played the role of a capital city, like Kalisz for the heroine of *Nights and Days*[15] – and, most certainly, that of the ultimate repository of culture and everything modern and progressive. Their residents looked down upon the 'villagers', and the 'villagers' rarely gazed up at the lofty heights where the people of Kalisz and Włocławek perched.

These provincial towns accommodated a disproportionate number of intelligentsia – of people with a broad education, on a par with that of intelligentsia from big cities, and most certainly with comparable ambitions – not to mention their sense of social calling. My father reminded me that if I was looking for God, I would find Him only in a small synagogue; I personally think that towns like Włocławek should be the first stage in the journey to uncover the ethos of the native intelligentsia. Claustrophobia exponentially multiplied the effect of condensation: the handful of Włocławians, in the same ways as the people of Płock or the residents of Siedlce, Krzemieniec or Kowel – all culture-hungry locals – had to construct the 'complete civilization' on the spot. The towns had thriving theatres, with all the novelties staged just a few months after the capital; cafés that were not to be browbeaten by the big city havens of leisurely philosophical rumination and hot political debates.

These people were high school teachers that the most renowned universities would have been delighted to hire as professors, if there were more ample funds for education. The provinciality of these towns expressed itself mostly in the dead seriousness with which culture and education were treated; and in the sheer volume of the local 'intelligentsia'. A great part of the latter was Jewish. Well – Polish-Jewish, to be sure, or, more specifically, Jewish by fate, but Polish by choice; Polish in content and form, though Jewish in background.[16]

The great assimilatory spurt of the late nineteenth century still reverberated in these towns at the time my mother was putting together her image of the world and of the purpose of human life. The line of progress from the *shtetl* led straight into Polish culture, and the Polish language was the main vehicle of the journey. The cultural and educational impact of these towns gained much of its impetus from the zeal and dedication of the avidly Polish newcomers from the Jewish ghetto.

Their love was all the more fervent and devoted, the less they could count on the reciprocal feelings of their beloved – born of the ruins of the Polish Nation, which many of its founders preferred to see as a Nation of Poles that did not need recruits from the assimilated, in the way that these had been needed by those advocating and fighting for Polish independence, to strengthen resistance against the denationalizing intentions and actions of invaders during the Partitions. The managers of the newly created nation, in agreement with the majority of its people – still unsure of their freedom – and a meaningful portion of the nation's intelligentsia, were inclined, however, to perceive in the actions and avowals of the devoted suitors the wicked intention of taking over the cultural heritage whose guardians they yearned to be recognized as. They were not pleased that the blossoming of Polish culture and education in hundreds of small towns of the Rzeczpospolita[17] owed much to the energy and devotion of exiles from Jewish ghettoes. The assimilated, as immortalized by Kafka in his allegory, were therefore similar to a galloping stallion that had only just freed its hind legs from the bog in which they were mired mere moments before, while the front hooves were still hanging in the air, searching in vain for purchase. In this snapshot, the steed was captured by Kafka in full flight – in utter futility . . .

My mother's father was one of these 'pioneers of progress', whose confidence in the progressive character of their skills and deeds was reinforced and multiplied by their belief in the progressiveness of their newly acquired Polishness. My mother received a strictly Polish education, much like her four sisters and the only brother; she had only as much Yiddish as one could not help but imbibe from the clatter of the Włocławek streets – just enough to tell her husband, later, the secrets she did not want her children to overhear. She was also brought up in an atmosphere of seemliness and decorum more akin to the pattern of Polish gentility than to the *shtetl* tradition. She was introduced to romantic novels, the art of conducting conversations in the salon style – elegant and sparkling with humour. She was taught to appreciate opera, theatre, classical music.

Yet the patriarchality of her father was strictly biblical. I met him only once, during his only visit to Poznań. I was too young to remember the details. What has remained in my memory was a wooden horse he brought me – but much more vivid, indeed overshadowing everything else, is the memory of long weeks of tense expectation and preparation for his arrival. Everything in our life was turned upside down: mother was suddenly inattentive; she was endlessly busy scrubbing and buffing up the floor, dusting, shining up glasses and polishing the silver; and, above all, she was terrified – a fear that I never saw before or after in situations far more threatening than a paternal inspection ... From my mother's behaviour, then, and a handful of fragments of other memories, I deduce that her father treated her with a 'cruel benevolence'. As if it was not a father coming to see his daughter, but a sinister Reviser; or Royalty, forgiving not the slightest deviation from the strict ceremony of submission and obedience. My mother's father infused his daughters with high expectations; at the same time, he kept them on a very short leash. It was a cruel benevolence, which envelops everything and brooks no dissent. The outcome was a lot of pent-up energy, unrelieved dreaming, and perhaps one or two broken lives. My mother's younger sister was forced into a marriage she deeply resented; immediately after grandfather's death, she divorced her unwanted husband and married the man she had loved since her teenage years. The other sisters accepted without murmur – or at least accepted – the husbands their father selected. They all married moderately successful and relatively well-off businessmen.

So did my mother. Or so, at least, it was hoped. As my father came from a respectable business family, he must have been assumed to be a good business prospect. My mother's dowry was to provide the take-off. The rest was to be up to him.

Perhaps no one took a closer look. So it went unnoticed, I suppose, that my father combined a rich spiritual life with an appalling dearth of practical sense and a revulsion towards hypocrisy. That man dreamed of being a scholar; they wanted him to be a merchant. Brilliance was mistaken for business acumen.

The ill-matched couple married, and moved to Poznań, at the enthusing moment of the city's return to Polish administration after more than 100 years of unbroken Prussian–German rule. When Poznań became a Polish city again, the residents were offered the right to opt for either Polish or German citizenship. Almost all the Poznań Jews – and practically all rich Poznań Jews – opted for Germany and left (only to be forced back through the Polish border 20 years later).[18] In Poznań, there remained just a few hundred families, counting between themselves no more than 2,000 souls. All of them were relatively poor, or just poor – mostly craftsmen and shopkeepers, some hawkers, a few *Luftmenschen*.[19] They all lived in the centre of the city, along a few streets occupied by the Jews since late medieval times. There was a sprinkling of educated men – mostly to exercise pastoral supervision over the community and to serve its religious needs.

My mother's life-long defiance of reality was to remain unabated through her life – yet it did not take much time to grow, either. From the start, it manifested itself in renting a flat in a residential area which avoided harbouring Jews through the centuries of the city's tormented history. It was a quiet, clean, bright, self-respecting and respectable district, with all the streets named after national or local luminaries of Polish culture, inhabited by professionals, civil servants, military men, gentlemen and gentlewomen – a few widows left by their illustrious husbands to glow with their past glory. Looking back, I gather that the only thing in our life which matched the aura of the district was my mother's ambition. Everything else about us must have seemed – and was – out of place. We belonged to the category of those who were looked down upon, with barely concealed contempt and mockery, by the intelligentsia and the descendants of nobility who together shaped the character of the neighbourhood. We were Jews, of course, among the people who for generations had struggled to keep their city Polish against successive waves of *Kulturkämpfe*.[20] We were also, for all practical intents and purposes, shopkeepers – members of the breed which offered the up-and-coming professional intelligentsia and the nostalgic scions of the once powerful squirearchy one of their few chances of spiritual unity: the shared experience of disdain and contempt.

At the same time as my mother's daydreaming, so did my father's life-long silent suffering start. He was idolatrously in love with her, ready in all things to defer to her, and to surrender everything that was precious to him for the sake of her happiness. I suppose the flat had been selected against his wish. He could not possibly enjoy the prospect of living 3 miles away from the nearest Jewish family, let alone a Jewish institution. There was little he could enjoy at the time, anyway, apart from his wife – by all accounts, and by the testimony of old photographs, a truly enticing woman with a very un-Jewish Slavic face, stately, with a beautifully curvy figure and bubbling temperament – and a daughter, to join them a little more than a year after the wedding. As to the rest, the discomfiting foreignness of the district must have been among the least of his worries. As a source of agony, it could not compete with what he was expected to dedicate his life to – by his parents, by his wife's parents, by his ethnicity, by the economic logic of the land, by fate. The mercer's shop he opened in the trading area of the city was his hell and his prison. There, his dreams burnt out, his hopes dried out – to be replaced by a gnawing feeling of personal inadequacy, of failing himself and the family. The shop became a place of humiliation and penitence. Not for long, though. Not all mercers in Poznań were unfulfilled scholars, and they on the whole fared better. Even before the start of the Great Depression, my father was declared bankrupt. The remaining stock was seized; all the furniture in our flat was stamped by the bailiffs to be auctioned on behalf of unpaid creditors.

My father put together every penny left from the debacle, took out some loans to top them up, and set off to Paris – not the first and not the last among the many who think that they can escape themselves by relocating. During his absence, we fed for several weeks on cabbage soup – courtesy of the janitor's wife, who kindly lent us a barrel of pickled cabbage from her own supply. After a while, a telegram arrived, and I heard my mother – until then, her normal, boisterous self – sobbing. I never read the telegram, but I know its content by heart. Cheated of all his money by the smart Parisian guys who pretended to rent him a shop while laughing up their sleeves at the sight of the unworldly, hapless sucker, my father asked my mother whether she still wanted him back.

This is my first, fully my own, vivid, unfading recollection – loud knocking on the door, and then the stretcher, and my father – unshaven, in a coat soaked through and dripping with dirty water, covered with weeds and slime.

Upon his return from Paris, and after a few days of pointless wandering around the offices of the better-off Jewish merchants, begging for a job, my father walked onto the beautiful, historic bridge spanning the river Warta and jumped off. But the unfortunate are not allowed to escape misfortune – whatever they try to do, even if it's suicide. A squad of boy-scouts passed by. They dived into the freezing water and fished my father out – against his will.

A cutting from the local press was kept among the family memorabilia (to be lost, like everything else, in 1939): 'A Jew attempted suicide. Saved by Polish scouts'. My father's misfortune had now become public knowledge and a public issue. The communal feelings of the local Jewry had been challenged. No sooner had my father recovered from the pneumonia he contracted in the wintery waters than he was offered the position of bookkeeper in the biggest Jewish wholesale business in town. My father moved to another prison. At least he was not now required to be his own warden.

For my mother, I was her only companion for most of the day, and perhaps the only promise that life could be still more interesting and enjoyable in the future. She did not invest much hope in my sister; my sister was a girl – the only thing a girl could look forward to was a good marriage, and finding one meant first and foremost not having to see her parents any more . . .

My mother's love for her daughter expressed itself therefore in a feverish search for a proper husband. It started in earnest very early – when my sister was barely 18 years old. My mother must have felt that the matter bore no delay, and it must have been given an unconditional priority. We were poor and my sister had no dowry. This could only mean that she would marry for love rather than reason, and that would mean in turn a life on a shoestring, a hand-to-mouth existence just like my mother's own. A loving mother would not wish her daughter a fate like that, and my mother did love her daughter.

And thus the price my sister paid for the modesty of our means was to be an early marriage, an arranged one – loveless if it could not be helped, but carrying material security if it could. I was a child then and not a reliable judge of female beauty, but I could sense that my sister was growing into a gorgeous girl with a slim, gently curved body and large burning eyes. She added exotic spice to our uniformly blond-haired and pale-faced district. Male friends started knocking at our door fairly early in her life, which only added urgency to my mother's feeling that something had to be done, and done fast, to lay my sister's future on secure foundations.

I was normally locked out during the long hours my mother and sister spent whispering to each other at the start of the campaign, and thus I cannot tell exactly how my mother went about her task. But for a while it consumed all her thoughts and all her energy. I was let in on one occasion only. I was allowed to join my mother and sister on a train ride to a place away from the town, some hundred miles south of Poznań,[21] to the big country estate of a member of an extremely rare breed: a Jewish landowner, a relict of a once more populous class of

Germanized Jews who settled on land during Prussian–German rule. In surroundings which, for us, implacable town-dwellers, looked like the nearest thing to a bucolic paradise, we found a fat, bald, ugly man in his late forties, a widower with children my sister's age, trying to impress upon us the grandeur of his possessions in a droning monologue delivered in a nondescript, bastardized Polish, heavily infused with German words which I at least could not understand. I remember my sister crying on the train all the way home. Well, I believe my mother did not love her as much as to force her into that marriage.

After this visit, Tosia rebelled and refused to cooperate in any further matchmaking efforts. She wanted (and this was by no means a desire that was widespread among women of the time) to learn a trade and take control over her own life. She also successfully finished gardening school – but her chances of getting hired in this line of work were close to non-existent.[22] She knew that she could not be supported financially by her parents for long; money was hardly flowing already and, to make matters worse, her little brother was setting off for high school and, if he got in, the meagre family finances would be further strained by the need for uniforms, school supplies and the massive – in relation to the family budget – tuition costs.

As it happened, my mother's worries were solved and my sister's fate sealed purely by accident. In 1938, a big national exhibition was held in Poznań. The City fathers went out of their way to advertise the event throughout Europe and to replenish the empty city coffers with the money from foreign tourists this event could attract – the 1930s were the years of the exhibitions, and visiting them was a favourite pastime for young, wealthy idlers who were only too eager to accept that 'travel broadens the mind'. Among the guests visiting the Poznań exhibition was a youngish scion of an old Sephardic clan settled for centuries in Jerusalem. As a good Jew, he first called at the Board of the local Jewish community. The

Secretary of the Board, a distant relative of my mother, advised him to rent a room in our flat – we lived close to the exhibition site, and my mother bulked up the household budget by letting a room to students; the exhibition was held in the summer months when students were away. The guest from Jerusalem duly arrived, and duly fell in love with my sister.

And so my sister, as Polish as they come, never giving a thought to the land of the Forefathers, found herself married into Palestine. I guess the sudden turn of events warmed my father's heart: here, at last, a foothold was to be established in the country of his dreams. My mother was surely happy: someone who could afford to gad about Europe with no clear purpose could be relied upon to provide her daughter with all those comforts she herself badly missed. To my sister, the visitor must have seemed an Angel-saviour shielding her from all those yet unknown fat, bald and ugly widowers eager to buy her charms at a good price. For the newcomer – love at first sight. For Tosia – the chance to get out of her parents' hair. For mother – the feeling of a successfully fulfilled mother's responsibility. And, finally, for my father – a foot in the door of the dreamed-of Zion. A few weeks later, my sister disappeared from my life. But not for long.

The wedding, and an exit visa to Palestine, came with lightning speed – but right afterwards, matters took a turn that neither the newly wedded bride, nor her family, had anticipated. The clan that had been residing for many years in the Holy Land turned out to be a centuries-old relic, in which women were kept behind walls under the watchful eye of the Clan mother and released only at the summons of their spouse for the purposes of engaging in another round of marital obligations. Camps and *lagers* were still an unknown phenomenon, and this is probably the only reason why Tosia did not associate her vegetation in this new locale, behind the walls of the women's ghetto, with one or the other. Call it what you will, but she suffered horribly. Except that, as the natural-born daughter of her mother, she was not willing to suffer in silence. She rebelled, fought with both her husband and the Clan mother, who was infuriated by this unheard-of rebelliousness and, in blatant disregard of these harsh strictures, Tosia escaped beyond the walls of the *Frauenzimmer*[23] whenever she wanted. When rebukes and ever harsher punishments failed, and hopes of the conversion or repentance of the sinner proved futile, she was acknowledged as the disgrace of the ancestral line, which marked the prisoner with the shameful status of a dissenter or black sheep, and increased the severity of the regime she was subjected to. The 19-year-old girl would not give up. She was seized by a plan: perhaps she could convince her husband to visit Poznań, tempting him with a sizeable sum of money that her parents planned to bestow upon him upon the birth of their first granddaughter? And once they found themselves in Poznań, no power on heaven or earth could force her to leave again. The gamble on her husband's avarice proved effective, the plan succeeded. Near the end of August 1939, Tosia's dream – dreamed against, and in spite of, everyone – came true: she returned to her home-city and family house.

Weeks of horror began – a different one from what she had escaped. Having realized that he had been cruelly tricked, that the munificent dowry was only in the young woman's imagination and was invented to lure him into the trap of an expensive and futile trip that was crowned with the loss of a wife and daughter, Tosia's husband was seized with a fit of madness that had been previously known in Poznań only in medieval lore and stories about exotic ancestral vendettas. The house shook with yells and the thumps of improvised projectiles. Tosia was covered in bruises; father (in despair, but also of course without success, searched throughout the city for a loan to pay off and appease the enraged man) and mother (condemned to staying in the house) were afraid for their daughter and for their own lives. Everyone was saved by another chance event: the date

that Hitler set for the invasion of Poland came two weeks after
Tosia's return to Poznań.

Now we must go thirteen years back in time.

Business debts were already mounting up, the prospects did
not look bright at all, and my mother did everything she could
to get rid of her unwanted pregnancy. At the time, however,
one could not do much, and the supply of new members to the
human race looked much more like the will of God than an
exercise in mother's freedom.

Homeric efforts to end the unwanted pregnancy have been
enshrined in family legend – but to the end of her life, even on
her deathbed in 1956, struggling against the complications of
many years of severe diabetes, my mother assured me fervently
that the failure of her efforts made her happy. I bet many other
mothers would be similarly happy, were they not prevented
from finding out by the much improved technology.

Once the available technology proved inadequate and I was
born, both my parents seemed to have been overwhelmed
with joy, which filled my sister, almost seven years older,
with despair. She rightly sensed a dangerous competitor in
someone who was both male and a younger (in all probability,
the youngest) child. She could not relish sharing the formerly
undivided attention of our parents. As it turned out, her worst
premonitions came true. The attention remained undivided,
only it now turned the other way. This remains one of those
guilts I will never be able to expiate. Through my childhood, I
swam in warm parental love. It kept the cold outside. Come to
think of it, there were all sorts of reasons to feel cold.

To start with, I was fat. I entered the world outside in a
shape which makes one an outcast at a distance, and which
renders what one does irrelevant by comparison with what
one is. Or, rather, a shape which makes the 'is' so blatantly
evident that the 'does' can attempt little, and accomplish still
less. Among my friends, I had a role I did not need to seek for

myself and fight for. My bad luck if I did not like it. It was going to take a big effort to be seen as something other than what I already was: 'the fat boy'.

My fat was made of love. My mother loved me dearly and naturally wanted there to be more of me. My mother was an exquisite cook. Her products were not exactly *cordon bleu* – she would have needed much richer resources at her disposal to let her culinary imagination roam free. In the absence of such resources, her culinary art expressed itself in asking the basest of foodstuff to taste delicious, or a slice of meat to fill the stomachs of four earnest eaters. There are two ways of making excellent food: one can buy dainty and expensive ingredients, or one can spend a lot of time in the kitchen. Having little money but rather too much otherwise unengaged time, my mother had grown into the mistress supreme of the second method. This stood her in good stead later, when society as a whole found itself in her situation – in wartime Russia or in post-war Poland: her cooking talents were much sought after and she made a quite brilliant career as a cooking instructor and manager, an acknowledged expert on shoe-string cookery. Before that happened, however, my fat was the only tangible testimony to her art. My mother spent most of the day in the kitchen, with me sitting at the kitchen table – drawing, reading, making noise or just moping. I was employed as the food taster, and asked to pass judgement on the quality of dishes as they emerged from the spellbinding liturgy of creation.

In the successive stages of many-hours-long culinary mysteries, I served my mother as an *adjutant gourmand*, which, in combination with the extreme infrequency of my leaving the house (my one possibility for a place to go was the sandbox on Asnyk Plaza, which my mother took me to every few days) and my not being engaged in any sports, disqualified me even more in the eyes of my peers and potential friends: it added the shame of obesity to the shame of my birth.

I was also Jewish. Being a Jew set me apart as much as my fatness did. In fact, more than my fatness. In the first twelve years
of my life, I saw quite a few other fat boys (fat boys fish each
other out unerringly from any crowd, however dense – much
as pregnant women do), but I hardly met another Jewish boy.
Jewishness was to me almost a family matter – other members
of the family were the only Jews I saw and knew about. This
made my Jewishness a practical issue, rather than a theoretical
one. What made it more practical still was the world outside
the family. Seldom did I hear other boys passed by in the street
making comments on my fatness; yet very few of them failed to
notify me that they duly noted my Jewishness.

By Polish standards, Poznań was a truly exceptional city. It
managed to combine a virtual absence of Jews with the most
vituperative antisemitic sentiments. Unbridled by any practi-
calities of cohabitation, local antisemites could focus fully on
their own refinement; they reached theoretical subtlety and
religious fervour only the totally otherworldly, millenarian
faith is able to achieve. Poznań became the driving force and
the fortress of National Democracy – a party which sought to
captivate the hearts and mind of the rest of the country with
the enchanting vision of a Jew-free life. The sophistication of
the theoretical blueprints benefitted enormously from the lack
of opportunity for their practical application.

Well, I was such an opportunity – one of the very, very few,
and hence particularly precious. I guess for the antisemites in
my part of the town, I must have been a godsent gift; they probably told each other that, were I not there, I would need to have
been invented. They seemed to compete between themselves
for the hunting privilege. I was too rare a prey to be shared
with others. The gangs which currently gained the upper hand
in the competition served a double role as my hunters and my
protectors – against the poaching schemes of the rival gangs.
The top gang would study my living habits, await patiently my
appearance on the street, and then follow me all the way up

to school, to the shop, to the library and back home, drawling precisely targeted terms of abuse or shouting a cruder one, occasionally slapping, kicking or stone-throwing. To be fair, they never went over the top. They were not just hunters, but reasonable gamekeepers as well. When two gangs secured their monopoly for somewhat longer stretches of time, our relations grew truly personal. We greeted each other with something akin to joy: a foretaste of the all-too-familiar ritual, in which all the actors know their roles by heart, which cannot go wrong and which will in the end confirm once more that the world is an orderly, and by and large secure, place to be.

For some reason, I do not remember that experience with horror. Dwarfed by what I learned later, the drama of my childhood looks more like something grotesque. A cottage-industry kind of antisemitism, so to speak. Inept, amateurish and ineffective. A superfluous pastime, leisurely – on occasion, good-humoured. Since that time, I have seen many other ritualized hatreds. Many other people cast in roles not of their moulding. Trained and drilled to discharge the poisonous alluvia of a hard life against targets not of their selection. Most of the rituals of hatred I witnessed were much more sinister than my childhood experience.

The most traumatic of encounters with my appointed persecutors bore heavily on the rest of my childhood, tearing apart once and for all the veil of false security. My mother, having done her shopping, came once to collect me from school. The current holders of the hunting privilege – two unemployed teenagers, one tall, slightly stooping, with the listless, shifty gait of a thief, the other thickly set, with the low skull of a sub-standard ape – were at their usual post. The four of us took the road home together. The couple kept, this time, a few steps behind, but otherwise their demeanour was unaffected by my mother's presence. They duly went through their by then traditional motions, and produced, in the predictable order, all their by then familiar sounds.

I looked at my mother: she kept me closer, but pulled her head between her shoulders, fixed her eyes on the cobblestones, studiously avoided looking back at our escort. It suddenly dawned upon me: my mother, the all-powerful and all-knowing, had no power to defend me, did not know what to do! She was humiliated, and she was afraid! From then on, and for many years to come, I lived in fear.

My parents did not normally go out in the evenings, but occasionally my father had to stay out longer at work or at meetings he sometimes attended. In a few cases, he missed the last tram and, unable to afford a taxi, walked all the way home on foot. With my trust in my parents' omnipotence crushed, I could not fall asleep when he was away. I remember standing in my nightclothes at the window for hours on end, peering into the dark and silent street beneath, waiting with bated breath for the familiar sound of my father's heels around the corner. I remember sobs of relief bursting out of my clenched throat once I heard the sound. I remember tiptoeing back to my bed and wrapping myself tight in the soft warmth of my repossessed happiness.

In the years immediately preceding the war, antisemitism grew more venomous, and more and more sought practical outlets. The death of Piłsudski,[24] who never allowed antisemitism to run out of control, and who was powerful enough to keep it in check; a continuously deteriorating economic situation in a country with a chronically overpopulated peasant countryside and industry much too weak to absorb rural poverty; Nazism triumphant on the other side of the border – at one and the same time, a trendsetting example and a gathering cloud over the insecure freedom of the country; all these and perhaps many other factors added urgency to anti-Jewish demands. With the government still stiffly opposed to the adoption of violent methods, but presiding over an economic boycott of the Jews and preaching massive emigration of the Jews from Poland, the mushrooming antisemitic movements grew both confident and impatient. We read of the mounting physical violence – of the beatings of Jewish students in the universities; of mini-pogroms in a rising number of rural areas and in small provincial towns; of self-styled fascist troopers marching through the Jewish *shtetls* while watched, rather apathetically, by the police, who were not particularly eager to be involved. One day, a couple of craftsmen appeared in our flat; my mother called them to fix two heavy iron crossbars at the front door. From that day on, our flat was to be barricaded each night – not against thieves (there was little they could steal from our home), but against the hoodlums heard to descend on Jewish homes just to frighten their inhabitants out of their wits and thus encourage them to leave. From that day on, I also developed an obsession. I could not go to bed without first opening the front door and sneaking silently outside to make sure that no bandits were keeping vigil on the staircase. Yet even this effort to allay my fears was not enough to ward off nightmares.

I was also poor. That is, my parents were. We did not live in poverty. Not by comparison with the abject misery and squalor a few blocks down, where shoddy workshops waited in vain for a stray customer and the children of unemployed workers and rural migrants churned the mud of unpaved roads with their bare feet. I do not remember being hungry – even during the memorable 'cabbage weeks'. And yet our life was a continuous struggle for survival, with my mother fighting desperately to make ends meet, with cash always short in the second half of every month, with even the simplest luxury strictly out of bounds, and everything but bare necessities being a luxury. After my father's bankruptcy, my parents stopped going out altogether, or receiving guests. Something had to be given up – and everything serving my parents' enjoyment was the first to go. I remember my father travelling each day several miles on the tram for lunch. He ate his meal sitting alone at the table, then saying 'Also' ('so be it' in German), crossing his arms on the table, laying his head on his right arm, and immediately starting to snore. After a fifteen-minute nap, he rose and left, to return at eight in the evening. Then he had a couple of sandwiches and went to bed. At nine, our family was asleep. And so it was, day by day, year by year. The father bore his cross without murmur. I guess he was happy that he could support his family after all. He felt guilty that survival was the only thing he could offer, and so he saw his life as an attempt to expiate this guilt. His colourless, insipid, joyless existence seemed to him an obvious part of the expiation. With my mother, it was different. She would not give up her dreams easily. Daily engrossed in her household magic – conjuring up nourishing meals out of means which a less frugal or prudent housewife would hardly consider sufficient for a snack – she still sometimes surrendered to temptation and took my sister, and soon myself as well, to the cinema round the corner. From her childhood, my sister certainly remembered better times. Myself, I did not know of any other life. Hence, I did not have dreams and did not suffer. I considered it natural that books and shoes and socks were things one gets as birthday presents. I do not remember having toys – books, which for many years were my only friends, I borrowed from a library a few blocks away.

And I read. A lot, and eagerly, though our house was not piled with books, nor with any other treats. I learned to read, so I am told, somewhere between the ages of 4 and 5, and almost entirely through my own efforts, without encouragement or reminders. I read whatever crossed my path – mainly newspapers, *IKC*[25] every day, and, once a week, *Nasz Przegląd*[26] (with a special supplement for children edited by Janusz Korczak,[27] which I devoured from cover to cover). For the purchase of 'literature for children and young people', there was not a penny to spare. For Karl May, Jack London and James Fenimore Cooper, the time came later, when (in my schooldays) I joined the nearby library of the Towarzystwo Czytelni Ludowych.

This 'Association for Popular Reading' was a non-profit organ-ization aimed at making books accessible to people who could not afford to buy them. It maintained a network of libraries, where one could borrow regularly for a nominal monthly pay-ment (equivalent to the price of two eggs). The Librarian of the local branch (a taciturn, spinsterish, constantly blushing and evidently book-loving girl) seemed to value highly my keen custom, and sent my way the best she had in her rather modest collection.

But before that, for my bedtime stories, father would read me Sven Hedin's blood-chilling accounts of his polar escapades (chilling mainly, though not only, because of the endless snow-drifts and icebergs they described). In this way, he instilled in me my persistent – still unsatisfied today – drive towards everything that is 'at the top of the map', maybe because the Arctic explorer and landscape were associated with the only moments of bonding with father – far rarer than I would have wanted . . . When the gates of the library's Sesame opened to me, I threw myself into everything that glittered with snow and glistened with frost, and which emanated the warmth of humans clinging to each other – a warmth that in the Arctic aura appeared to glow brighter and warm more gently than in the temperate climate of Greater Poland. Aside from Jack London, I devoured anything by Andersen and Selma Lagerloef I could get my hands on, and, eluding the watchfulness of the Librarian, a devoted protector of children's virtue, I was even able to share the experience of the protagonist of Hamsun's *Hunger*, Pontoppidan's 'The Royal Guest'[28] and Ibsen's *Peer Gynt*.

I suppose my love of reading led my father to relive his hopes again, vicariously, through me; I was to become all that he dreamed of being but was not. Thirty years later, he would die in a distant kibbutz serenely, at peace with his life at last: under his pillow, my first book would be found – a gift he received two days before.

I also read during the breaks between classes at the public school on Słowacki Street – a few hundred yards down the road. I was the only Jew, and one of the very few fat boys. My exceptional status was therefore blatantly evident and never in dispute, which rendered my situation secure and, in a curious way, pleasurable. To my schoolmates, I was 'our own Jew' and 'our own fatty', which gave them duties along with rights. Except for an occasional gratuitous sneer or pinch, they tolerated my presence with good grace; often I felt they were pleased I was there, and would miss me if I were not. I did not feel victimized, or even singled out for special treatment. Most of the teachers seemed to like me and value my good progress; they often asked me to coach weaker pupils, which I did gladly.

Aware of the dangers threatening me in the playground, our teachers allowed me (actually, recommended to me – and, more accurately, ordered me) to remain in the classroom during breaks.

It was worst in the early years, when I was small, and of an inferior type: clumsy, unable to run, jump or play ball, and not adept at interacting with peers, forming friendships or fending off attacks (or at least keeping my distance from malice and avoiding trouble). I was an unparalleled candidate for the role of school wimp, an object of torment for the risk-free frolics of the older boys looking to blow off steam – boys against whom the gradually growing group of friendly classmates, all of them just as small as me, could not stand a chance. My tormentors dominated over the scrawny snot-noses in the lower grades thanks to the size of their biceps and the self-confidence (read: impunity) they derived from them. They were far more gifted than we were in inflicting pain and concocting ever new and creative ways to produce it. With time, however, my situation improved. The most threatening of the schoolyard demons left school, one after another, and my friends and I were gradually transformed into the 'older', and finally the 'oldest', students in the school. This was an entirely different situation from that of earlier years, when I was, for school veterans, a newly discovered object of amusement and opportunity for release – all the more appealing for being, until recently, rarely encountered, and too fresh for the promised delights to become commonplace and lose their appeal.

I had quite a few good colleagues, and yet very few friends. The way my mates spent their free time was off limits for me. I could not roam nearby woods, stroll in the parks. I did not ride a bike, I did not swim, I did not go skating. Playing ball was out of the question – because no team would accept me as a member. Most social facilities for the young were run by the Catholic Church and I would not be welcomed there either. So, where could I play? On the street? The street was full of dangers . . . A few boys from neighbouring houses seemed to have agreed among themselves to seize every opportunity offered by the neighbourhood's only 'kike'[29] to unleash their tongues or make use of their muscles. This kike was fat, ungainly and certainly unable to put up any kind of fight. I did not make all that many friends in school, but the ones I did make were characterized by a rare loyalty; our friendship went through many difficult trials and outlasted the most difficult of them – war, occupation, Holocaust – and General Moczar.[30] Today, unfortunately, due to the cruel injustice of fate, I am the only one of us still alive. A few weeks ago, I mourned the loss of Edmund Melosik, the last of my school friends.[31]

The few friends I did have were all 'special cases' like myself. One was a frail, physically (though not mentally) retarded boy, who was too shy and frightened to join the outdoor games and preferred the kind of life I had to bear. We met in his or my flat to read, play or do our homework together. Another was a highly intelligent son of a captain serving in the nearby regiment. A professional soldier, yet a superbly educated man, his father was fastidiously choosy in selecting his son's friends; he virtually goaded me into befriending his son. He carefully scrutinized all other classmates and picked me out as the only one likely to sustain his son's interests in literature and history, which he wished to cultivate. My third – and, as far as I remember, the last – friend was the very handsome son of a widowed mother, who moved in the middle of the 1930s into a flat in a house next to ours. I suppose this was a mutual 'friendship at first sight'. We shared a love for books; we liked to talk about them, and to try our own pens and discuss the inept results of our efforts. This was the only friend from my childhood years whom I met again, albeit briefly, after the war. He was then one of the most promising young poets of the new, communist, Poland.

I completed my elementary education in 1938. My parents could ill afford the high fees of a gymnasium (the secondary school in the Polish education system), but there was not a moment of doubt that they would make whatever sacrifice was necessary to see me through. So the true problem was to get admitted. And this was indeed a problem. All but one of the state gymnasia in Poznań practised *numerus nullus* – complete exclusion of Jewish children. The Berger State Gymnasium was the only secondary school which settled for *numerus clausus* – restricting the number of Jewish pupils so that it would not exceed the percentage of Jews in the total population of the area. In the context of Poznań, this meant less than 1 per cent. I graduated from my primary school with excellent marks, but the chances of admission were still very slim indeed. The anxiety about the outcome of the entrance examinations came on top of my sister's whirlwind romance, marriage and abrupt departure. It was a long, hot and consequential summer.

First came written exams in Polish literature and in mathematics. The candidates reaching the top marks in both were to be admitted; the rest had to take competitive oral examinations. I attended both written examinations. A week later, my turn at the orals had arrived. The Director of the Gymnasium, with the written exams in front of him, sat on the podium;

I was invited to sit on a bench next to the professor (this is how the gymnasia's teachers were titled) conducting the orals. I was out of my wits with fear, shaking all over and hardly aware of what was going on around me. The examiner was coolly cordial, yet did not seem to care much about my mental state (as my older classmates did not fail to inform me shortly thereafter, he was the cruellest and most merciless attacker of the 'Jewish element' among the teaching staff).

The question was simple: 'Describe your daily journey to school'. Having expected a profound debate about the subtleties of one of the gems of Polish literature or the intricacies of the convoluted Polish history – something more akin to my lofty image of that temple of wisdom I hoped the gymnasium to be – I sat aghast, trying hard to reassemble my shattered thoughts. My first sentence was disastrous: by a slip of the tongue, instead of saying 'I live in a house on a street corner', I said 'I live in a corner street.' I saw with horror a smile crawling all over my tormentor's face. He was clearly relieved – 'it was easy to get rid of this one'. In a moment, he will send me home. Before he had time to do that, however, the Director spoke: 'Excuse me, Sir, this boy needs no orals. Both written exams were excellent, he has already been admitted.' The Director's words, the examiner's suddenly sour and disappointed face, the deafening sounding of my heart, the tears of my mother who waited, half alive, outside – all melted into the experience of an excruciating happiness: the happiest memory of my childhood years. My first achievement – by my efforts alone, and against overwhelming, indomitable odds.

A few weeks later, the great day came. Proudly donning my Berger Gymnasium cap, that visible and indisputable pass into the ranks of the glorious Polish intelligentsia, I arrived at the door of the first form. I had no time to cross it before I was submerged in an avalanche of kicks and punches. Pushed and pulled from all sides, I lost control over my legs and found myself moving – moved, rather – towards the distant left rear corner of the room. Someone's arms thrust me finally on the last bench. 'Here is your place, Jew! And don't you dare look elsewhere.'

It took me a few minutes to come round – all the more so as the din in the classroom continued unabated. Only when I recovered my senses did I notice that I was not to be alone in the ghetto to which I had been assigned. From the whirling cloud of angry and contemptuous faces, twisted bodies, flying fists, some other limp figures emerged, dumped one by one on the benches near me. When the entry of the form-master restored calm, I looked around. There were four more pale faces around me. Four other boys looked furtively at each other. Four pairs of eyes filled with tears of shame, trying not to look in the eyes of the others who witnessed their humiliation.

And so now, for the first time in my school career, I was not alone; I was to share my fate with others. There were five of us – the Jews who wished to be Poles; the Jews who arrogantly behaved as if they were Poles. Who, like all the others in the classroom – but evidently without the rights the others had – wanted to make their own the magnificent tradition of Polish language, history, culture. For the first time, such a will and the ensuing determination ceased to be my personal oddity. I belonged now to a group, to a category, which could be classified and branded and summarily treated.

In that classroom, there were five of us (or so the rest of the class decided). One of the five was to perish in the Holocaust; one lives in Warsaw to this very day. The remaining three, myself included, left their country. At least, bodily they did.

Three of us, as I soon learned, had failed their exams a year before and were left in the first form for the second year. Thus, only two had been admitted to Berger Gymnasium in 1938. And since the Berger Gymnasium was the only one in the whole city which did not practise *numerus nullus*, only two Jewish boys had been allowed into secondary education that year in the whole of Poznań. That year, the roads leading from the ghetto to Treblinka had not yet been built – and no one, neither the kickers nor the kicked, had any idea that those roads had already been planned out, and that construction had actually begun – though there was also a wall of sorts around this ghetto of school-benches. Built, for now, from hateful looks, mockery and insults, a leg stuck out to trip someone up, and left or right hooks. A home-spun style, dating back to the pre-industrial era, improvised – but no less airtight for all that.

As far as I am aware, not one of our teachers objected to our forceful confinement to a ghetto. Some took care to manifest their approval by selecting the residents of the ghetto for special treatment. The teacher of Polish literature,[32] for example, having posited in front of the class a particularly beguiling question, would begin by addressing, one by one, the ghetto dwellers; he would do it, like the judges in beauty contests, 'in the reverse order' of assumed ability to answer, to make sure that the ignorance of the Jews was duly exposed. I am pleased to report that I was the last of the Jews so to be called, and that the raillery normally ended there – for the lack of more Jews, of course, but also for the fact that the thesis of the collective inability of the Jewish race to fathom Polish literary lore had been seriously undermined.

A similar tactic was deployed by the teacher of mathematics – though what axe a maths teacher could grind in such a way was less immediately obvious. The teacher of geography made it publicly known that knowledge possessed by the Jews must have been obtained in a not entirely honest way, and thus took care to mark it lower than a similar knowledge revealed by non-Jewish pupils. I found it impossible to repent the only mistake I made in the year-long study of geography (wrongly naming the minerals of which one of the Polish mountain ranges was built) and ended the year with a barely 'satisfactory' mark in the subject.

After many years, I was to learn that Jasia[33] had identical experiences. Her Polish teacher took her aside after grades were given and explained: 'Of course you understand, Jasia, I could not give you a different grade, because it is unheard of for a Jew to receive a 5 (the Warsaw equivalent of Poznań's 1)[34] in the Polish class.'

Also after many years, now with Jasia, I experienced, together with Władysław Kowalski (him under the lights on the stage of the Ateneum Theatre, as Andri in Max Frisch's play *Andorra*; me in the darkness, in the audience), the tragedy of the apprentice in love with carpentry, whose master failed him in the exam not because the chair he made was worse than those made by others, but because 'Jews are made only to be merchants', and because *'Das ist's, was deinesgleichen im Blut hat . . . du kannst Geld verdienen'* ('Those like you have it in your blood . . . all you can do is make money'), and therefore they are incapable of making a proper chair . . . They are unable to be able . . . And because Arni went up against the laws of creation, and dared, with the impudence proper to his kind, to take the journeyman's exam, the Doctor in the play could attest, with disgust: *'Ich kenne den Jud . . . das Schlimme am Jud ist sein Ehrgeiz'* ('I know about Jews . . . the worst thing about them is their ambition').

The Doctor was not alone in his assessments; they were shared by people more enlightened than he – even if, like the great Maria Dąbrowska, they recognized that their consciences were not entirely clear as a result. Within the walls of the Berger Gymnasium, and long before Jasia and I went to the Ateneum – and long, long before I began to read the confessions of Maria Dąbrowska – it came to me, slowly but inexorably, that I was destined to be (but probably also chose, inspired by this destiny), and would likely remain, one of those who are 'not entirely one of them', who are condemned to 'irritate people' . . . And that I was condemned to irritate 'people' not necessarily because there were more 'creative and free thoughts' bubbling within me than in them, nor because I was 'braver' than they, but precisely because I was 'not entirely one of them'. Because (similarly to the son of the landowner in Tadeusz Kotarbiński's *Joyful Sorrows*, who, despite all of his virtues – inherited and acquired – and his most upright devotion to the cause of socialism and honest intentions towards it, could not stop being the descendant of a landowner) I could not stop being a Jew. And because I could not, my only remaining option was to embrace the gloomy prediction of Tuwim's hunchback: that, even if he had hanged himself with the most beautiful of cravats, no one would say 'what a beautiful cravat!' – everyone would declare, 'what a disgusting hunchback'.

Snot-nosed Zygmunt was informed that, in order to receive the same grade as the *others*, he had to work much harder than those others did. And that if he did exactly that, it would be perceived as arrogance, overzealousness, obtrusiveness, and thus as a reason to withhold recognition, consideration. Heads – '*theirs*', irritated by me, won; tails – '*ours*', irritated them, lost.

The labels of 'us' and 'them' were probably introduced into human language as part of the punishment handed down by God to the sinful know-it-alls at the construction site of the Tower of Babel.

However, some other teachers studiously disavowed the invisible ghetto walls. One or two – the teacher of history, in particular – seemed to be ashamed to teach in a classroom so divided. The gradation of teachers' attitudes was roughly replicated among the pupils. No one, however, either among the teachers or among our non-Jewish classmates, tried to defy the 'facts of life'. The division was solid and permanent, as those who wished it to remain so acted, while those who did not like it just watched.

Being now a member of a group, of a category, sharing my predicament with others in a 'preordained' way neither they nor I could challenge, changed my life in a most radical fashion. Suddenly, I stopped being a solitary case, a person left to

my own devices and able to rely on no one but myself. There
was now a curious thing called 'common interest', or another
called 'joint defence'. I remember that at first I found thinking
in these terms rather hard, but that soon I got the taste for it
and even came to enjoy it. The most profound change, however,
was to find myself surrounded by secure – because 'appointed'
– friends: ones who could not stop being my friends, who had
no choice but to remain friends, much as I could not stop being
theirs. Our respective destinies were, so to speak, tied together,
for better or worse. It did not even matter if we liked or disliked
each other. We were in it together *ex officio*. What held us
together was not painstakingly constructed out of feelings and
sympathies; rather, it preceded all emotion. This made it solid
in a way I did not know of before. But also, perhaps, somewhat
less human.

Little did I know what was yet to follow. It came in the
inauspicious shape of one of my new 'appointed' friends. In
passing, he asked me whether I would be interested in joining
him at a get-together he attended on two afternoons every
week. I was interested – I had never attended a get-together
before, on mornings, afternoons, or at any other time. The one
I did attend, at my friend's invitation, was held in a derelict,
shoddy room in one of the buildings quietly living out their old
age in the few streets left of the old Jewish quarter. Inside that
room, I found several boys and girls of more or less my age.
Together, they constituted the Poznań branch of *Hashomer
Hatzair*.[35]

The rest was a maelstrom. I was now in a group which
accepted me for a reason other than its inability to get rid of
me. The other boys and girls were not 'special cases' like me;
myself, I was not a special case any more. We talked, we quar-
relled, we danced, we fought, we behaved in a way I thought
was reserved only for normal people, of which I evidently was
not one. Inside these flaking walls, I was all I could not be
outside. I ate the forbidden fruit of the tree of freedom, and it

dawned upon me that life could be different from how it was –
not just on two afternoons every week. Suddenly, the world did
not look unshakeable and preordained. Neither did the choice
seem to be, as before, 'take it or leave it'. I felt I would not take
it any more. And I did not intend to leave it.

The world I wished to put in place of the existing one was
conceived after the pattern of the *Hashomer Hatzair* branch.
Looking back, I think it was the life we practised, rather than
the life we fantasized about, which sedimented in the lasting
image of a just world which, from then on and up to this day, I
was to dream of, run after, delude myself I would find.

This alluring world was given the name of Zion, yet I do not
believe that the name referred to any particular geographically
defined place. As far as I was concerned, Zion was located in
the Winiary woods,[36] where, for the first time in my life, I had
my own share of May Day delights in the secure company of my
new friends. Zion was a curious world without bullies. A world
in which people were liked or disliked for what they did, rather
than for what they were. In Zion, people were equal unless they
made themselves otherwise. There were no Jews and Gentiles,
no rich and poor, no haves and have-nots. Everyone had the
right to be respected. No one was ridiculed for being different.

From my brief, barely half-a-year long, *Hashomer Hatzair*
experience, I emerged determined to change the world. And
a socialist. And slim. Indeed, during these fateful six months,
I lost all my fat. Soon after, I lost my home – forever. And my
homeland – for the first time.

3

The Fate of a Refugee and Soldier

On 1 September, the Germans invaded Poland. Poznań was 60 miles from the border. The first big city on the Nazi road to victory.

The bombs began to fall on the city from the early hours of the first day of war, and did not stop until we left Poznań in one of the last trains leaving the beleaguered town on the night of 2 September. We made our way to the station stealthily in complete darkness, hiding in the doorways when a successive wave of enemy planes approached. We took only as much as we could carry in our hands. My sister lost the few belongings she brought from Palestine – she had her daughter to carry. The station lay in ruins, and people flocked into already tightly packed carriages with no one in sight to stop or guide them.

The bombers pursued our train all along the way. We stopped several times to scatter and hide beneath the tracks. Finally, in Inowrocław, 100 miles away from Poznań, the train ground to its final halt. The tracks farther east had been pulverized, and the railway network did not operate any more. The buildings of Inowrocław station no longer existed. Emboldened by the total lack of resistance, German planes strafed the stuck trains with bullets. German pilots clearly enjoyed the chance to display their flying skills. They flew just a few yards above the ground, then drew whimsical loops and circles in the sky, only to dive again. Time and again, they flew over so close that I can bet I saw the malicious grin on the pilot's face. In between bombs and fire, we stayed in the train waiting for my father to return. He could not stand the thought that we travelled all this way without paying for tickets. He returned to lead us out of danger only when he had satisfied himself that no railwayman was left to collect what was owed. Even so, I guess, he suffered. He could not stand dishonesty – his own, least of all.

The remaining distance from Inowrocław to Włocławek, where most of my mother's family lived, we travelled on a peasant's horse cart. My aunts seemed to have expected our arrival, though I cannot remember them rejoicing at the news of our lucky escape. We were put in a flat vacated by a family who had escaped farther east, and left to look after ourselves.

Not that we were in control of our fate. The hard-pressed remnants of the defeated army rushed to the East – on horseback, in horse carriages, on foot. Soon the streets were empty of soldiers and an uncanny, frightening silence followed. And then the Germans came. On motorcycles, in trucks, in tanks.

A few days later, my mother cut my yellow pyjamas into pieces in order to sew triangles on the backs of our coats – the signs of our Jewish distinction now officially recognized by our new rulers. Sporting these signs, we now walked on the roadways – symbolically just a few inches below the level of ordinary people, who walked, as before, on the pavements.

My sister and her husband held British Commonwealth passports. As such, they were exempt from punitive regulations – for a time, at least. My sister's choice took now, however, a different form. On one side, there was the tedious and dreary routine of the oriental version of the *Frauenzimmer*; on the other, an existence equally humiliating, but in addition also cruel, frightening and unpredictable. Somehow the first choice, so repulsive yesterday, seemed now less repugnant. And so my sister called at the local Commandant's office and expressed her desire to return to Palestine.

A minor miracle followed. In the mad world in which the fist was the only passport, the gun the only title to respect, and the Jews were barred from holding either, an elegant motorcar pulled up in front of our door, two smartly dressed high-ranking officers emerged and – bowing and saluting non-stop – handed over to my sister tickets for the train to Berlin and a booking for a chic Berlin hotel, all courtesy of the Reich. They profusely apologized for not yet having obtained clearance for the rest of the journey (these English, you know, they are so inefficient!), but hastened to assure that everything would be done to speed things up and that the German Government would extend its protection for as long as necessary.

What happened next was fit for the theatre of the absurd.

And so, three Jews with yellow triangles on their backs saw off at the Włocławek station three Jews without badges. Well, they did not exactly see the train departing. Just before my sister, with her daughter in her arms and her husband at her side, was shown (with a lot of further bowing and saluting) into the carriage reserved for German officers, a German patrolman pointed his finger at my father: You, Jew, come here and sweep this filthy platform clean! With his back to the train taking his daughter away, tears in his eyes, his hands full of soggy papers and the mouldy leftovers of soldiers' snacks, kept on the move by the prodding of the rifle butt – this was the image of my father that my sister took with her on her journey to what was now her only home.

I remember returning to our flat shattered, but desperate: I would not stay here any more. I would not see my father laughed at and humiliated. Being shouted at and bullied was not exactly a new experience, for either my father or myself. And yet I seemed to sense a danger that my father, resigned as he had been to his fate, was reluctant to admit: life is going to be unpleasant, he agreed, they do not like us, they will make our lot nastier than before, and there is little we can do to resist; one needs to survive to the end of the war, however difficult life might be; so let us handle it together, let us settle in a small Jewish town – perhaps Izbica, that is not far from here, and almost all the inhabitants are Jewish, a well-established community, strong, we will help each other and survive . . . I remember everything in me militating against this idea (we received the news, not too much later, that Izbica was one of the first Jewish villages where there was a mass murder of residents[1]). A child's instinct? Or the standard stubbornness of a youngster – or maybe a childish naivety, the faith of Kipling's butterfly: that it's enough to stomp your feet to change your fate, to banish all unpleasantness? Maybe a premonition? A rebellious streak suddenly developed during the evenings spent in the *Hashomer Hatzair* room? A new conviction that the world could be better, and that one ought to help it to be such? I would not know. I do not remember any thoughts – just the feelings. The feelings were strong, however. So strong, as a matter of fact, that they did prevail in the end over my father's nostalgic solution. And thus my parents survived the war.

And I am writing these words, forty-odd years after Hitler's death.

I could easily convince my mother. She grew up in Congress Poland, the territory controlled by the Russian Empire, and was comfortable with Russians; she probably imagined life among the Soviets as a return to her childhood years – sometimes hilly and sometimes cloudy, but always full of dreams, and hopes that were all the more exciting because they had not yet been disappointed. There, too, there was a foreign power; there was occupation; Jews were harassed, people were attacked – but, still, how did that compare to the present barbarism of the Germans! As for me, Russians were as foreign to me as Germans. I was not expecting paradise on the other side of the green border. What urged me on? Probably the thought

that, under Russian rule, there would not be Jews or Poles, and
we would all suffer together. Captivity would make us equal,
instead of dividing us with a wall that could not be scaled.
There would not be roads for some, pavements for others.
There would not be yellow patches 'only for a select few'. It
would not be that some were placed on the pillory as others
watched – sometimes sympathizing, sometimes with a glimmer of joy in their eyes, sometimes with eyes lacking any kind
of feeling – because it didn't, for now at least, concern them.
That such reflections were not based only in the experiences of
a child and cannot be explained purely as a child's yearnings
was confirmed for me recently by reading Joseph Roth's *Juden
auf Wanderschaft*,[2] a book published eleven years before the
episode in Włocławek, in which, after completing a journalistic
scrutiny and survey of Jewish agglomerations in Europe and
across the ocean, Roth asserted that '[. . .] while anti-Semitism
has become a subject for study in the West, and blood lust
a political point of view, in the new Russia, it remains a disgrace'.[3] And he predicted – how very naively, as it was to turn
out many years later with regard to antisemitism in Russia
– 'What will ultimately kill it off is public shame'; 'The victim
is freed from his torments and the bully from his compulsion.
This is a great accomplishment of the Russian Revolution.'[4]

It is in non-Jewish Poles' sense of their own 'added value', in
the conviction not shared by those of their compatriots who
also happened to be Jews (or, more specifically, by those who
had a special defect, not to be found in other Poles), that we
should seek the origins of the difference between how Jews and
non-Jewish Poles perceived the two occupations.[5] For Poles
who were not tainted by the stigma of Jewishness, nothing
distinguished the Russian occupation from the German one.
Here and there was captivity; here and there were persecution,
deportations and camps; here and there were humiliation, the
refusal of rights and human dignity. But for Poles burdened
with Jewishness, one occupation differed from the other in

the same way that the chance of survival differs from certain extermination. Under Soviet power, they faced the same threat as everyone else. Under German rule, they were threatened with a fate that others were spared from. Non-Jewish Poles behind the new border resented their Jewish neighbours for greeting the Soviet conquerors with flowers. But in September of 1941, a ZWZ[6] officer reported to London that 'Poles on the ground (newly occupied by Germans) see the Germans as their redeemers, have everywhere accepted German soldiers enthusiastically, with flowers, sometimes with triumphal arches, and offered them their assistance.'[7]

The percentage of Polish Jews who paid with their lives for the German occupation was roughly equal to the percentage of non-Jewish Poles who survived it intact.

Once we declared our intention to move east, to the part of Poland now occupied by the Russians, my mother's sisters and brother sighed with relief – they had enough problems of their own, holding on to their property against ever more greedy German extortions. They made a collection, 200 złotys each – enough to hire a peasant driver, a pair of horses, a horse cart, to deliver us safely to the new border and out of sight. My father found a few other uprooted people to share in our journey – and in the middle of October, we took off.

The 200 miles to the new border took us ten days. Well before reaching our destination, we had to abandon our primitive transport and continue our journey on foot; both horses, not particularly boisterous specimens from the start, collapsed before we did. By the end of October, we finally arrived at Wojciechowice – a tiny village a few hundred yards from the frontier which now ran between Ostrołęka (on the German side) and Łomża (on the Russian). We rented a room in a peasant farmhouse. We were lucky to find one, as all the buildings in the village were filled to the brim with other refugees like us, counting, just like us, on permission to cross the border 'to the other side'. That day, we saw one of my Włocław uncles on a cart drawn by a single horse crossing the border in the direction opposite to the one we intended to take. He had set off for the 'Soviet side' to check where it was more tolerable, and, having decided that the Soviets were calling for an end to the 'bourgeois and landowners' and setting out to seize the fortunes of those who were, like him, owners of property or mills, he decided that, between the two evils, he would prefer the Germans . . .

On the first day, my father paid a visit to the Wehrmacht captain in command of the unit garrisoned in the village. The captain must have been deeply impressed by my father's refined, literary German, as he asked him politely to act as the spokesman for the rest of the refugees, and promised a whole-hearted cooperation. He kept his word. The next day, through my father, he asked all refugees to gather at the crossing point, which we did, our hearts pounding with great expectations. We watched our captain driving his military black *Horch* the half-mile distance between the two frontier posts. We strained our eyes to follow his negotiations with Russian border troops. We waited impatiently for the Russian answer when the captain returned to discuss with my father the poems of Heine. Our waiting took a long time. Only after a couple of hours did two human figures detach themselves from the group of soldiers on the other side of the border. They started on a leisurely walk in our direction; the closer they came, the better we saw their ill-fitted uniforms, loosely hanging buttons, unpolished and well-worn shoes. They looked like angels to me. Or messengers of Zion.

The Russian officer whispered briefly with our captain, saluted and turned back. The captain was truly saddened to report to my father: the Russians have new and strict orders, the border exchange is over, no one will be let in from now on; I am sorry, there is nothing I can do, all this is now out of my hands, I must consult my superiors in Ostrołęka . . .

My mother would not stand idle while other people decided her fate. My mother's beauty was always Slavic, rather than Jewish. Now, in rough clothes and with an enormous shawl around her head, she was virtually indistinguishable from peasant women. She removed the only trace of her Jewishness – the yellow triangle – and coaxed our landlady, whom she befriended from the first day, to harness a horse and drive her to Ostrołęka, where she hoped to use her power of persuasion to enlist the cooperation of the German district commandant. She promised to return in the evening.

This was not to be, however. A few hours after her departure, the captain walked briskly into our room, pale and trembling. He told my father that the regular troops had been called away, that the *Grenzschutz*[8] was taking over the border, and that from now on things were going to be tough and he had no power to help. Indeed, shortly afterwards, we heard a loud command reverberating through the village: 'Alle Juden raus!'[9] From houses, barns and stables, men, women and children emerged, pushed and kicked by soldiers in strange uniforms towards the buildings of the village head. When we joined the crowd, we heard the *Grenzschutz* officer say that we were to be transported to Ostrów Mazowiecka, where all Jews wishing to pass to the Russian side were gathered.

A few months later, the news arrived that the refugees assembled in Ostrów Mazowiecka were annihilated on the spot – as soon as they finished digging their mass grave. It was the first groundwork laid for *Endlösung*, which, after two years, was transformed into a routine procedure in occupied territory in the East.[10]

In any case, we could not go to Ostrów. We could not go anywhere, as long as my mother was away. We had to wait for her return. I did not discuss this with my father, yet I knew he thought the same. We understood each other without words when we sneaked behind the nearest building and ran towards the woods which stretched over both sides of the border. Soon we saw a solitary Russian border guard, sitting on a tree-trunk, watching birds, humming, a rifle lying on the ground at his feet. Gasping for his breath, my father declared: 'I am here to wait for my wife. I am not going anywhere until she comes.'

I think this was the longest day of my life.

When the change of guard arrived, the humming soldier engaged in a long discussion with my father, trying to convince him that it would be much better to wait for one's wife in the village than in the woods; she might not find us here, but all people who cross the border end up eventually in the village. Besides – he tempted in a Russian reduced to our inferior level of comprehension – there is warm food in the village, and a warm bed . . .

We found in the village several other people – all men – who, like us, ran away from the round-up. On a chilly, yet sunny, November day, we sat on a few benches in front of the military quarters. The early night descended, and the clear air was fast turning freezing. Yet only late in the evening, already shaking with cold, were we commanded to get up and follow the guard, who would take us to the house where we had been billeted for the night.

Our silent walk lasted half an hour before we realized that we left the village long ago, that we were drawn into total darkness and that no house was in sight. It took us a few minutes more to notice that, for a time now, we were walking across a freshly ploughed field, away from roads or footpaths. Finally, we understood: we had been led back to the Germans. We were to be smuggled through the border.

I do not remember who was the first to fall on the ground and refuse to move. But I do remember myself clutching the wet soil with both my hands, and shouting in what I presumed (wrongly, as I was to find later) to be Russian: 'My mother is here, I won't go!' I was the only child in the company, and my cries must have particularly deeply impressed our guard, clearly untrained to smuggle people through borders, and less still to send children to their death. Our protest was perhaps in excess of the need. The soldier stopped obediently. He did not even try to make us change our minds. Instead, he signalled his distress with a rocket flare. We were still lying on the ground, now frozen to the bones and soaked with mud, when we heard distant hoof-beats. Shortly afterwards, a mounted officer emerged from the night. He stood his horse on its hind legs, raising its front hoofs over the heads of the prostrated bodies. He must have been a virtuoso of the equestrian art. For several minutes, he danced over us on horseback, making his intention to trample us into the soil as credible as possible, and yet managing not to hurt anybody. Nevertheless, the crescendo of the choral lamentation was the only appreciation of his skills. The officer whispered something into the soldier's ear and dissolved again in the darkness from which he emerged. In the silence which followed, we heard the soldier's words: 'Now I will turn the other way. When I look back, I do not want to see any trace of you.' Somehow, we understood without repeating.

It was 10 miles from there to Łomża.[11] It was dark, and we had to keep away from the roads. And yet by dawn we entered the town. Gathering his last strength, my father buttonholed the first passers-by on their way to the synagogue asking for a place to stay. Łomża was bursting at the seams with refugees. There was no hope for a room – but there was a lady nearby who already rented square inches of the floor to a few dozens of the homeless and would not mind renting a few more. We shuffled our feet – these were perhaps the longest hundred yards I remember. The first person I saw inside was my mother, still in her peasant shawl, nestling in the corner of a big room empty of furniture and filled from wall to wall with snoring, groaning and panting people. From the ninth circle of hell, I was suddenly transported to paradise.

Łomża was small, overcrowded, and with no prospects of a
job or lodging. And so we took the train to Białystok, the biggest town in this part of Russian-occupied Poland. We found
Białystok not very different, though – the same homeless
crowds, sky-high rents, thousands of uprooted people searching for lost relatives and the means to survive another day. We
had spent all the money brought from Włocławek, and father
desperately tried to earn some more. Everybody in Białystok
was a tradesman, and to join the jostling throngs of peddlers in
the marketplace seemed the only way to earn one's living. My
father obtained some leather from a wholesaler with a promise
of commission on retail sales. He went to the market once or
twice, clutching a few sheets of shoe-leather in his hands, only
to find out that, once more, he had fallen victim to those more
clever than he was and had any hope of becoming: the leather
crumbled and cracked when as much as touched with a finger.
My mother took our fate in her own hands. 'You will never be a
merchant, my dear', she told my father, in a voice brooking no
objection. 'It is high time you understood it for a change.' My
father agreed with glee and enthusiasm.

This meant, however, that Białystok was not for us. We had
to move elsewhere – away from the buying and selling crowds.
But where? Here my love of geography came in handy (*Romer's
Atlas* was the only treasure that I was able to preserve and
keep whole in my endless wanderings; I slept clutching it in
my arms). To me, the right place seemed to be Mołodeczno,
a small town, but not a village, removed far enough from the
German border not to be easily reached by the refugees. It
was also situated in the romantic lands of Wileńszczyzna,
among – as one would expect – Mickiewicz's buckwheat and
clovers.[12] Our last remaining pennies we spent on rail tickets
to Mołodeczno.

It was a garrison town, and not much more than that.
Rambling barracks, scattered over a vast fenced-off flat terrain,
occupied most of the space. The rest of the town consisted

mostly of two perpendicular, long, wide roads, covered with cobblestones and adorned on both sides with strings of squat and sunken, rural rather than urban, houses. Like in the rest of the poverty-stricken country, low life cohabited there with high spirits. The local gymnasium was famous for its exquisite scholarship and proud of its distinguished graduates. Its already elevated standing had now received a further lift from a good number of Jewish and Belorussian intellectuals, allowed to reinforce the teaching staff.

Rooms for rent were aplenty when we arrived, and we found one in no time in one of the peasant households. Jobs were also plentiful; location of a Soviet regiment in the town brought in its wake a great number of servicing institutions and companies. The next day after our arrival, my father was offered the first position he asked for: he became – what else? – an accountant in a big trade warehouse serving the local garrison. His first impression was one of horror and dismay: 'Everybody steals! They ask me to enter in the books goods which evaporated before being put on the shelves; or delete, as faulty, things of perfectly usable quality. How can a state be made of theft?' Uncharacteristically, my father could not keep silent – this time, after all, it was a matter of honesty, one matter which for my father was not open to negotiation. And so he shared his disgust with the director of the warehouse, a Jew from Minsk and a seasoned dignitary of Soviet commerce. 'You know what this man told me?', my father asked me, his face contorted in mental agony. 'He told me: don't you worry, it is true we all steal, but think how much just one capitalist is stealing over there!' For a long time, my father fumed over the answer. He never made peace with either the idea or the practice of 'thieving democracy', the argument against the monopoly of theft having failed to convince him. He continued to suffer – but, as was his habit, he now suffered in silence.

Well, my father was once again a bookkeeper, even if the books he now kept were fantasy books rather than exercises in realism, socialist or otherwise. A veritable revolution took place, however, in my mother's life. She went to the garrison mess and offered her services as a cook. She was put to the test, made a few titbits out of atrociously looking and smelling stuff, and was enthusiastically accepted. Her conjuring talents fit the thieving democracy very well. From that moment on, for many years to come, she was to cook meals out of nothing.

She had done it for a long time before – but now the number of grateful beneficiaries of her skills expanded radically. Her art was acclaimed, praised, cherished. My mother was happy. She loved her new life, the sleepy town, the army whose officers looked at her with the eyes of loving dogs, the country which kept such an army.

I was also happy. No one, it seemed, questioned my credentials. For my new colleagues, I was the most Polish person of them all. Here, at the far outskirts of the interwar Republic, Polishness as such was continually in doubt. The vernacular was a curious mixture of Russian, Polish, Yiddish and that uncodified peasant dialect which some intellectuals dreamt to elevate into the literary Belorussian. There were Poles, Russians, Jews, Belorussians among my new classmates, but this did not seem to matter. The category to which one belonged seemed to some a matter of accident, for some others a question of self-definition and choice. No one around spoke Polish as pure and refined as mine. No one moved with equal ease through Polish literature and history. In the new context, I looked so frightfully Polish that I aroused the suspicion, and then hatred, of the deputy headmaster – a militant Belorussian nationalist and a Pole-baiter. A few days after I joined the school, he called me to his office and told me in no uncertain words that the rule of the Polish invaders was over, and that I and my ilk had better take note, and that his was a Belorussian school with no room for Polish speakers, and that I should either learn Belorussian by Christmas or forget about my education. I was shattered, but continued to give my answers in the classroom in Polish. I had enough trouble with mastering the basics of Russian; there were no 'teach yourself' books of any kind, and I learned Russian the most harrowing way – reading through the articles of *Pravda*, dictionary in my hand. The encounter with the deputy headmaster did, however, have an effect – though not the one he hoped for. Setting the Belorussian language as the enemy of Polish made me hate the former. I never managed to force myself to learn it. At the first opportunity, I moved to a newly opened gymnasium with Russian as the language of teaching.

The Soviet government declared all the inhabitants of the occupied Polish territory Soviet citizens. As we were refugees, however, from the part of Poland over which the Russians did not yet proclaim their jurisdiction, a special paragraph had been inserted in our passports forbidding us to stay within 60 miles of the state border. Mołodeczno was a mere 40 miles from the then independent Lithuania. We faced deportation. Among the high-ranking admirers of my mother's culinary art, the news had a bombshell effect. The prospect of unappetizing, unimaginative canteen fare mattered to them more than respect for Soviet law, or – in this case – the threat to national security arising from the presence of three people of doubtful origin. The fatal paragraph was never deleted from our passports, and yet the deportation order did not arrive either.

To me, these episodes were mere hiccups. The eighteen months in Mołodeczno wrote themselves into my memory as an experience of constant bliss. With both parents at work, we were, for the first time, truly well-off – by the standards set by my childhood, at least. I was surrounded by friends and generally liked. Apparently, I was also handsome. Girls became restless in my company. Some were downright aggressive. It was frightening, but pleasant. I felt free and needed. I found my Zion in Mołodeczno. I joined the local equivalent of *Hashomer Hatzair* – the Komsomol.[13]

On the morning of 22 June 1941, I was lying on the sand by the bank of the local river, surrounded by friends, basking in the sun and mulling over some topics I wished to crack during the summer holiday. Suddenly, I saw my mother running towards me. 'Come home immediately! War has broken out!'

Mołodeczno was too small a target to be bothered with. During the first day of the German invasion, there were few signs that the country was at war. I saw the war first in the eyes of our landlady's nephew. Born on the Soviet side of the old border and brought up in a *kolkhoz*,[14] he moved after the Soviet invasion to Mołodeczno and settled in his aunt's household. He clearly liked what he found there; he relished possessing 'his own' cow and horse; he paraded his newly acquired small-holder status around, and became the hidden but indomitable force behind his aunt's resolute refusal to join the collective farm. On 22 June, his eyes filled with joy and hope. And with hatred, when turned in our direction. 'The Germans will do no harm to honest people, but some people they do not like – Jews above all – and they are right', he announced, thought-fully, his eyes resting firmly on my father's face. Swarms of ants ran over my back. We admittedly had no idea about the procedures of *Einsatzgruppen*,[15] or about the fact that the Jews of Mołodeczno would be slaughtered upon the arrival of the Nazis, but the memories of a few weeks in German-occupied Włocławek, in combination with the joyful mood of our host, sufficed to make us only too aware of the fate that awaited us.

The quietly forgotten reality was coming back to stake its claim.

The next day my mother returned from her work early. By this time, German planes were already flying over the town, though on the whole carrying their bombs to more attrac-tive targets. Only occasionally did they shower the barracks with machine-gun rounds. Like in the Polish war, the planes encountered no resistance. They were free to do whatever they liked. My mother returned to tell us that the families of the army personnel were to be evacuated from the town, and that she had been offered a place on the special train. There was little time to lose.

We lived far from the station and our landlady's nephew refused to drive us there. And so we took as much as we could squeeze into three bags (*Romer's Atlas* could not be crammed in) and started on our next exodus. When I turned back after a few minutes, unable to reconcile myself to the thought of abandoning the friend I had saved from Poznań, I found the nephew in our room, ransacking what we had left behind. He refused to let me in and kept hurling curses at me when I ran back to join my parents.

Unlike the Poznań train, this one was not full. Apart from the wives and children of the officers, only a few local people decided to move. The Soviets, apparently, had not made many friends. Or perhaps people did not think there was much to choose between the two occupiers. We knew the Germans at first hand. Not all did, however. During the months of the Stalin–Hitler pact, all the might of Soviet propaganda was deployed to paint an angelic portrait of the awesome ally. Now the Soviets gathered the fruits of their lie. Many of those who cheerfully bade them farewell were to perish a few days after the arrival of the German troops. Only they did not know it yet. And would not believe, if told. Molotov's voice announcing on the radio the act of German treachery was full of wounded love and incomprehension: How come they have betrayed our friendship? We wished them no harm . . .

It was a long, long way – first through the westernmost territories already ravaged by German bombers, then through the deep interior of Russia, far away from the frontline yet already in a state of war. The war, in its very first weeks, already showed itself in the haggard, tired look of men in uniform, in the absence of men in civilian clothes, in the bewildered faces of women suddenly left to look after themselves. Trains full of men in uniforms ran west; our train uncertainly, haltingly, crawled east. Garrison families disappeared one by one as they reached their hometowns. The train slowly shrank until a few carriages were left, filled with the homeless. People like us, with nowhere to go. We were shunted around, attached to ever new trains, left for days on sidetracks. Finally, somewhere halfway between Moscow and Ural, we were told to disembark. Someone had decided that we should be settled in local *kolkhozs* – having lost their men, they badly needed extra labour.

The station was called Krasnye Baki, and was a regional centre north of Gorki,[16] a huge sprawling city encircling the point where the largest rivers of European Russia met. Horse carts took us to a village still farther north. As an advance against our future labour, we were offered some flour, potatoes and oil.

The next morning, my mother and I joined a long column of women and children taking to the fields. Only the two of us wore shoes. The rest walked in bast shoes, or strange moccasins made of straw. We walked for several miles before we reached the plot where the harvesting was scheduled for the day: a vast field covered with overripe rye which had already started seeding. Some women worked with scythes; one rode a tractor, which moved a few yards with ear-shattering noise, only to grind to an abrupt halt and emit an enormous cloud of acrid smoke. From that point on, only scythes set apart the badly needed bread from hectares of rotten rye. Tall for my age, I was offered a scythe, but the woman in charge soon concluded that this would be a waste of the precious tool. I was assigned to a large group of women and children who raked and tied cut stalks. We worked in grim determination, in complete silence, disturbed only by the constant buzz of gnats hungry for animal blood. I remember them sitting tight on every bare inch of my skin. Having sunk their darts deep in my body they were too busy sucking my blood to notice my desperate attempts to shake them off. There was no way of getting rid of them; the few I managed to destroy were immediately replaced with new and hungry ones. The swarm evidently was getting regular reinforcements. Apart from my mother and myself, nobody seemed to mind them. Gnats were clearly part of life, like the broken tractor, like the rotting rye, like the job obviously beyond human capacity, like the work from sunrise to sunset rewarded in the evening by a few boiled potatoes and hot water sprinkled with flour and salt.

After several days I fell ill and had to stay home. My body was swollen, covered with blisters, boils and festering sores. The innumerable bites and bruises were infected. I was in pain, unable to move, to sit, to lie down. My mother proved stronger; she stayed in the field one day longer.

While we were working in the fields, father walked every day 10 miles to the regional centre in a vain attempt to find employment and lodgings. Each morning, mother boiled a pot of soup for the evening meal. The day I stayed alone in the house, she prepared two plates of soup – one for me, another for my father. He might have had to stay away for a night, though, as he intended to call at another town and could miss the last train back. I stood in the window which overlooked a long stretch of the road, up to the top of the low hill 2 miles away. It was getting dark. There was no sign of my father. He must have missed his train. I ate his soup. A few minutes later, in the last rays of the setting sun, my father appeared on the hill. There was nothing left for him in the house to eat. This was another of those sins I will never live to atone for.

I was hungry. I was to be hungry for the next two and a half years, till my army life started. Not occasionally hungry, but hungry twenty-four hours a day, seven days a week. I was hungry waiting for a meal, and hungry after finishing the meal. I imagined the blissful life after the end of the war as one huge baker's shop open all hours. I starved along with tens of millions of people 'behind the front lines', with all those who survived the war on leftovers of cabbage pickled for the army or on scraps of a heavy wet bread baked from a flour of unknown origins, mixed with bran, chaff and grass.

The country was hungry. I know some people high up ate better – but we did not see them. Shared hunger hurt less. But it was painful all the same. And the pain remained long after hunger ended. To this very day, I cannot fall asleep if there is no bread in the house. And I can never feel as enthusiastic about any – however refined – food as I feel about bread. It is bread, after all, which truly matters. If you do not know it, you are lucky. Or, perhaps, not lucky at all, but naive. Or spoiled. And not truly tested.

Father returned with good news. In another regional centre – Shakhunia – located farther to the north, closer to Wiatka (then called Kirow), he had finally found a position as a bookkeeper, and a room to rent. What he did not yet know on that day was that the war, which did not seem to put a high premium on bookkeepers, added glitter and well-nigh metaphysical significance to my mother's cooking skills. In Shakhunia, my mother was put in charge of feeding the railwaymen. Shakhunia was a railway junction first, and a town as a distant second. So my mother was put in charge of the survival of that small particle of the vast country at war. And my father became, for many years to come, his wife's husband, hidden and invisible in her giant shadow. I think my father was relieved, and happy. All his life he tried to be true to the advice of Shemaiah:[17] 'Love work and hate mastery, and make not thyself known to the government.' All his life, he believed, with Rabbi Hillel, that 'who so makes great his name loses his name'. Now he had the chance to live up to his principles. He disappeared from view – melted into his desk in his bookkeeper's office, buried in his readings in the evening, soundlessly cooking the evening meal so that mother could eat when she returned from work.

I went back to school. I had been admitted to the last form of the secondary school. As most of the teachers had been enlisted, several old ones were recalled from retirement, or for-given crimes for which they had been dismissed before time. To those teachers, my knowledge and attitude to learning – both bred and drilled in a good-quality, old-fashioned gymnasium – seemed to feel somewhat other-worldly. The teacher of Russian, an old man frightened out of his wits by his past trials, clung convulsively to every word in the last edition of the official schoolbook, with its latest and binding assessment of the meritorious and the unmentionable – though it was obvious that his experiences in the camps had not shattered him entirely, and a love for the genius and beauty of Russian literature could not be entirely destroyed by the concentration camp guards. I was his only relief from the mental slavery he had no courage left to resist. Almost every day, he called me to the blackboard and asked me to discuss a novel or recite a piece of poetry. He did not interrupt. He sat with his head in his hands. Once, having finished a long poem by Tyutchev,[18] I could swear I saw tears in his eyes.

I finished school with a gold medal. This gave me the right of admission to any faculty of any university of my choice. I was 16 – the youngest among the graduates. On graduation day, I went, together with all the other boys, to the local military office and handed over an application for an army school.

Shortly, all the other boys were called up, but my appli-cation remained without reply. Perhaps I was under age. More probably, the army school had no room for an untrust-worthy foreigner. As the waiting grew longer and the hope faded, I applied for admission to the Faculty of Physics and Mathematics at Gorki University. For the three summer months, I volunteered to work in the Shakhunia Railway Workshops – a large plant dedicated to keeping the loco-motives of the whole region between Niżny Nowogród and Wiatka on the tracks. This was a serious and difficult matter, as the rolling stock, not replaced since the beginning of the war yet used beyond capacity, was fast growing old and needed more than the ordinary servicing. I lacked any mechanical skills and was sent to learn the elements of the job from an old, experienced tinsmith, recently recalled from retirement. I learned to weld leaking oilcans and make new ones from scratch, as well as other similar minor and less responsible jobs. More important things, like filing the burnt bearings or forging the spares for broken parts of the engine, I was allowed only to watch and, from time to time, to help with under the unflaggingly vigilant eye of my master.

Things on the frontline (at those lucky moments when there was a definite frontline) went from bad to worse. It seemed that, at any moment, the Germans[19] would cross the Volga and advance into the Ural Mountains. Almost everywhere, the Red Army was in retreat, losing most of its men and its arms. Nowhere else was the might of Germany resisted. Russia fought alone the united industrial might of Europe. In our workshops, the few old men, and keen but inept adolescents of my age and still younger, took it upon themselves to do the job of non-existent factories, of dozens of other specialized plants now bombed out of existence or hastily refurbished without complaint, yet with a lot of intense, obstinate passion. If an important part of the ingredients was missing, they would conjure up a substitute. We worked in buildings which themselves badly needed repair. The ventilators had long ceased to work, and the shops were filled with corrosive smoke and poisonous fumes. No one seemed to mind – least of all, the old craftsmen, who knew only too well what all this meant for their lungs. For me, awe and admiration were the feelings I remember best. I felt overwhelmed by the spectacle of human solidarity and dedication. I heard no grumbling and I did not grumble myself. We were all hungry and tired. We all spoke in hoarse voices and coughed up phlegm. We strained our eyes, bloodied and itching. Our hands were covered with burns and scars. Yet there was meaning in everything we did, and we had our share of joy and happiness when we achieved the impossible and a dead locomotive was restored to life. After three months, I left the workshops with an injection of romantic utopia which was, for better and for worse, to outlast the war and the strange unusual world in which it did not look utopian at all. Not all inhuman conditions de-humanize. Some disclose humanity in man.

In the north of Russia, winter starts early, and in the middle of October Gorki was a frozen city. There was no fuel, and central heating was set at a level barely sufficient to prevent the water-pipes bursting. We stayed in our coats all day long, and did not take them off when we went to bed. I remember the difficulty of turning the pages of a book with hands never taken out of thick fingerless gloves. Together with nineteen other students, I was allocated a bed in a room meant to accommodate four; most of the student halls had been converted into military hos-pitals. We did not mind the overcrowding – on the contrary, this added a degree or two to the temperature of the room. The focal point of the room was an electric kettle, always kept boil-ing unless the electricity was cut off (as it was for at least eight hours every day). When writing essays or doing our equations, we warmed our hands by pressing them against the kettle or a cupful of hot water.

Among the students, I was again the youngest. All the others were either war veterans with wounds which disqualified them from further military service, or the physically unfit who could not be enlisted. I was the only fit and healthy person – a cir-cumstance which would have made me feel guilty, if not for the hope that my share of the war effort was still in front of me. I was not to be given time to contemplate my position, however. After two months of studying and freezing, the house administrator called me to her office to tell me that I had no right to live in a big and important city like Gorki and I must return to Shakhunia immediately. I could come occasionally, for a day or two, to sit my exams, though. . . . The latter chance

I grasped: I visited Gorki twice more, to pass my first- and second-year exams.

During the two months I stayed in Gorki, my parents left Shakhunia and moved to Vakhtan, where mother was offered the supervision of the awesome task of feeding hundreds of lumberjacks spread in small groups all over the huge territory of the north-Russian forest. To reach Vakhtan, one had to take a train (or walk) from Shakhunia to another station 15 miles farther north, and then travel several hours along a narrow-gauge track. The track was built to carry timber to the main railroad, but once a day, at night when the timber trains were resting, two doll-like carriages with a samovar-like engine provided passenger services. Vakhtan itself was a small settlement lost amidst woods and marshes. Houses, roads, pavements were all made of wood – the only good available in abundance.

Just how far Vakhtan was from everywhere else, I learned the moment I entered the local library. To my utter amazement, I found there a 'full, unexpurgated' chronicle of Soviet literary life since the early 1920s. The successive waves of purges and autos-da-fé which maimed and truncated all public libraries I had visited before had clearly bypassed this one. Nobody seemed to have cared about the danger of poisoning the minds of the forest people who communicated with the rest of the country only through trainloads of timber. The few months I spent in Vakhtan remained in my memory, above all, as a time of constant excitement and elation. In no other period of my life have I devoured so many books. I swallowed complete editions of Russian classics, printed in the times of scarcity and high hopes on newsprint, now yellow and crumbling. I devoured the Soviet literature of the 1920s and the early 1930s. I pored over long-forgotten philosophical and historical debates from when the country was still free enough to disagree and debate. I read the authors whose very names had acquired the awesome power of sucking the person who pronounced them in public into the same non-existence into which they themselves had been cast. This was harsh winter, with temperatures never rising above minus 30 °C for several months. During the day, I worked in an office or walked long forest paths to reach distant lumberjack outposts and collect reports on the number of trees felled and volume of logs cut. But the nights belonged to books. I just imbibed them without digesting; I guess they needed time to incubate. But incubate they did. Slowly, yet inexorably, I began to see around me things I did not see before, even when looking them straight in the face.

And there was something else which happened in Vakhtan. I heard on the radio (there were loudspeakers in every house, connected by cable to the only wireless set, kept in the local library) that in Moscow a Union of Polish Patriots had formed, and that the first action it undertook was to publish a newspaper, *Free Poland*, and a journal, *New Horizons*.[20] Immediately, I sent an application for membership and my subscription for both publications. The first copies soon arrived. I vividly remember the shock. The intoxication. The wild explosion of feverish fantasy. I read what I received from the first page to the last, and back again. The titles of both publications merged in my mind, became one: Poland free, horizons new. Free Poland became my new horizon. With bated breath, I read about the future dignity of my country. I read about things I knew before, yet poorly understood: about community strife and hatred arising out of poverty and injustice; about life without prospects and dreariness without end which rebounded in mutual suspicion and jealousy; about the nation tearing itself apart instead of coming to grips with its true problems, like lack of freedom and democratic rights. I read about things I did not think about before – about Poland of the future, a loving mother for her suffering children, a country of liberty and justice. I read about a dream country for everybody, however weak and wan. A country without hunger, misery and unemployment. A country in which one man's success would not mean another man's defeat (as Wieniawa-Długoszewski put it:[21] one in which a tailor from Poznań would not lay himself to sleep, overwhelmed with envy at the news that a canon from Białystok had become a prelate). A new Poland, yet at the same time a Poland which for the first time would be true to herself. In an equal and confident society, Polish culture, Polish letters, Polish language would finally blossom and reach heights never dreamt of before. A Free Poland of new horizons would be the pride of the free world. I had my share of the glasshouses . . .[22]

I relished previously unimaginable visions: a future Poland – a country of freedom and fairness, without hunger, poverty or unemployment; a country in which the success of one person did not equal the failure of another.

I was shaken out of this state – half-dream, half-fever – by my call-up notice, which finally arrived several weeks before my eighteenth birthday. It was not what I expected, though. Much to my amazement and dismay, I had been mobilized to the Moscow police. I found myself in the 'Seventh Division of the Regulation of Street Traffic' on the Arbat[23] when I arrived in Moscow. Apparently, Stalin – or someone standing close to him and reading his thoughts – had come up with a felicitous idea: to make sure that the police stand fast and do not fraternize with the natives, let us compose it of people who are unlikely to find a common language with the local population. It seemed, anyway, that such an idea did occur to someone on high, as I found around me, in a newly formed police traffic division, men of all sorts except the kind one would naturally expect in the local police force. There were men from Poland proper, like myself; Latvians; Lithuanians – men with heavily stained personal files, some guilty of well-recorded and still unrepented crimes. We were, so to speak, thieves enrolled to guard the safe. One could hardly imagine people like us taking the side of the Muscovites in the case of trouble . . . They probably hoped that we would not hesitate to seize any opportunity for retaliation and would hold by the throats any local rebels, with whom, after all, we had nothing in common.

In haste, we had been taught the elements of traffic regulations and sent to the streets to acquire experience – while being incessantly watched from the pavements by superior officers. The success of our training was to be measured by the amount of penalties we imposed on rule-breakers during the day. Those of us who brought in the evening the highest amount of traffic ticket counterfoils and court summons were praised at the briefings and set as the patterns to emulate. I, a slouch, never found myself among them. The chance of a career in the police was close to zero.

At the beginning of winter 1943, Muscovites were at the end of their tether. Women and war invalids were working ten or twelve hours a day on rations barely sufficient to feed a child. Tired and emaciated, with grey faces and bleary eyes, they hurried along the streets – to catch an overcrowded tram, to join another never-ending queue, to be back at home in time to put the child to bed. Some stopped running, and strolled aimlessly, with nowhere to go and nowhere they wished to arrive. It was such people we had been enlisted to keep in check. The others – better fed, confident and in control of themselves – passed by in fast cars which we had no right to stop, or even to look at too closely.

I hated my new job – a rude awakening, indeed, from the Vakhtan world of dreams. After several weeks of training and a few first days of street practice, I applied for permission to leave the force. 'I am a Pole, I want to join the Polish Army which the Union of Polish Patriots has just begun to form', I said. Permission was granted, together with a rank-stripping ceremony. I was dressed in a motley assortment of antique and threadbare parts of uniforms worn by past generations of Moscow policemen, given an ounce of caviar (to replace the pound of sausage due, but 'temporarily unavailable') and sent

on a 500-mile-long journey to Sumy in Ukraine, where the new
Polish Army was being put together.

At the gates of the pre-revolutionary Cadet School in Sumy,
I arrived on my last legs, barefoot and practically naked; most
of my officially allocated clothes fell apart, together with their
long-past glory, and at the station in Kharkiv I had literally
traded the proverbial 'shirt off my back', covered in patches
from the cuffs to the collar, for a potato pancake. The first thing
I heard at the gate was the Polish language. The first thing I saw
was the Polish Eagle adorning the gate and the sentry's cap. I
felt I had reached the end of my wanderings. I was home.

This was a strange army, if ever there was one. The Red Army
had recently recaptured Pokuttia, Podilia, Volhynia, and a few
other scraps of the pre-war Polish territory from the Germans,
and, eager to have a Polish ally at his side as soon as possible,
Stalin took a somewhat illogical step and ordered the mobilization of local peasants – whom he had transformed a few years
earlier into Soviet citizens, without asking for their consent –
into the Polish Army. And so the enclosure of the former Cadet
School swarmed with fresh recruits of nondescript identity –
themselves unsure where they truly belonged, speaking a sort
of Polish heavily infused with Ukrainian words, and spoken in
the tuneful, meditative Ukrainian fashion. Above this crowd,
only superficially sprinkled with a few 'true Poles' like myself,
there were some NCOs[24] from the old Polish Army, painstakingly gathered from the nooks and crannies of Siberia or
Central Asia, where they scattered after they were released
from POW camps. Higher up still, only Russian was spoken.
Polish commissioned officers had been murdered en masse
in Katyń.[25] Those who were lucky enough to escape that fate
had left Russia with Anders' Army after Stalin's attempted,
but unconsummated, romance with the Polish government-
in-exile. And so, to command the new Polish troops, the Red
Army lent its own officers. Some of them could trace Polish

ancestors and still bore Polish-sounding names. Many Poles settled in Russia after their term of Siberian exile, or having involved themselves in Russian revolutionary struggles. Most of the 'borrowed' officers did not aspire to any Polish connection whatsoever. Virtually none of them – Pole or not Pole – spoke any Polish or was willing to admit that he now served in an army which differed from the Red one in anything but the design of the uniforms.

Like a handful of raisins added to a bowl of dough, roaming the grasslands were a comparatively small number of Polish civilians – including me – who had been exiled or transported, and some actual Polish officers, mainly those from the pre-war Polish Army who had not managed to join Anders' Army; by 1942, that army had already been relocated to Persia.[26]

Political hues, the ideological orientation of the new army, was what they cared the least about: that the army arose on Russian soil, that it was led by Soviet officers, that it prepared for battle on the Russian front under the leadership of the heads of the Red Army – all this was unquestionable.

The founders of the Union of Polish Patriots, old Polish communists and socialists or veterans of the Spanish Civil War, now dressed in generals' and colonels' uniforms, faced the mind-boggling task of making that awesome concoction into a Polish Army. Polishness was what they were after. What was not clear was the Polish identity of that army. This is why the generals and the colonels searched for anybody who could inject a Polish spirit into this army. Everyone with a good grounding in Polish culture and some higher education was set aside for this task. With my first year of physics completed and the second well advanced, and with my experience of a solid Polish education, I was fished out almost immediately after crossing the threshold.

I found myself among a bizarre group of people – of all ages, all types of biographies, all religious and political denominations, all shades of the ideological spectrum. The only thing which united them was unswerving loyalty to their Polish identity and perfect command of Polish. No one had a military training worth speaking about, unlike most of the generals and colonels who selected them. Yet, in the span of three weeks, we were to be trained into the officers of the Polish Army. We were to serve as 'deputy commanders for political affairs' – a Polish antidote for the Russian allegiance of the commanders.

Our three-week-long course consisted almost entirely of lectures about Polish history and literature – something I enjoyed enormously. What I enjoyed less was the 'military' part of our training, conducted exclusively by a pre-war sergeant who, of all the mysteries of military art, remembered only the marching drill, and sang military songs about Kasia who herded the oxen. His theoretical instruction he finished after the first attempt – when he failed to convince his overly intellectual riff-raff of soldiers that 'a command is a strict fulfillment of command'.

The day I remember best was a visit from the army theatre troupe. And, from the visit, I recall most vividly one song. The huge ballroom of the old Cadet School was tightly packed with hundreds of soldiers; for many of them, this was perhaps the first experience of a live performer on stage. A brittle, dark-haired girl climbed on stage and began to sing – in a thin, almost childish, yet soft and velvety voice. The song was dedicated to Warsaw. The lyrics spoke of the beauty of Warsaw streets, and the joy of walking them again, of breathing the air of that most loved of all cities. I had never been to Warsaw. I had never heard about Warsaw streets. In my part of the country, Warsaw was not held in high esteem: a dirty, disorderly oriental place, unlike the neat, tidy, civilized and Western Poznań. And yet I wept. I could not stop myself, although I did try very hard – I was, after all, at that under-defined age when one has to prove one's still uncertain manhood. Apparently, one can feel nostalgia for the future. I felt it, anyway. The little girl on the stage sang of my dreams of new horizons, of free

Poland, of the new horizons the freedom of my country would open.

A day or two after the concert, I was called to one of the staff offices. I was met there by a woman in a captain's uniform. She asked about my past, my present thoughts, my intentions. It was a long, leisurely, pleasant conversation. When I thought we had finished and prepared to leave, she said something which made me freeze in my chair: I thought I misunderstood and asked her to repeat. There was no mistake, though. I was asked to change my name. 'You know, your name does not sound 100 per cent Polish. It is not an awful name, of course, there are other names much worse, much more foreign-sounding and ridiculous. But still . . . We are a Polish Army, you see. And you yourself have said that you feel Polish. So what about a nice Polish name?' I do not remember my answer. I was too discomposed and agitated to control my words and to record them in my memory. But I flatly refused the offer. I was not ashamed of my name. And I did not feel my Polishness was something like a badge, or a name. It was inside me, where it was safe, and it did not need a certificate.

On the last day of the course, we were summoned to our final briefing. We were told that we would all be appointed deputy commanders of companies, with full powers, yet without commission. To deserve a commission, we must still pass the practical test. Some of us were nonplussed – this was not what we expected. One person asked the question which I guess was on everybody else's lips: without rank, how can we gain the authority we need to command? The Colonel Grosz in charge of the briefing, a veteran of the Spanish War, an old communist and a high-calibre intellectual, responded: 'If you do not gain authority without rank, the rank will not help either . . .' Looking back, I believe this last, curt lesson was more important than all the lectures and the exercises the course had to offer. And perhaps not just that one course.

Anyway, there I was – an 18-year-old still to receive his commission, but already in charge of fifty-odd souls, most of them seated in bodies twice my age. I was the only commander trying to impress it upon those souls that the language through which they made themselves audible should be Polish, rather than Russian, Ukrainian or 'local'. The only person in the 5th Battery of the 6th PAL trying to achieve this with, at best, the condescending disdain or ironic indifference of platoon commanders – nominally my subordinates, but in fact by far my superiors: truly trained and experienced military men.

How did they see me, my soldiers? As an alien, I presume. Yet, alien as a Jew? Or as a Pole? Or as a man in power – something they learned not to expect anything good from and were thoroughly fed up with, whether it came in a Polish, Russian or German disguise. I did not know then, and I would never know. One thing I knew was that – rank or no rank – I was a Polish officer, fighting for the Polish cause. In the 5th Battery, 6th PAL, 4th Division of Jan Kiliński to which I was assigned, I was Poland.

A military train took us to the other end of already fully reconquered Ukraine. We disembarked at Olyka woods, not far from Kowel, which belonged to Poland before the war, but was now annexed to the Soviet Ukraine. For a few days, we stayed in the woods and went through the final preparation for joining the war action.

Late one evening, I sat in the tent with my Battery commander and the commander of the first platoon. We had our order for the next day: to cross the river Bug, into the undisputed Polish territory. For me, this meant far more than it did to my colleagues, for whom the Bug was just one more river to cross. But I think that all three of us, although possibly for different reasons, were excited and restless, full of joyful expectations mixed with fears. My Battery commander turned to me. 'Tomorrow, we will be in Poland. I wonder – what do you think? Did you like it in Russia? You are a member of the *Komsomol* like me; I bet you would like to return to Russia when the war is over.' 'No', I answered. 'I am a Pole, and I am about to return to my country.' 'But wouldn't Poland be much like Soviet Russia? What is the difference?', my commander pressed on.

For many years, I shivered when recalling what did happen later, and what could have happened after that. Engrossed in my sweet anticipations, disarmed by hope of dreams coming true, I let my tongue loose. My tongue said: 'Poland will be a free country. Unlike Russia, where everyone repeats what they are told to say, and instead of using their own brains, just shouts in a chorus "Stalin, Stalin, Stalin".' I do not think I said this because I was a hero, though saying this did call for heroism. The truth is less flattering. I said what I did because I was still (and was to remain for quite a few years more) green and naive. I was about to enter my mature life armed with romantic dreams, world-shattering energy, but little wisdom. When not tempered with wisdom, dreams and energy make a dangerous mixture. Dangerous for the dreamer. Worse than that: not just for the dreamer alone . . .

Well, this time the dreamer escaped the danger. My Battery commander and the commander of the first platoon did not betray me, though not betraying me put themselves in danger. The names of the just and the righteous ought to be remembered. The name of my Battery commander, the son of Siberian exiles, was Lange. The name of the first platoon commander, 'nastojaszczewo russkowo parnia',[27] was Bormotov – or that of, in our language, a real Russian guy.

The name of my father was Maurycy (Moshe) Bauman.

Then there was Hrubieszów, Chełm, Lublin – the joy on people's faces at the sight of Polish Eagles on soldiers' caps, the joy on mine at the sight of them. And, finally, Szembek's Square in Praga, where the 5th Battery was commanded to entrench, and from which, for the first time, it fired on the Germans . . . On the other side of the Vistula, the Warsaw Uprising was dying out. I watched with trepidation and a feeling of powerlessness as our infantry, which had managed to cross to the other bank, deprived of air support (fighter planes from the 1st Polish Army in the USSR had not been sent) and supported only by artillery fire, defended itself fiercely and unsuccessfully from the onslaught of German divisions redeployed from other parts of the front.

After the final defeat (and almost total annihilation) of our landing troops, my troop was transferred to Radość,[28] where, as it turned out, we were to entrench ourselves and to stay until the beginning of the January offensive, only rarely firing at German positions that were not visible from this distance.

At the beginning of January, the commander of the 4th Division, General Kieniewicz – yet another descendant of exiles – arrived in Radość for an inspection. Unlike many, he had not forgotten his mother tongue, or perhaps he had recalled it through strenuous efforts; in any case, he spoke with the soldiers comfortably, though with a clear Russian accent, reminding them that the fight was only beginning, because nearly all of Poland was still under German occupation, and there had been enough lazy lounging in dugouts. On 16 January, the Battery, loaded into Studebakers[29] supplied by the Americans, crossed a pontoon bridge hastily put up between the right bank of the Vistula and a beachhead at Warka. And from there, a snow-covered road led north to Warsaw . . .

It was already dark when the engine of the Studebaker in whose cab I was riding growled, coughed and stopped. Before we were able to repair the damage, the rest of the column passed us and disappeared into the darkness. We needed to catch up with it – blindly, because we had not yet received orders as to which direction we were to proceed in. I assumed that we were on the way to capture Warsaw – and I headed directly north, relying on German road signs.

There were more and more buildings on either side of the road, but all of them were deserted. There was not a living soul on the streets. It was only after travelling some number of miles that I realized that there were no tyre-marks on the road ahead of us. Somewhere along the way, the column must have turned off the road . . . I had probably dozed off and missed the turn, and the driver ignored it, hurrying to Warsaw. From the bed of the truck came the sounds of the rhythmic snores of the crew. But where had the rest of the regiment gone?! I stopped the car, went into the first house I saw; there was no one inside, but there were the remnants of an uneaten supper on the table, along with scattered evidence, clearly abandoned in a hurry, that it was officers of the Wehrmacht who had been sitting at the table. The food hadn't fully cooled, they couldn't have got far. We were surrounded by darkness, the sky was clouded over, snow fell thickly. It was time to set a night watch, send soldiers from the frozen Studebaker to sleep in the previous officers' quarters, wait until dawn.

This is how one quarter of the 5th Battery – or, more precisely, one 3-inch cannon and its crew – captured Warsaw on the day before its official liberation. It was only on the morning of the 17th that I realized that we had spent the night in Czerniaków, where, months earlier, the survivors of the unsuccessful landing had perished.

Later, there was a sharp dressing-down and a reprimand from Colonel Kumpicki, the commander of the regiment, for going AWOL from the column . . . And even later was the Pomeranian Line – freezing nights, and torrential rain during the day, soldier's greatcoats soaked through during the day and cooling into an icy shell at dusk, Germans shooting from time to time during the day, and fleeing from us (from us!) under the cover of night. And, finally, Kołobrzeg.[30]

The leader of the 5th Battery, which had entrenched on a railroad embankment about a third of a mile south of a locomotive shed, was the aforementioned Lieutenant Lange

– a terrific artillerist, feisty, and with a lively imagination, but extremely caring towards his soldiers and genuinely liked by them. At stops, he could be found on improvised lookout points together with the scouting platoon; whereas my place, as his nominal deputy, was with the cannons and firing platoons. When we were capturing the Pomeranian Line, the stops were rare – and if there were any, they were short: the Germans fled without putting up much of a resistance, abandoning their camps and heavier cargo, and we chased them day and night, almost without stopping and often sleeping on the march, saved from freezing by the necessity of a constant process of setting up the cannons and then immediately mobilizing again – sometimes before firing a single round. Actually, after crossing the Vistula, we stopped for the first time only in Kołobrzeg, from which the German divisions, cut off from the rest of the Wehrmacht by the Soviet Army, had nowhere to escape. It was still cold and wet – every night we were bothered by freezing temperatures; the locomotive shed was the only relatively complete building in sight (there were glimmers of some houses at the edge of the forest by the sea, but that was where the Germans who were shooting at us, and at whom we returned fire, were hiding) – nonetheless, as I remember, after two weeks of non-stop movement and without a roof over our heads, we were relieved to stop – to rest a bit . . .

The regiment commander, Colonel Kumpicki, and the division commander, Major Lemiesz (who were both also descendants of Polish exiles or Polish soldiers of the Russian Revolution, but, unlike General Kieniewicz, had a weak command of Polish despite diligent attempts to repair the gaps in their knowledge) set up their headquarters in the locomotive shed. Lieutenant Lange was there as well, with the commanding platoon; the artillery platoons had dug in their cannons alongside the railway embankment. The exchange of fire was sporadic; from our observation point (also in the locomotive shed), it was hard to see, through field glasses, the enemy hidden in the neighbouring forest, and potential targets rarely appeared in firing range. One such rare experience has particularly burned itself into my memory: a single Wehrmacht soldier ran out of the woods with a Panzerfaust[31] on his shoulder and ran through the empty field, pockmarked with artillery fire, in the direction of the locomotive shed, probably with the mission or intention of unloading it into the headquarters established there. The officers pulled out their guns; the daredevil was showered with dozens of bullets, but none of them hit him (even the best of artillerymen turn out not to be the best shooters, it seems, when they need to use their sidearms). There were enough of them, however, to dissuade the daredevil from his objective. He turned around and darted back into the forest. Well, it was March 1945. The air smelled of spring (thinly), and the approaching end of the war (thickly!). From a distance, it seemed to me, that the would-be hero-suicide was not even 20 years old – just like me. Bravery is bravery, but he probably wanted to live to experience the approaching world, now close, in which bullets would cease to whistle . . .

I spent just over two days in Kołobrzeg. On the third day, during another, short but intense, exchange of fire with German artillerymen, I was wounded in the shoulder by a shard from an artillery shell and transported to a field hospital for surgery. Up to that point, my soldiers had not regained a single foot of ground in Kołobrzeg. They would do so only a few days later. To this day, I do not understand why my deeds in Kołobrzeg were granted a Cross of Valour.

I underwent the operation in Starogard, at a 'Soviet hospital for Polish wounded' constructed at lightning speed (despite the hurried mobilization on the liberated terrain, there were not enough Polish doctors called for service to supply a Polish field hospital). In spite of a horribly painful split shoulder blade, the Russian surgeon forbade me from keeping my aching arm in a sling ('it will heal badly, it will produce random growths of proud flesh') and sent me to treat it by rowing on a nearby lake. The prescribed torture turned out to be extremely effective. The shoulder recovered perfectly, the wound healed in the course of a week, and the use of my right arm was barely impacted (with the exception of regular, though transitory, aches and pains when the weather is changing).

In the '1st May Day Deed',[32] a few friends and I requested early release from the hospital. Already by 3 May, thanks to the helpful drivers of many army trucks, I was able to reach 'Kumpicki's farm' (as the improvised military road signs called it) and join the Battery just past Berlin, after crossing the burning city – now on foot – from its eastern to its western suburbs.

In the field camp, it smelled of spring, the end of war, freedom. For all of us, it was clear that this time Hitler was really *kaputt*[33] and that it was a matter of days, if not hours, for him to admit it (we did not know yet about his suicide and were eagerly delighting in thoughts of a ceremony of tar and feathers). It was only a question of how to survive those few days or hours – and then everything, really everything, would be simple, bright and wonderful . . .

Colonel Kumpicki was the final casualty of the 6th Division of the PAL. On 6 May, he set off, at night, for the division headquarters – the first time since the outbreak of war that the headlights on the Jeep were turned on. Thus, what was probably the last plane in the Luftwaffe still capable of flight had no particular difficulties in finding a target for what was probably the last bomb that the Luftwaffe had.

Half a century had to pass for me to learn from the newspapers of my native land that everything that I was doing with my brothers in arms was done in the name of enslaving, and not liberating, the homeland.[34] This slander hurt terribly, as it must (if one believes in life after death) have hurt the tens of thousands of Poles who paid for this liberation/enslavement with their lives. Because, after all, as we were reminded relatively recently (15 April 2007) by Jerzy Urban:

in the course of the few months from August 1944 to the end of April 1945, more members of the Polish Army perished fighting on the Soviet front than had been lost in the entire campaign of September 1939 and in all the Polish armies fighting alongside western allies taken together. Those pre-Soviet fighters did not know that they were leaving this world for the sake of enslaving their country.

And, as he added, 'Even today's students of the IPN [Instytut Pamięci Narodowej, the Institute of National Remembrance] should ask a few questions: for instance, whether the 1st and 2nd Polish Army occupying Eastern Prussia, Western Pomerania, Lower Silesia, etc., also enslaved those German territories, or whether those were being liberated. Poland after all still benefits from their occupation.'[35]

4

Maturation

On the day of the Third Reich's capitulation, I, a second lieutenant in the Polish Army, was still a year and a half away from the age of maturity (which, as I had been taught in pre-war times, I would only achieve on my twenty-first birthday).

I do not remember losing much sleep over this thought. Quite the opposite: my youth and immaturity seemed to me to pair beautifully with the state of the country and the world (however broad or narrow my vision was at the time). And, within me and all around me, everything was just beginning: beginning *anew*. And both here and there, it was only the future that counted. The war and the occupation – with their daily portion of humiliations, hunger and fear, the relentless presence of death, the terrible and indivisible workings of a blind fate – were a nightmare, which here and now, at this moment, came to an end, and whose dark fumes it was necessary to shake off as quickly as possible. Everything was once again within human power, and there was no justification for inaction. After years of idle dreams, plentiful fantasies only meagrely stocked with hope, the time had come for plans, and thus, also, for words – but, finally, powerful ones, words that, as never before, could, should and ought to become flesh.

Maybe it really was so, or maybe it only seemed that way to me. But for me at least, it came to the same thing. I do not remember concerning myself, in May 1945, with the Spencerian clash between the interests of the 'individual' and 'society'. I encountered Herbert Spencer only much later, while studying the history of British socialism, and it did not happen without a shock and a feeling of almost an Archimedean *eureka*; and a little later, I also fell under the spell of what today's philosophical fashion calls 'subjectivity', when I found my way to John Stuart Mill. Several years of military service did not prepare me to separate the individual from the dense marching column, and my former Russian spiritual counsellors – Plechanov, with his contempt for individuals, and Mayakovsky with his 'What's an individual? No earthly good. One man, even the most important of all, can't raise a ten-yard log of wood, to say nothing of a house ten stories tall'[1] – harmonized far better with the day-to-day experiences of barracks life. Even if I had clearly distinguished the individual from the human group in general (and I don't think that, back then, I would have been able to), I probably would have said that their fates could not be separated. And if I had already experienced Professor Kotarbiński's exam in logic, I would have nipped this inquiry in the bud as a pointlessly circling tautology. Only in a good country can a person live well, and a good country is one in which people live well.

I remembered my country from before the war as having left much to be desired in this regard, and my own life there as similarly far from ideal. I can repeat the words written by Czesław Miłosz towards the end of the century: 'That Poland does not correspond at all to the ideal image that the new generation can create for itself. Getting to know that Poland will be for many readers a difficult experience, maybe a shock, and they will ask: "How is it possible?" But it was possible. . .'[2]

I did not have to ask whether it was possible; I remembered that it was. A few years younger than Miłosz, I was, however, born and raised in 'that' Poland, the same one as his. And 'that' Poland was a country of unbelievable poverty, which settled down a few steps away from my house, on the other side of Dąbrowski Street, and from time to time it sprouted along the prim and proper streets of Prus and Słowacki that were seemingly content with themselves and their fates. For a few years, it even reached into our apartment, and in every village that I visited as a child, poverty, unemployment and hopelessness multiplied without any restraints, openly mocking our pretences, masks and appearances. There was also the Poland that was hospitable to those with means but merciless and lacking compassion for those who depended on their good graces, forcing those others, like my father, to trade human dignity for bread for their family. I remembered all of this the way I remembered the cuffs, kicks and pokes, the memory of which hurt long after the bruises disappeared and the physical pain had ceased. I remembered all this the way I remembered the jeers and insults designed to last forever and to be so much more resistant than the bumps and bruises to the healing work of memory. In her unique study of post-war attitudes of Polish Jews who survived the Holocaust, Irena Nowakowska cites an anonymous officer who, in answer to her questions, stated that, instead of remembering past tortures and harms, it is necessary to occupy oneself with building a future in which they could not be repeated. I will divulge a secret: I was this swaggering officer.[3]

From the studies of Małgorzata Melchior,[4] we learn – and, indeed, it 'stands to reason' – that the experiences of Jews who survived the war in occupied Poland are different from the experiences of Polish Jews who avoided this fate. Jews concealing themselves with 'Aryan papers' remembered their fears of 'non-Jewish' Poles – a fear that Jews who found themselves beyond the borders of the occupied country, me along with them, did not have the opportunity to experience. Joanna Beata Michlic, the author of a foundational text about the changing idea of the Jew in Polish consciousness, presents the following description of a typical experience of a Jew hiding among Poles: 'I myself lived in constant fear that the Germans would kill me, but I was even more afraid of Poles who were able to recognize that I was a Jew. [. . .] However, telling a stranger or even an acquaintance that I was a Jew [. . .] would simply mean committing suicide.'5 And Emanuel, the hero of Adolf Rudnicki's story *Regina, Regina Borkowska*, when he emerged from the livestock railcar headed for Treblinka, thought: 'The time of the elements. Woe to the human, when they gain power.' Hiding in a basement, he understood what a house is. Observing the police, he understood what a Judas is. The forest was a stranger, the fields were strangers, and he was most afraid of people. 'From that first hut, a person will emerge who will be my murderer.'6

Of course, one can understand the widespread reluctance of non-Jews to give a helping hand to Jews, condemned to death en masse, and therefore singled out by the invaders from the rest of the occupied populace who were threatened with death only individually. Even the decision not to report a Jew who was in hiding, and, all the more so, a decision to come to their aid and to seek out or offer a hiding place, would subject a person, and their family, to a mortal danger. It required a downright heroic bravery, as well as a readiness to sacrifice that is only given to saints, and rarely accessible to regular people. Those who have been spared such inhuman tests of their moral strength cannot fully comprehend their atrocity. They will never be certain (just as I cannot be certain) whether, if they were subjected to a similar test, they would pass it with dignity, and in accordance with the moral principles that they genuinely, honestly espouse. Following the moral impulse could cost too much; the real difficulty, however, is that it would be equally costly to refuse to save a life, even if the price in such a case would 'only' be a guilty conscience. This dilemma had no good solution. No amount of arguments, even if they were logically airtight, could suppress the pangs of conscience.

Jerzy Jastrzębowski, cited by Jan Błoński[7] (in the immortal study entitled 'The poor Poles look at the ghetto'), recalled a history he heard from an older relative. His family decided to rescue an old friend, a Jew, of irreproachable Polish appearance, speaking perfect Polish, seemingly of noble birth – but they would not hide his three sisters, who looked like Jews, and spoke Polish with a clear Yiddish accent. But this friend would not accept the offer: he did not want to save himself if his sisters were going to their deaths.

> If my family's decision had been different, there was a 90 per cent probability that we would have been discovered and executed for hiding Jews. There was probably less than a 10 per cent chance that the family of Eljasz Parzynski could at all be saved in those conditions. The person relating this family drama to me said again and again: 'What were we to do? There was nothing we could do!' And yet, she did not look me in the eye. She knew I sensed the insincerity of the argument even though the facts were true.[8]

But the person Jerzy Jastrzębowski was speaking to was at least conscious of the dilemma, and in the conflict between reason and conscience opted for the latter, even though they acknowledged the rightness of the former. Most people facing a similar dilemma cannot stand such clarity of vision, nor the torments caused by the confusion of their thoughts and feelings that such a clarity of vision would doubtless give them. As psychologists tell us, the majority chooses the less spiritually costly option: most avoid the dilemma as much as possible and, to that end, deny its existence. They decide in advance in favour of the instinct of self-preservation above all other obligations, in order to defend themselves from their conscience. Or they flee to an even better option, denying that such obligations burdened them at that moment, because, after all, the victims met the fate that they had earned with their own sinful deeds.

Insulting the victims, accusing them of crimes that called for punishment, and therefore removing them *ex post facto* from the realm of moral obligation are reactions to which people experiencing a strong cognitive dissonance have recourse most frequently – and also most eagerly.[9] In the admittedly complex realities of life, there is generally no shortage of grist for the mill of such reactions, and if sometimes the supply of facts is insufficient, the human imagination readily fills the gap. If, for example, the crimes cannot be perceived with the naked eye, you can always claim that the guilty are especially clever at hiding them – which provides another reason to accuse the victims, and to guard against helping them. Thanks to such reactions, and similar ones, the moral impulse is suppressed. But its silencing does not mean that it disappears. Pushed into the dark corners of the subconscious, it withers and rots there, adding venom to the trauma, fuelling resentment and motivating an even more active search for reasons why the victims were not worthy of being included within the sphere of moral obligation. The stronger the pangs of conscience, and the harder it is for us to quell them, the more loudly we insult the memories of the victims; but the more loudly we shout, the smaller are our chances of extricating ourselves from the darkness, of uncovering and treating the injuries that led us to shout.

The splinter left by the failed exam in ethics is not the only reason for cognitive dissonance and for the beyond-rational, violent and bitter reactions. In a book about the post-war 'moral collapse', Jan Gross cites, among others, Bożena Szaynok, whose pioneering study of antisemitic excesses in Poland reminds us that 'Jewish property changed hands during the war.'[10] The acquisition of Jewish property was a real social advance for the new Polish owners, and the return of the former owners was a personal catastrophe, which was to be resisted with all available means. As if anticipating Leon Festinger's theory of 'cognitive dissonance', Stanisław Ossowski, in connection with this very issue, presented one of the most penetrating and accurate interpretations of the defensive reactions to such a turn of events: 'When someone's tragedy becomes someone else's gain, there appears a need to persuade oneself and others that the tragedy was morally justified. Such was the situation of the owners of stores formerly belonging to Jewish owners, or of those who had previously been competing against Jewish shop-owners.'[11]

The bitter experience of Emanuel in Rudnicki's story, or of the 'typical Polish Jew' of Joanna Beata Michlic, could be accounted for by the general properties of the human psyche, thereby absolving the perpetrators of moral offences, at least in part (though – oh, paradox – it would be easier for those held at gunpoint to understand and accept such explanations than it would be to persuade the gunman to acknowledge and accept them). We could understand the reasons for the even bitterer experiences awaiting 'typical Polish Jews' – those Jews who, in stark contradiction with realities and elementary sociological knowledge, naively imagined that the fear of neighbours and its causes would disappear from Polish lands along with those German occupiers who were now escaping in panic. This is how Jasia remembers one of the first devastating experiences she had after coming out of hiding. It happened in one of those trucks that took on the function of public transport, non-existent in the recently liberated, but decidedly ruined, capital:

Riding in a terrible crowd with these strangers, I suddenly realized that this is the first opportunity I had of looking people in Warsaw directly in the eyes. I lifted my head and smiled at my nearest neighbour, as if to say, 'Look, I returned, I'm alive!' And then I heard as one man said to another, 'Unbelievable! Some of them still remain. The German bunglers didn't gas them all.'[12]

The truck was full, but the critic of the 'bungled work' didn't even lower his voice – certain that none of his fellow passengers would pay attention or protest.

I repeat: I did not live through the German occupation of Poland. Only for a few days did I wander the streets of occupied Włocławek with the yellow stigma of a still-living corpse, like a mute accusation for some, but a cause for joy to other passers-by – those on the pavement. But those passers-by were not then threatened with death for extending the vegetation of the condemned, nor were the belongings of those headed for death available for divvying up; I managed to avoid the shame of pitying or conflicted looks, or the threat of vengeful ones, from passers-by. Unlike Emanuel [in Rudnicki's story], I was afraid of *Germans*, and not *people*. Though, when I returned to Polish streets and pavements, I was also no longer afraid of Germans. Fear had fled along with the missiles fired at them.

I returned to my native country from my Russian exile/shelter without the baggage of *that* allergy and *that* complex. I encountered many fears during my exile, but they were different. I did not experience *that* fear. And even if I had wanted to imagine the exile in all its atrocious, dehumanizing awfulness, I would probably have been inclined to ascribe it to conditions that, along with the occupiers, with their wrongdoing and their tendency to turn others into wrongdoers, were departing into the past before my eyes, and not without my participation. I did not experience Poland under German occupation; I returned to a Poland that was the one I had left while getting onto a train on 2 September 1939. It was the project of transforming *that* Poland into 'something better' in which I longed to participate. We will talk, we will come to an understanding, agree; together we will roll up our sleeves, and together we will dress the unhealed wounds and prevent new ones; together we will cleanse the country that is ours, once and for all, of envy and hatred, degradation and humiliation ... Today's reader will probably frown contemptuously: how naive . . . I expect a similar reaction to the one that was anticipated by Tadeusz Konwicki, when, in a conversation with Stanisław Bereś,[13] he confessed to his own post-war attitudes, similar to mine:

> I did not belong to the generation of businessmen making shady deals, but to the generation of people exhausted by a terrible war . . . I lived in a moral ecosphere, in an atmosphere of tensions. So it was easy for me to accept such a proposal for a better world order; all the more so as I was convinced it was the stupid world that had led to this hecatomb. If I said to a Polish businessman today that we needed to repair the world, he would laugh at me, but at the time, it was no joke.[14]

The idea that the world can be transformed into a better one comes to the mind of 19-year-olds in every generation. They paint for themselves the image of this 'better world' in various ways, every generation with its own colours, but they never give up painting it. That it must be so is guaranteed by the 19-year-olds' audaciousness, their lack of life experience and unburnt fingers, and also by their awareness that everything important in life still lies ahead, and everything that surrounds them is temporary, transitory. And 19-year-olds cannot escape thinking about a better world, even if the world they enter is as tough as granite and is resistant to all their whims. Even in such a world, as in any other, young people must climb – and when a person is climbing, a new view unfolds with every step. And the change *of* what is perceived is easy to confuse with the change *in* what is looked at . . . And, in addition, the weight of the past, which in normal times would bode for bold young people – as Nietzsche warned – only 'gnashing of teeth and loneliest misery',[15] was flimsy to my 19-year-old's reckoning, and moreover appeared to me to already be in a strained condition: the war that was now coming to an end was doing away with a big part of it, thus challenging faith in the immovability of what to other generations seemed immovable. All of this together (in a perverse way, it's true) gave some confidence to those who dreamed about taking the world apart and sewing it up anew.

In one of his recent TV interviews, Leszek Kołakowski said that he was driven at that time by similar desires. And that, comparing different ideas for a better Poland circulating during those days, he came to the conclusion that the communists had, comparatively, the best programme. He was not alone in this view. People who were thinking and feeling intensely during those times, patriots not necessarily sympathetic to communism, believed (not without reason, after all) that the roots of Poland's wretchedness ran deep – and a radical wretchedness, as they rightly considered, required a radical medicine. They shuddered at the idea that Poland could return to its pre-War state – to the class divisions, mass unemployment and equally mass poverty that called out to the heavens for vengeance . . . Many years later, not long before his death, Stanisław Ossowski confessed to me that when the news spread, in August 1939 in Modlin, where he was sent during mobilization, that Beck had reconciled with Ribbentrop and there would be no war, he was alarmed and fell into despair: so everything would stay just as it was?

The communists promised to end the 'old ways', and they did it more fervently than anyone else. They claimed to have a programme for radical eradication of class oppression, for returning the land to the peasants and factories to the workers, and for restoring dignity to both peasants and workers – and everyone else. With this programme, they believed they were the only ones who could create the conditions for the freedom, equality and brotherhood demanded by all the greatest intellects since the time of the Enlightenment, and sought, thus far unsuccessfully, by each generation of reformers and revolutionaries. And, under the influence of the bitter and sobering experiences of defeat and occupation, the masses of Poles who shared Ossowski's fears grew uncontrollably. In March 1944, Jan Rzepecki, the head of the Bureau of Information and Propaganda of the AK, an attentive and diligent investigator of the occupied nation's pulse, warned General Bór-Komorowski, and, through him, the government-in-exile, that:

> there has undoubtedly been a radicalization of groups pre- viously oppressed . . . There has been a popular demand for eliminating the great concentration of goods in the hands of private citizens or groups of people and for eradicating all material, cultural and political privilege . . . all efforts to reverse this process or at least to stop it are hopeless, and even harmful. This is the passionate pursuit of the masses that nothing will be able to stifle . . .[16]

I spent a few years among the Soviets, where the commu- nists had a full twenty years to prove their claims through practice. So I should have known better: that their promises did not pave the path to actions, and the path of action was a bloody one . . . But I did not know – or I preferred not to know. I suppressed my doubts and did not allow them to speak up, attributing anything that alarmed me or put me off to avoidable mistakes, which we, wise after the fact, would be able to prevent in Poland, or so I believed (a little more than twenty years later, my English friend Ralph Miliband[17] tried to persuade me, in the same way, that in realizing this smart programme, so noble in its premises, the English would avoid the mistakes made by both Russians and Poles . . . he consid- ered me a renegade when I tried, in vain, to explain to him that such hopes are inclined to prove futile when put to a practical test). I cannot be sure today with what thoughts – or to what extent without thinking – I entered those next twenty years that Celina Budzyńska called in hindsight 'years of hope and defeat'.[18] Budzyńska *could* know even more, much more than I did, and she knew it from first-hand experience, not just from rumours and secret confessions. She lost those closest to her in Stalinist purges, and was herself for years in Soviet camps as the 'wife of an enemy of the people'. But even she admitted:

> I am asked by my grandchildren and young friends, how could you, after everything you lived through and with all you knew, 'build socialism' again, and in your own country at that. It is hard to answer this, not only for others but, above all – for myself. I cannot escape it, as did Konwicki in 'The rising and setting of the moon', pretending it was not me but someone entirely different. No, it was certainly me, with all of my experiences and thoughts, which somehow co-existed with a deep faith in socialism, in the idea of justice, etc. It is funny, but maybe not entirely. And the point here is not to confess your fault, but to ask how it could happen.[19]

Much to my disappointment, and probably to that of many readers, in the remainder of her memoirs, in the effort to answer the question 'how could this happen?', Budzyńska simply lists events, often entirely incidental and having little to do with life choices: 'meeting friends, old and new'; 'burned-out houses, ruins, roads, cinders' that turn out to constitute Jerusalem Avenue in Warsaw; a chance encounter with an acquaintance who proposes a ride to Łódź, and there, as it happens, at that exact moment, the Central School of the PPR[20] is founded, etc., etc. Events followed one after another quickly, at a dizzying speed, not leaving a moment to catch one's breath, not leaving space for reflection; and they appeared one after another in such a way that it was not possible to distinguish 'what happened to me' from 'what I did myself'. One would want to say the string of events was due to 'blind chance', like in Kieślowski's film of the same title, though every chance event,[21] just like in the film, was brimming with consequences neither planned nor foreseen, nor consciously desired, nor possible to figure out in advance. And 'blind chance' just means that if what happened had not happened, the sequence of things could have been entirely different, and an entirely different life could have followed.

An example of such a consequential 'blind chance' in my own life was the news that reached the regiment a few days after the surrender of the Germans, as I was expecting a speedy demobilization, and my intention of returning to my interrupted studies in physics was reincarnating from a dream into a plan: the 4th Division, along with a few other military units, was to be reorganized, entering the newly formed 'Korpus Bezpieczenstwa Wewnętrznego' (KBW), the 'Internal Security Corps'.[22] Overnight, we all became – from soldiers to colonels – soldiers of the KBW. Because there was no plan for an artillery in the KBW, those who were, like me, political and educational officers in the 6th PAL – artillery-men by designation but not at all by skill, or especially by profession – were sent to the protective battalions forming in the capital cities of voivodeships. As we were told, the task of the KBW was to protect objects that needed protecting and to disarm the armed 'bands' when, and if, they appeared. After a short transition period in Łódź, I was assigned to Bydgoszcz.

That it was the 4th Division that was chosen for the role of the 'skeleton' of the newly created KBW was, from the perspective of my life's journey, a chance event . . . But it was not an accident that I seized the accidental opportunity without a murmur. Remaining in the army was not, admittedly, a part of my plans; I wanted above all to return to my studies as quickly as possible – but this, or some other, contribution to 'building socialism' figured high on my list of desires. I took the role I was appointed to as a delay in demobilization and a signal that a return to civilian life and my personal preferences needed to wait.

In the same spirit I perceived the proposal of joining the PPR, the Polska Partia Robotnicza, and the one of cooperating with 'military information'. Typically for a novice, I knew about these issues only from books, and I assumed that assisting in counter-espionage was officers' obvious patriotic duty towards the military forces and to the people they protected. (My obligation to cooperate, as short-lived as it was, was one part of my autobiography that I did not speak about; I remained silent simply because signing up included a promise to keep it secret. I was not allowed to break this promise. And it was not I who eventually broke it . . .) I took all that was happening en masse, considering it as the call to 'contribute to building socialism', the order that I yearned for. I complied, even though these unplanned events came at an unexpected time. Relatively quickly, it became clear that this was not how I had envisioned it . . . because what I was doing did not have much in common with how I imagined 'building socialism'.

There were no 'bands', either in Łódź or in Pomerania, and as an officer I did not have guard duty. I thus passed the time chatting with soldiers, inspecting the kitchen and preventing people from stealing from it, raising public funds for the battalion's banner and organizing a public ceremony to bless it,[23] and . . . establishing a soccer team that I signed up for local tournaments under the name 'WKS Sztorm' (it was quickly promoted to the Pomeranian A-class, before it was incorporated, to my despair, into the 'Gwardia', the newly established national sports club of the Ministry of the Interior).[24] In this last project, I was fortunate to have the devoted professional help of Lieutenant Bojczuk, a pre-war soccer player and later the coach of Resovia who, by happy chance, had been assigned to the battalion in the role of paymaster. As I remember, acquiring soccer jerseys, shorts and cleats was not an easy matter in 1946, and consumed a lot of my time and energy.

When the battalion had expanded to the size of a regiment, I became an instructor in the regiment's political and educational department. This was not a labour-intensive post. For me, its primary virtue was the plenitude of time left available for observing soccer training. And when an officers' school was created in Szczytno,[25] I was transferred there to a similar position as instructor – except that, in addition to delivering my lectures, I came up with the idea of publishing (by mimeograph) a weekly bulletin for everyone in the school. After the disastrous results in Bydgoszcz, I did not attempt to organize a soccer team. All the more so as the newly minted officers were leaving Szczytno for their new units every three months, with a new course then opening for freshly recruited students. The conditions were thus not conducive to creating and training a proper team. Besides, Szczytno lacked the invaluable Bojczuk.

Near the end of 1947, I was called down to Warsaw, to the Division of Propaganda in the Political Department of the KBW, on the initiative of its head, Colonel Zdzisław Bibrowski. As he confessed to me later, Bibrowski was impressed by my monthly accounts of political and educational work, written in a style which was absolutely not suited to such accounts, but which possibly signalled some virtues (or vices) that could prove useful in writing lectures. From then on, until the end, I was a 'clerk'. Day after day, I sat at a desk; every day, to my unhappiness, dragged sluggishly on, try as I might – usually with very little success – to lend it vigour by finding relatively sensible and comparatively less boring tasks. The only variety in my office routine was the not very exciting briefings from the political and education instructors in the voivodeship units. But all this did leave a lot of time for my studies, to which – as I will elaborate in a moment – I eagerly returned.

As far as I remember, I was sent into the 'field' – the rural area of Podlachia – only once, in the winter of 1945 and 1946. Armed troops, sometimes originating in underground organizations but mostly just in regular criminal gangs, were scattered around Białystok. The remnants of the occupation-inflicted demoralization, these people attacked police stations and stopped trains, dragging out the passengers and exacting tributes, often executing the victims they chose on the spot.

The aim of our action was to arrest the attackers: soldiers were given a list of addresses where the aggressors were allegedly residing. As far as I know, none, or almost none, of the suspects was ever found at the addresses provided by local denunciations. Either they were never there, or they had sufficient advanced warning to hide in the forest. The soldiers' actions were nothing in comparison to the more successful 'Sanacja' expeditions to pacify Volhynia, Podolia or Pokuttia.[26] The two were incomparable, either with regard to the radicalism of the means used, or in the effects of their use . . . We were led by a 'specialist in hunting terrorists' sent from Russia, but his expertise turned out to be not very useful in Polish conditions. I have no idea what the 'expert' wrote in his report on the expedition, but I do not think that he praised my bravery (not much remains in my memory from this trip into the field aside from the terrible cold and a thrilling experience: the premiere of *Forbidden Songs* in a Białystok movie theatre).[27] Indeed, I was never again sent into 'the field'. In fact, I was kept far from any of the more 'responsible' tasks requiring people with nerves stronger than mine and with fewer scruples. For instance, I was not included in the 'election commissions' that were called for the referendum and parliamentary elections not long after my 'field' experience.

Next to this 'expert', by the way, I played a role that mirrored my function next to other political and education officers of the 4th Division: I was an antidote for the blatant Russianness of the leaders. The need for such a function in the KBW soon ended, because all the 'experts' were sent back to Russia and replaced with a cadre of Polish officers. Not many remember today that the KBW was the first almost totally 'de-Russified' military formation in Poland. In this respect, the Corps contrasted sharply with the rest of the Polish Army, especially at the moment when Konstanty Rokossowski assumed command of the army subordinated to the Ministry of National Defence.[28] During the 'Polish October', it was only the 'internal army' – not the

one under Rokossowski's control, but the one under the joint
leadership of Wacław Komar and Juliusz Hübner – that could
be, and was, sent to prepare the defence of Warsaw against
a possible Soviet attack.[29] These armies were the only armed
group of whose patriotism and loyalty in a conflict with Big
Brother the Polish authorities could be certain.

Two further 'blind chance' events happened in my life when,
near the end of 1947, I finally settled in Warsaw together with
my parents, happily repatriated from the Soviet Union a year
earlier.

The first chance event: in the fall of 1947, as I sped to
the University of Warsaw with a transcript testifying to my
completion of the first two years of studies in physics at the
university in Gorki (it was carefully preserved in spite of the
front, and wounds, and the hospital), I was told that Soviet
studies were not accredited by the University of Warsaw. I
was also informed that, in the following academic year, I could
apply to start university from the beginning. This accident
turned out to be, so to speak, a happy one ... In my years in
Bydgoszcz and Szczytno, I had dreamed of returning to my scientific studies, but, rather than exploring cosmic 'black holes'
and even discovering new laws of physics, I was increasingly
drawn to studies more directly engaged in 'fixing society' and
improving human lives. I hesitated, however, because I was
also drawn to the studies I had already started. I was unable to
make a decision; the rejection from the physics department of
the University of Warsaw solved my problem and freed me, in
some sense, from the torments of a choice. Because it was still
possible to be admitted to the Academy of Political Sciences, I
applied and was accepted. From then on, nearly every evening
for the next three years was spent at lectures or tutorials on
Rej and Rejtan Streets; and a significant portion of my days
passed at the office, with evenings at home devoted to reading. It was my first real encounter with philosophy, sociology,

social history. They immediately captivated me; it was love at first sight. So it was no longer an accident, but a choice, that I remained faithful to that first love until the end. And that I was never to fall out of love.

The second chance event: I met Janina at the Academy of Political Sciences. But it was not by chance that I fell in love with her at first sight. And it was certainly no accident that I never fell out of love during the next sixty years.

A stifling, smothering atmosphere dominated in the political division of the KBW, as can be, and often is, the case behind walls with no windows and with doors rarely opened. A visitor from Mars would be hard pressed to understand the reason for the KBW's existence; it would seem like a collective whose own existence – or rather self-annihilation – was its only goal, fate and task. In the second half of 1948, an intense Stalinization of the 'socialist camp' began, initiated by the anathema on Tito. It was accompanied by what proved to be a permanent 'great purge', the aim of which was to eliminate 'suspicious elements' from the (already 'unified') Party, and thus also from institutions symbiotically connected to the Party, such as the political division of the KBW. 'Suspicious elements' included those who had joined the Polish Workers' Party, and later the Polish United Workers' Party, with hopes that were 'not the ones they were supposed to be' – hopes that were untimely and naive, and, as was now about to be revealed, entirely unsuited to the new tasks. These 'elements' were people on whose obedience (not to mention motivation) the Party could not count in the coming period of 'sharpening class conflict' and introducing the 'dictatorship of the proletariat'.

And just on the basis of who I was, as if 'by nature', I was suspected of all of these sins in practically every respect. I was the son of a former shopkeeper and of a woman related to owners of factories or sawmills, thus caught by birth in the hazy space between the petty bourgeoisie and the bourgeoisie. Although still insufficiently educated, I was a student – a person who was actively educating himself, and thus aspired to the 'pseudo-elite' of the 'educatedets'.[30] In times in which 'your drive rather than a high school diploma will make you into an officer',[31] and when 'individuality', individualism and independence of judgement, characteristic of the educatedets, were irreconcil-able with the idea of a disciplined 'collective', these disgraces were known under different names, yet with intentions and results similar to those to be found in the recent conflicts over the 4th Republic. Let us note that, in those times, the bearers of diplomas were not born, like today, under every roadside stone, but on a seemingly sky-high rock. Or so it appeared from the perspective of the uneducated nation, stripped of its intel-ligentsia by the occupation. For many reasons, I was an obvious target for those on the prowl, and for the regularly repeated ritual of persecution, the hunt and collecting hunting trophies.

For my being able to avoid, for a few years, the increasing numbers of hunters, and poachers aspiring to the role of hunt-ers, I am probably indebted to Colonel Zdzisław Bibrowski,[32] who, just like me, was a 'foreign body' in this group – a wise person, a man of remarkable intelligence, impressive with the breadth of his learning and knowledge, a rare life wisdom and humour, together with the scepticism and reflection practically of a Seneca, and an ethics probably related most to the studies of Marcus Aurelius. Zdzisław Bibrowski was a rare phenomenon – a remnant of the generation of visionary communist intelligentsia, rapidly crumbling (or, rather, being crumbled) from the Party ranks and disappearing from public view. For some reason, Bibrowski took a liking to me and did what he could to protect me. This accident meant that my pres-ence in the ranks of the KBW lasted until the end of 1952. My turn to be culled came inexorably after Bibrowski's departure from the leadership of the Division. It is worth remembering that, twenty-something years later, Bibrowski was to become the initiator, organizer, driving force and brain of the section of Solidarity composed of academic workers.

The need for a direct pretext for removing me from the KBW was served by the 'doctors' plot'[33] and my 'Zionism', apparently obvious to my supervisors. I am not sure whether the concept of 'Zionism' was already the code word for Jew in the Polish Party lexicon at that time, as it was among the Soviets – but the leaders of the Polish People's Republic espoused a principle of trans-generational heredity of sin (as was the father, so is the son), and my father indeed had the habit of visiting the – admittedly entirely legal – Israeli embassy in Warsaw. That, at least, was the reason I was given for letting me go from my job – but for years I had been considered a 'foreign body' by the KBW and felt that I was 'on the outs', expecting to be expelled long before my father first crossed the threshold of the Israeli embassy and the first Moscow doctor was accused of poisonous aspirations stemming from Zionist beliefs.

When the many-years-old predictions finally materialized and I was expelled, I reacted with contradictory feelings: a sense of tragedy and relief.

Tragedy: the three of us, Jasia and I and 3-year-old Ania, were left practically without bread and with the threat of losing our staff housing hanging over our heads. A young military couple with an infant moved in with us immediately after my parents relocated to a different staff apartment at the Warsaw Food Cooperative, where my mother worked. Jasia's earnings in Polish Film were far too meagre to support a three-person family. The staff manager at the KBW offered me a referral for a job in . . . the training division of the Ministry of State Farms, designated at the time as the Polish substitute for Siberia, where disloyal, thus fallen, 'elements' were exiled and isolated. I did not take the referral and thus remained unemployed. Accustomed to a salary that I received regularly on the first of every month, I also remained without money.

And relief: years of fear, of a life of being permanently on call and subject to the same blunt standards as everyone else, were finally behind me. After a seven-year long delay, I finally received the right (and obligation!) to make a choice of what to do with my life; a choice that would be my own, incontrovertibly, and my own responsibility. One more accident was that a two-year master's degree programme had been established at the Department of Philosophy of the University of Warsaw a year earlier and that my dismissal from the army coincided with the completion of my first year of studies. Yet it was no longer an accident but the result of a choice that I went to the dean's office and placed into the hands of the dean, Professor Emil Adler, an application for the position of assistant in the Department of Philosophy (as it turned out, this was not only the first, but also the last, application for a job that I ever submitted in my academic life; after that, there were only invitations). To my surprise and complete relief, the application was accepted. It was a surprise, because a firm residue of many years of 'life in purge' was my equally firm belief that, in accordance with a modernized version of Archimedes' law, a body once expelled will be expelled constantly and from everywhere. It was a relief, regardless of the meagreness of assistants' salaries.

The question circulated within Party circles in the Polish People's Republic, and especially among the persistently and inexorably growing troop of 'former Party members': how is a communist different from an apple? And the answer: an apple falls when it matures, but a communist matures upon falling . . . I have often wondered whether the vicissitudes of my life, caught succinctly but accurately in that disguised-as-a-joke assertion, reflected this rule. I was plagued and tormented by this question, and even now, in the twilight of my life, I am unable to get rid of it completely. How would my life have gone, how would my consciousness have developed and matured, if I had not 'fallen' – or, more accurately, if I had not been made to fall?

I console myself as much as I can that, after all, the next fifteen years of my life did not quite follow this rule, though I admit with regret that they did not deviate from it strongly enough to immunize me entirely against being forced into it. On the one hand, a few more years were to pass from the first 'fall' before the process of 'maturation' really began in earnest. On the other hand, the next 'fall', which took place fifteen years later, this time with the active involvement of my Alma Mater, was, without a doubt, the result and not the cause of 'maturation'.

In 1953, I was still a committed communist. Whatever disgusted or repelled me in the practices of the 'powers that be' I attributed to what two years later would be called by Khrushchev 'errors and excesses'.[34] I perceived a growing number of human harms, unjust accusations and evil deeds, but they did not form a whole for me. I did not think they were intended, or, even less, that they were inherent to the 'order' that was being introduced to Poland. And it certainly did not cross my mind that they could be in a causal relationship to the 'building of socialism' or that they were inextricably linked to it in any other way. My doubts were not about the idea, but about the way it was being realized, or more specifically, about the moves that were attributed to it. It was not 'the system' that was to be blamed, I thought, but its faulty functioning. I believed that the people at the top, in accordance with their assurances, were indeed driven by the desire for social justice, except that – whether out of incomprehension or for a lack of ability – they made mistakes using means that were not conducive to accomplishing this goal (after all, the call for social justice presaged the emergence of the idea of socialism and demanded turning it into flesh). These people wanted the right thing, but made errors. They tried, but it didn't work. They erred. But they wanted the same thing as I did, so we were on the same road; and those who strayed could still be brought back onto the right track if we only appealed to their reason. In the end, if it didn't work, it would be possible to replace them with other people, more reasonable ones, more honest, equipped with a lot of good will. Assuming, of course, as I did, that they wanted to repair their mistakes, and that, if they didn't want it fervently enough, then many others would be found who would want to do all that is necessary to avoid 'errors and excesses'.

I admit: I 'matured' slowly. There was a stubborn hope that the 'Party would understand' and acknowledge its 'errors', would turn away from the wrong path and, to use the words that could be heard after the 'Prague Spring', 'restore a human face to socialism'. It persisted for yet some time after my smarter friends, such as Leszek Kołakowski, had already come to the conclusion that this was not about errors, but about the underlying premises of the system; that the people who were drawn into the Party and wanted to serve it were doing so not despite its 'errors', but because what others considered as errors, or even as the wickedness and crimes of the rulers, actually suited them; and that, with such a 'Party', there is nothing to discuss, and it is not even worth trying. That any 'repairs' could be done only in spite of the ruling party, and not with its initiative and participation.

I was convinced of the sense, rightness and righteousness of the 'great project'. There was, after all, something to base this conviction on. Poland was growing, and its people with it. In those days, progress in Poland, as in the rest of the world, was measured by the number of factory chimneys and tons of steel or coal produced, and in that regard its pace in the so far predominantly agricultural country could only be described as dizzying. Before our eyes, Warsaw rose from the dead, and, from month to month, it became more beautiful (during our Sunday walks, with Jasia, we delighted in the sights of the charming Old Town, the MDM, Muranów[35] rising from the ruins, or – yes, yes! – from day to day, climbing ever higher towards the clouds, the Palace of Culture and Science). After the agricultural reforms promised by pre-war governments, but never undertaken by them seriously, were finally completed, rural Poland emerged from the misery and cultural backwardness that had plagued it for only too long. In contrast to the capitalist West, it was not the unemployed who lined up in front of employment offices, but directors of factories who lined for workers (even if, also in a stark contrast to the West, customers waited in vain for goods, rather than goods for clientele). In universities, one could now see boys and girls who before the war would have not dreamed of crossing the threshold of such schools (as Miłosz wrote, a year and a half before, in a bulletin posted on the day he decided to stay abroad, the 'semi-feudal structure of Poland was broken' and 'working-class and peasant youth filled universities').[36] Although there was still much to wish for when it came to education, healthcare, housing or leisure resorts (for now, for now!), they were all free or nearly free, and accessible to all. To cite Miłosz once more: 'for someone who understood the dynamic of transformations taking place in Poland, the conflicts of several small parties [in exile – ZB] gave the impression of a futile game, with these politicians looking like vaudeville figures'.[37]

And still, always in the background, there was that feeling that the worst was behind us, that the atrocities of war and bestiality of the occupation would not return, and the fact that (to cite Camus), 'The leveling-out that death's imminence had failed in practice to accomplish was realized at last, for a few gay hours, in the rapture of escape.'[38] . . . For now, for 'at least a few hours' that stretched over a few years, there was something with which to delight the eye and exhilarate the heart. Only Doctor Rieux, the hero of Camus's *The Plague*, knew 'that the plague bacillus never dies or disappears for good; that it can lie dormant for years and years in furniture and linen-chests; that it bides its time in bedrooms, cellars, trunks, and bookshelves; and that perhaps the day would come when, for the bane and enlightening of men, it would rouse up its rats again.'[39] . . . Well, I lacked his wisdom.

I cannot fully explain why I was doing what I was doing, though it would probably be easier for me to explain it to others than to myself. My life lacked the *experimentum crucis* – final proofs, brooking no objection. I am sometimes jealous of people who can solve dilemmas readily, without deliberating, mainly for the public good, and who, by so doing, rid themselves of problems (and also of their own suspicions and doubts?). I admire, though I do not envy, people who insist that they would do things more wisely than others if they found themselves in such a situation – and who are even able to say that they would behave nobly in situations that they have never experienced, and that they would do this in accordance with the wisdom that they have at the moment when they are making such claims. And I definitely, decidedly, prefer my own doubts to the impudence of those who are inclined to believe – or at least claim to believe – that people's opposition to eavesdropping on citizens and to mandatory public confessions can only be explained by their having something to hide; or that opposition to sending to galleys those who have stolen a loaf of bread could only be the work of those who have stolen plenty of bread themselves. I cannot compete with these people in ingenuity and finding peace of mind . . . and I thank God that I can't.

The English writer Thomas Hardy convincingly demonstrated in his numerous novels that one's fate is a person's character. But what is my character? Fate saved me (stinted?) a reliable test, in which I could discover my character – check it truly and without a shadow of a doubt. Unlike many of my peers, I was spared the experience of the camps and *lagers*, in which, as Primo Levi concisely summed up, 'everyone is desperately and ferociously alone', 'everything is hostile' and 'all are enemies or rivals'.[40] I was spared the camps in which, I would say, people awaken to their own solitude; realize that they are face to face with their existence, stripped of covers, whether presented or acquired, deprived of the possibility of lying to others or, what is more important, of lying to themselves; unable to ignore or misinterpret the truth about themselves. They are thus unable to pretend to be what they are not; they cannot pretend in front of others, but mainly and above all, for the first time in their life completely and finally, they stand without fig leaves before themselves.

A few decades ago, there was a wave of hijacking planes and taking hostages. Every new attack was trumpeted in the news (which, of course, earned the pioneers imitators, inviting others to further attacks and abductions), but for a few days only, as is generally the case with our homeless attention span, wandering and refusing to rest. The victims of the kidnappings disappeared from the public sight just as swiftly as they were pushed into it. With only one exception: a certain journalist from *Le Monde*[41] found the addresses of former hostages and visited them years later, to refresh memories of bygone, nearly forgotten, media spectacles. To his surprise, he discovered that a significant portion of married couples who were both victims of such an attack and experienced it together divorced soon after being set free . . . why? Because to the husband and wife, the partner they had ostensibly known for a long time revealed a face that they had never seen before; and, once having seen this visage, they saw it as villainous, worthy of contempt and not to be tolerated. For example, the caring, affectionate and capable husband and father, a man carefully guarding his dignity, turned out in a moment of danger to be an egoist and coward, fell to his knees before the kidnappers and was ready to sacrifice his entire family in order to save his own skin. But if that couple had boarded a different plane, or if either had got onto the plane alone, they would have never seen this heretofore unknown side of their partner; they might have not even suspected its existence, and they would have lived out their years together in harmony, in a blissful shared ignorance, through golden and perhaps diamond anniversaries. Other discoveries, perhaps even the opposite, can probably be made when a capricious accident tears to shreds the thin, comforting cloak of daily routine; deprived of imagination, the callous

partner can find in himself a stockpile of courage and the propensity for self-sacrifice that neither he, nor those around him,
certain that they knew him through and through, would have
even suspected he had. Different situations present a person
with different challenges, and different challenges demand different virtues and reveal different faults.

Hardy is probably right when he says that a person's character is their fate, and thus that the key to a person's character
is also the key to their fate. The thing is, however, that not
every life provides the keys to all the locks of character. For
the truth of any judgement beginning with 'what if' cannot be
guaranteed. And the least worthy of trust are those judgements
that begin with 'If I were in his place'.

The main protagonists of the movie *The Lives of Others*,
directed by Florian Henckel von Donnersmarck, are crammed
into the same tight corner of a totalitarian nation, in which
no strap of land and no crevice will escape diligent surveillance, in which every free choice is considered to be a crime
against the state precisely because it is free, and is treated
accordingly by the state. The main *dramatis personae* are artists in the theatre – playwrights, directors or actors – namely,
people who by dint of their profession become personifica-
tions of imagination, inventiveness, originality, experiment,
or, in short, of free choice. They are not, however, alone in
this corner. Big Brother never sleeps. The eyes of Big Brother
are always open; his ears are always perked up. The random
(frivolous, capricious, unpredictable) moves of Big Brother in
the endless game of grace and disgrace, favour and humiliation, reach artists' workspaces, theatrical scenes and bedrooms
disguised as accidents or 'chance occurrences of fate'. There
are too many accidents and caprices of fate to feel safe in this
corner, to protect oneself from surprises and effectively ward
off the blows. A difficult situation, to put it mildly: difficult for
all residents of this corner, both the cowards and the brave
ones, for the careerists and those who are fighters by nature.

You might say that being moved time and again from one police file to another, the artists, those pawns in a game that they are not playing, have no choice but to stick to the role of a billiard ball: they have to move when pushed and then roll in the direction determined in advance by the placement of the cue and at the distance dictated by the power of the shot. But do they really have no other choice?

All of the protagonists of Donnersmarck's film are crowded into the same corner and pushed by the same pool cues. But this is where the resemblances between them end . . . One of them, a blacklisted director, from the first moment opts for a clean conscience and fidelity to his artistic vision – and, later, even suicide – rather than dishonesty and the betrayal of ideals that would buy him a return to the stage. Another, a playwright, a favourite of Big Brother and his model intellectual, chooses being published and on display, applauded and feted in national award ceremonies, and gives up the satisfaction of speaking the truth, the whole truth, and nothing but the truth. The third character in the drama, a much-loved artist, agrees under threat of being banned from public appearances to sell her body to a dignitary of the regime and betray her artist friends. She discloses to her inquisitors the hiding place of the typewriter that has been used in writing a pamphlet against the tyranny of the state. If found, this typewriter would have served as evidence against the playwright whom she loved, thereby condemning him to prison. But her inquisitor, famous for his insidious, refined methods of interrogating his victims, removes the machine and prevents a catastrophe. Probably moved by the couple's love and willing to save them, he does what he does at the cost of his own inevitable degradation; the police find only an empty space.

Before his suicide, the director changes his will and leaves the manuscript of his never-produced *Sonata for a Good Person* to the playwright. After the fall of the Stasi-run regime, the playwright dedicates his new play with the same title to the person who as an inquisitor opted for humanness rather than his superiors' approval or an advancement of his own career ... *Fate dictates the available choices. But it is character that makes the choices.*

I will run ahead now, to bring the history of my anti-romance with the security forces to an end. (Here I bit my own tongue ... To an end? Remember, all of you who are 'starting anew': once brought to life, security forces – whatever their colours – are by their own nature immortal. They will certainly outlive you. If their own vital forces do not suffice, the founders of the next 'security service' will certainly make sure of that.)

I was leaving the KBW with a red flag in my life-story. My being categorized as one of the 'usual suspects' – or, more simply, as wild game – became a fact: irreversible and indisputable fact. Just like the Moscow doctors, I was saved (from consequences more serious than losing my job) by another accident: the death of Stalin. But the sentence was noted in the archives of the security force and (by no fault of the hooded judges) only its execution was delayed.

In truth, it took another two and a half years before the suspicions of the security forces became justified by my behaviour. Finally, there was something to track, something to report on, something to fill the file with. That they had to wait so long for all this is one more proof of the shameful slowness of my 'maturation'.

Another set of scales would not fall from my eyes and I would not stop deluding myself that communism is one version of the 'road to socialism' (as winding, full of stumbles and erroneous as it was), until Khrushchev delivered his memorable speech and Stalinist crimes were explicitly named. I write 'another' set of scales and not 'the last', because I still believed that the *Polish* road, over which the fight was about to begin, would not follow the trajectory of the *Soviet* version and would not go astray. The story of my friend Ralph, an intelligent and upright person, is another testimony to how difficult it is to free oneself from this kind of delusion. Ralph visited Warsaw during the Polish October to imbibe with his own eyes and ears, with baited breath and true jealousy, the activities of the intelligentsia and workers who joined forces during the period of repairing the (people's) Republic. Later, Ralph believed that he and his fellow travellers would be able to protect the *English* road to socialism from straying and from repeating the *Polish* errors and mishaps . . . And at the time of the 'Prague Spring', Jiři Lederer, the editor of *Literárne Noviny* ('Literary News'), while in Warsaw, assured me warmly but honestly that Dubček was not Gomułka, and the Czechs were not the Poles, and they would manage perfectly all that the Poles tried to do but messed up, and what the Hungarians wanted to do but weren't allowed to.

The ideas inspired by the speech given by (the sociologically illiterate) Khrushchev resulted in my initially somewhat awkward 'revisionist manifestos': 'On the need for a sociology of the party', published, thanks to the censors' temporary paralysis, in *Studia Filozoficzne* ('Philosophical Studies'); 'Treatise on bureaucracy'[42] and 'Notes beyond time',[43] published in *Twórczość* ('Creativity'); the brochure 'On the democracy internal to the party'; and publications in *Po Prostu* ('Simply'). All these texts have been cut up by the censors, and a few months later this kind of publication would have been banned altogether.[44] Well, the Philosophy Department at UW[45] was a veritable nest of revisionism and of 'wrong-thinking' of all kinds.

Even practising sociology as an independent source of knowledge about the state of society was considered to be of an 'anti-state' and 'anti-socialist' nature, because it meant fulfilling a function over which the state demanded a complete monopoly. And, by their very nature, the sociologists guilty of practising it were seen as suspects. Constantly, officially, and almost certainly also unofficially, we were all objects of concern for those in power, as well as of surveillance by its 'organs'. The archives of the Department of Security (UB), today renamed the treasury of national memory, swelled with documents.

My personal contribution to instigating the rebellious spirit was, to put it mildly, second-rate in comparison to that of my departmental colleagues Leszek Kołakowski, with his tremendous authority, or Krzysztof Pomian, with his inexhaustible energy (not to mention self-abnegating and self-sacrificing people like Kuroń, Modzelewski, Lipski or Michnik).[46] It was limited to proclaiming heretical views in lectures and class discussions, refusing to participate in delegations to international congresses in cases where passports were denied to this or that non-Party non-Bolshevik friend (parenthetically speaking, plenty of such non-Party Bolsheviks were prepared to swallow any prescribed pill, however bitter it was, without complaint), or advocating, 'against the good of the institution', for a student held responsible for 'anti-State and anti-socialist activities' and actions by the university disciplinary court. But the dimensions of my file in the archive were nonetheless quite respectable (I cannot swear to this, I did not have a look at it either then or now).

Denunciations were the daily bread of the archives, but probably an insufficient one because secret services, with the passage of time, began to resort to provocation. One day, my department was visited by Benek Tejkowski, the erstwhile spiritual leader of Kraków's rebelling students and a prisoner of the UB. Rebellious circles accorded him the halo of the 'Red Tomato' which he bore right from the times of the Polish October in 1956. It should have raised our suspicions that a provincial rebel targeted by 'organs' was suddenly given an apartment in the centre of Warsaw, by Hoża Street, and allowed to open a salon that attracted the cream of Warsaw's independent-thinking students and young adepts of the humanities. But it did not . . . We embraced the hero with open arms. I arranged an assistantship for him, and agreed on a topic for a master's thesis on the theory and practices of bureaucracy. Tejkowski turned out to be, to say the least, a fiendishly (I use this word advisedly!) intelligent and diligent person; the dissertation was written at an astonishingly fast speed and proved exceptional in every sense of the word. Except that, before I received a copy to examine, the original landed by luck (but probably not) at the Commission for Party Control, launching a series of disciplinary proceedings under the leadership of Mrs Gomułka, and ending with a reprimand and warning. And again, in November of 1967, a group of friends gathered in my daughter Anna's room to celebrate her eighteenth birthday. As they were leaving, all of the guests were arrested, pushed down the stairs, brutally beaten, and kept overnight for 'interrogation' in Mostowski Palace. The arrest was overseen by the police major Lucjan Nowak, who sometime earlier had moved – or, as our doorwoman lamented, 'broke in by force' – into the apartment below us, designated for someone else, apparently legalizing this act by installing devices through which he could eavesdrop on us and follow all that was happening in our apartment.

The day after the student rally at the university on 8 March 1968, the knives came fully out of their sheaths. To this day, I believe that it was organized as a result of a series of intricate provocations by the Security Service, SB, at least in part (as I wrote then in the article 'On frustration and conjurers' published in the Parisian *Kultura*,[47] I believe it despite the fact that I still cannot prove it). TV screens and front pages of magazines were full of accusations against university professors, spreading moral desolation among the naive, gullible youth. Buckets of slops were pouring through TV programmes and newspaper columns from the lips or fountain pens of Kur, Kąkol, Gontarz[48] and other Party bards. Swarms of youthful adepts of the journalistic arts, and of future 'March docents'[49] (who remembers today their names or numbers?) tried to advance their sluggish careers, racing to solve puzzles of the type: 'What does the Catholic Kisielewski[50] have in common with the Zionist Bauman?' Sometimes, even a respectable, non-Party professor joined in the chorus, publishing a devastating critique of Bauman's theory of culture under a title that said it all: 'A disturbing phenomenon'. The article appeared in *Trybuna Ludu*,[51] which did not usually review the work of academics. The house phone, bugged already for a long time, rang with anonymous threats of the type, 'We will come soon, you scabby Jew, to take care of you'; and in the elevator of our building the words 'Bauman is the enemy' appeared. And because the 'Catholic Kisielewski' was severely beaten on the street by 'unknown' assailants, young friends in the Department would not let the 'Zionist Bauman', despite his protests, take a single step alone when he was walking to the Department or returning home from work.

Not a step alone was I permitted to take – whether on foot or by car, wherever I was going and for whatever reason – by the secret police, either. Since they probably did not expect to discover any additional information about my anti-state activities, they were just trying to scare me. As the banner displayed in one of the 'working people's demonstrations' made clear, they wanted to force me to leave Poland for 'Siam',[52] thereby satisfying the 'demands of the workers'. Or were just harassing me. We encountered a variation on such harassment-for-the-sake-of-harassment while leaving Poland: 'customs officers' confiscated all of my and Jasia's manuscripts. When, years later, I applied to the Customs Office for the return of the confiscated materials, I was told that the seized documents were turned over to the Academy of Sciences. In response to my subsequent inquiries, the head of the Academy of Sciences wrote that he had never received any of my manuscripts. I sent copies of both responses to the Chairman of the State Council with a request to resolve this dispute between two respectable state institutions. Professor Jabłoński did not repond to this letter. While rummaging the archives of the IPN, an acquaintance found the file with the confiscated manuscripts.

He notified me and sent me the number of the file. Unlike the head of the people's state, the IPN did respond to my request to return the confiscated documents it inherited from the UB.[53] But, like the authorities of the previous era, they did not return the manuscripts.[54] Instead, as I suspect, they published a public report by the 'historian' Gontarczyk, in which the author decided, for instance, that the Cross of Valour I was awarded in 1945 for taking Kołobrzeg was a medal for 'fighting against the patriotic underground' and 'for seizing many bandits'. He derived this 'historical fact' from arguments used in a certain application submitted by those who wished me well, but in the eyes of the 'higher ups' were not quite on the right side. In the application, they stated that the erring officer of the Political Directorate, Zygmunt Bauman, should be kept in his current position despite his errors. As I have said, security forces do not die. They are no less effective beyond the grave than when alive.

That it is so, I learned once more years later, when we lived in a quiet neighbourhood of Leeds, our home city for the last forty years. The only two burglaries that took place in our street during this time were of our house. In the first case, the 'thief' took Jasia's purse from her bedroom. The purse was subsequently dumped, retaining all of its contents, except for the address book in which Jasia kept phone numbers of our friends. As we learned from a show on the BBC years later, the theft of Jasia's address book was connected to the activities of a Stasi agent enrolled in Ph.D. studies at the department located next door to Sociology at the University of Leeds. This agent's task was to report on my conspiratorial actions in England. In the second case, the matter was more serious: while returning from a series of lectures abroad, we found our household torn apart, with all the furniture overturned. And yet nothing was missing. This time, I think, the burglary evidenced the attention paid by a different group of 'special forces' to my grandson. Michał Sfard,[55] a young but already renowned

lawyer, has been a thorn in the flesh of the Israeli establishment. Again and again, he has petitioned the highest court
on behalf of disinherited or otherwise harmed Palestinians,
and regularly 'publicized' issues that the establishment would
prefer to keep quiet. The 'burglary' took place right after he
paid us a visit. The Shin Bet[56] may have thought that Michał
was storing materials in preparation for further court cases at
our house.

I wonder how many protagonists there are in these memoirs
of mine. One named Zygmunt Bauman, or two men known
by the same name? The one from the first part of this con-
fabulation seems, after all, rather different from the one in
the second part. This brings to mind the story of the Polish
poet Wiktor Woroszylski and the suspicion that the W. W.
from before the expedition of 'helpful brothers'[57] to rebelling
Hungary and the W. W. from after that expedition were two
different people. Unlike Tadeusz Konwicki, whom I quoted
before, Wiktor Woroszylski insisted that he did not become
any different from how he was before. In this, he was much
like the hero of his own historical sketches. If he could become
'a new person', it was precisely because he was 'constantly the
same as in his earlier incarnation'. And because Wiktor was a
poet, and quite a good poet at that, he conveyed this thought
in a poem, 'The obstinacy of Martin Luther' – one I would not
be able to write, but would endorse unwaveringly, gladly and
humbly:

Do I recognize my writings as mine
or am I willing to retract them penitently
Wise Gentlemen, what is mine is mine
Fat fingers and heavy chin
This body a tub of beer and a conscience
In which my faith has built a nest
Writings also mine My fingers I will not retract

The double chin, the man parts I will not renounce[58]
The belly will always be belly, the conscience will remain
   conscience,
Wise Gentlemen[59]

5

Who Am I?

I am writing up these recollections in English. This is, simultaneously, fortunate and unfortunate. It is unfortunate, as
much of the problem which I, and other boys assigned to
share in my plight, faced on 1 September 1938[1] must be downright abstruse and incomprehensible – nay, inexpressible – for
a person grown up in the universe made of the English language.
Such a person would not understand (and if he understands,
he would not *feel*) how truly complex 'being Polish' is – that
idea which rolls into one the states of 'being English' and 'being
British', which he himself so prudently keeps carefully apart.
And yet it is fortunate that I am trying to make sense of that
experience in English; were I to try to do it in Polish – I would
not be able to prise a personal problem off its centuries-long,
convoluted, irreparably twisted history. Writing in English, I
can attempt a posture of emotional detachment, look at my
Polishness from aside, as one tends to look at any other object
of scrutiny. Well, I can try.

And yet I cannot avoid history. History decreed that the
state of 'being Polish' had been through centuries a question
of decision, choice and action. It has been something one had
to fight for, defend, consciously cultivate, vigilantly preserve.

'Being Polish' did not mean guarding the already well-formed and marked frontiers, but rather drawing the yet-not-existing boundaries – *making* realities rather than expressing them. There was in Polishness a constant streak of uncertainty, 'until-further-noticeness' – a kind of precarious provisionality other, more secure, nations know little about.

Under such circumstances, one could only expect that the besieged, incessantly threatened nation would obsessively test and re-test the loyalty of its rank. It would develop a well-nigh paranoic fear of being swamped, diluted, overrun, disarmed. It would look askance and with suspicion at all newcomers with less-than-foolproof credentials. It would see itself surrounded by enemies, and it would fear more than anybody else the 'enemy within'.

Under such circumstances, one should also accept that the decision to be a Pole (particularly if it was not made for one by ancestors so distant that the decision had time to petrify into rock-solid reality) was a decision to join in a struggle with no assured victory, and with no prospect of the victory ever being assured. For centuries, people did not define themselves as Poles for the want of an easy life. Those who did define themselves as Poles could rarely be accused of opting for comfort and security. In most cases, they deserved unqualified moral praise and whole-hearted welcome.

That the same circumstances should lead to consequences pointing in opposite directions, clashing with each other and ultimately coming into conflict – is illogical. Well, blame the circumstances.

It is one of the mysteries of social psychology that groups which ground their identity in will and decision tend to deny the right of self-definition to others; by questioning and denigrating the validity of self-determination, they wish perhaps to suppress and forget the frail foundation of their own existence. This is what happened in the inter-war Poland. After a long period of slavery and de-polonizing pressures, the forces dominating the new sovereign state hastened to make it a 'state of the Poles', rather than a 'Polish state'; an instrument for subordinating all not-fully Polish – ethnically, religiously or culturally distinct – groups; above all, an instrument to perpetuate their otherness and to deprive them of the same right to self-definition on which the reemergence of the Polish political presence ultimately rested.

So be it. However forceful and obtrusive, history does not absolve me from the responsibility for my own biography. How history defines me is History's problem. How I define myself is my problem. That the two problems meet and interfere with each other is my misfortune. Preoccupied as it is with statistics, history would not brook being bothered. I do not mind responsibility. I feel responsible for my Polishness in the same way I accept responsibility for my one-time communism, life-long socialism, rejection of Israel, decision to end my life as a displaced, exterritorial person and a loyal subject of the Crown.

I cannot shirk asking, and answering, the question: Am I a Pole? And if I am, what does this mean?

Yes, I am a Pole. Polishness is my spiritual home, Polish language is my world. This is my decision. You do not like it? I am sorry, but this is your decision. I am a Polish Jew. I'll never shed my Jewishness, membership of a tradition which gave the world its moral sense, its conscience, its thrust for perfection, its millennial dream. I do not see why my Jewishness should be difficult to square with my Polishness. This is my problem. You think it cannot be squared? I am sorry, but this is your problem.

Another Polish Jew, much more famous than myself, Julian Tuwim,[2] wrote once that, for him, 'being Polish' means, among other things, hating Polish antisemitism more than antisemitism of any other nationality. How true. I feel Polish when I hate Polish obscurantism while only disdaining obscurantism elsewhere (for the same reason, looking at Israel, I sense I am Jewish). I live deeply my Polishness when I view Moczar with abhorrence, while Pinochet only with disgust (for the same reason, I feel more Jewish the more I loathe Sharon or Kahane). Jan Józef Lipski,[3] the Pole with a big heart and equally big naivety, suggested that it is up to the Poles to criticize antisemitism, and up to the Jews to focus on their sin of anti-Polishness. As a Polish Jew – an entity with no place in Lipski's world chart – I refuse to observe this division of labour. This is refusal in another sense of being a Polish Jew.

As far as I am concerned, Polish antisemites – all those unthinking thugs and hoodlums who kicked me and pushed me into the improvised ghetto on 1 September 1938 – defied their own purpose. If anything, they ennobled my Polishness. They lent it the moral fullness it otherwise would not possess. Being a Pole always meant being ready to pay a price. Their forefathers, of whom they had probably only a vaguest of memories, suffered for stubbornly refusing to deny their Polishness. So did I – thanks to them. If I insist on being a Pole, let no one tell me that it has come easy. I am sorry to sadden you, my friendly Polish antisemites, but it has been partly thanks to you that I have earned my right to Polishness no less convincingly than your ancestors did.

And, like so many of your ancestors, I smuggled my Polishness out of the country, cheating the secret police disguised as customs officers. This is one legacy of forty years of my life which they – however hard they tried – failed to confiscate. For it was hidden, as the Poet suggested to the Bride in Wyspiański's *Wedding*:[4] 'in your heart, my girl, in your little heart'. Come and try to tear it out of there . . .

[The love letter from my father]

My non-smiling, self-effacing father never learned the vocabulary of love. Perhaps he did, but was too shy to speak it. No wonder I was shocked when, on the train taking me to my university life, I opened the letter he put in my pocket when seeing me off at the station. This was a love letter. I was leaving my parents now, starting my own and different life – and father hastened to let me know all he felt over the years, what role I played in his life and what sort of man he dreamt I'd be.

There was also fatherly advice. Life wisdom that my father wished to share with his son. The only capital he could bequeath. His only gift. Remember – he wrote: your people,[5] only your people, can appreciate you and your work. Remember – he wrote: you are a Jew, and you belong to the Jewish People.

I cannot recall my thoughts.

Since that journey from Shakhunia to Gorki, they have been submerged many times over, suffused with things I learned later, and dissolved in ideas I could not possess at the time. But I remember that I struggled with my father's message all the way to Gorki, and that in the end I refused to accept it.

My people? Who are my people? And why are they mine? Simply because 'I belong to them'? Must I belong? And do I really want to belong? And if I did want to belong – why, it ought to be a nation – something I have been cast into without my participation, by other people's selection. And why must there be a selection? Selection means rejection, division, antagonism – precisely the things I suffered from and found most repelling.

I would not know whether the Jews were in this respect different from other 'peoples'. The Jews have been trampled down and despised and slighted and persecuted, and they stood fast, and refused to surrender, and remained faithful to themselves, and never succumbed to the temptation of denying what they were even when lured to do so and promised a better life as a reward – and for all that, they deserve respect and veneration. Yet, for at least a century and a half, the same was true about the Poles – and the moment they won their freedom and found themselves in their own home again, they started to trample down and despise and slight and persecute the Ukrainians, the Belorussians, the Jews – everybody who came in handy and was close enough to receive their share of suffering. Would not the Jews do exactly the same, once given a chance? I would not wish to be party to it when it happened. I would not wish to 'belong' when, confident in their new power – that of the fist and the sword, not of ideas or clear conscience – they rapturously forget what they had been taught by their own, very own Talmud – that book of wisdom for the lowly and the suffering. When they forget that 'a man should always be of the pursued and not of the pursuers', that it is better 'to be the cursed than to be the curser'. When they refuse to listen to the old, wise Raba. (A man once came before Raba and said to him: 'The ruler of my city has ordered me to kill a certain person, and if I refuse he will kill me.' Raba told him, 'Be killed and do not kill; do you think that your blood is redder than his? Perhaps his is redder than yours.')

Perhaps all the suffering comes from the need to compare whose blood is redder. Perhaps the evil is in the comparing itself. Perhaps the real issue is to stop comparing altogether, once and for all. I guess the evil sits in the very compulsion to select, and in the curse of being selected. Once one wants to belong, one cannot help setting off others whom one refuses to admit as one's kin. Belonging cannot but mean dividing, and setting double standards. Where standards divide, morality ends. Drawing the line between us and them, we efface the line between good and evil.

Little did the Poles do to endear themselves to the people they refused to admit into their tribe. If I had embraced the Polish view of the world, culture, history and – so be it – the 'Polish identity', it was hardly by invitation. Most Poles I knew did everything to force me to change my mind; they tried really hard to make me feel unwelcomed, foreign and undeserving. Yet if I do what they wanted me to do, I will confirm the very principle of tribalism – the tribal right to reject and to persecute, the very reason of hatred and suffering. The cause of hatred may only rejoice once it evokes a mirror-image tribal hatred as its response. And who is more obliged to challenge the principle of tribalism and hatred, than I – the Jew and a Pole?

We, the Jews, supplied the world with the archetype of suffering; perhaps in that lies our greatest contribution to striving after moral perfection. One of us was crucified, uncounted others were beaten to death, burned, drowned, impaled, hatchetted. Our history reflects itself in the idea of suffering as redemption, and moral will as something which no coercion can create and no violence can destroy. Our history has been a never-ending lesson in what happens once the human race crumbles into tribes. The meaning of our history is all in that lesson. Setting ourselves as a tribe – as one tribe among many – we can only forfeit that meaning. Being truly Jewish means to strive for a world without tribes. A world which does not divide into mine and foreign people . . .

I cannot guarantee these were my thoughts on the road to Gorki. In all probability, the thoughts were different.

Thinking is the endless work of secondary processing (today widely known as 'recycling'), and a transformation sufficiently thorough that it would be dishonest to say it is capable of recreating the order of things *es is ist eigentlich gewesen*[6] – to break through the successive layers of palimpsest and lay out an alloy of successive geological strata. We are all reminiscent of the 'traditionalists' so accurately described by Stefan Czarnowski,[7] for whom the things that came from the distant past appeared to be on the same plane as their newest additions. Maybe my thinking then, on the train, took an entirely different course. I make no promises as to the fidelity of the recollection I just presented. That the reconstructive effort is 'true' means only that today's meaning has been ascribed to my old decision to reject father's advice (and I did make such a decision) and that, because of that, the entire later course of my life starts making sense. At the very least, it explains my absolute inability to ground myself in an Israeli reality. This reconstruction can attest only to how little I knew and understood then, in the train from Szachunia to Niżny Nowogród. I believed that moral will would be able to ward off the pressures of tribal attitudes and that it could strengthen one's resolve against these attitudes' temptations. I did not realize how capable human institutions were of transforming individual moral impulses into group egoism, heartlessness and cruelty.

Perhaps I would not know all this on the train in Gorki – forty-five years ago, and so many bitter experiences between. And yet there is some truth in their reconstruction. This reconstruction makes sense of the part of my life which followed. Above all, it shows how little I knew and understood at the time. I seemed to believe that moral will would overpower the dead weight of tribalism. And I seemed to be unaware that, in the fight against overwhelming odds, moral will may well lose its only source of strength and only title to respect: its ethical purity. If that happens, there is little to choose between inhumanity of the will and inhumanity of the tribe. All this I was still to learn – and learn the hard and unenviable way.

6

Before Dusk Falls

'Home is security', says Jean Améry.[1] Writing these words in 1966, the Frenchman, born in Austria in 1912 as Franz Meyer, knew what he was talking about. He had lost his homeland and waited twenty-seven years to fully grasp what that irreversible loss meant: he learned that 'the re-entrance into a place is never also a restoration of the lost time'.[2]

Safety is nothing other than certainty; and again, 'one feels secure . . . [w]here no chance occurrence is to be expected, nothing completely strange is to be feared'.[3] So safety means the absence of anything completely and utterly incomprehensible. As Wittgenstein would say, it is the absence of something that comes without instructions, or even just a hint, for how to behave towards it. Améry realized the loss of his fatherland when he found himself surrounded by signs 'as inscrutable [. . .] as Etruscan script',[4] at least for him: 'Faces, gestures, clothes, houses, words',[5] while remaining sensory impressions, ceased to be signs. If the homeland is the habitat of order, predictability and self-assurance, the foreign is the domain of disorder, surprise and confusion. If one stays in a foreign place long enough, one can learn ways to discover, or at least

speculate about, the order of meanings in the chaos of experience; but 'for the exiled person who came to the new country
already as an adult, penetrating the signs will not be spontane-
ous but rather an intellectual act, one combined with a certain
expenditure of mental effort'.[6]

We would probably remain unaware of the fact that our
mother tongue has a grammar, if not for the fact that teachers
informed us about it, first to our surprise, and then, somewhat
later, to our irritation. Grammar is the Cerberus guarding the
gates to all languages – *with the exception of our native tongue*
(it is precisely the lack of this Cerberus that makes it native).
In our native tongue, grammar is an easy and non-intrusive
guide, a concerned but not visible guardian angel; in all others,
it is a demon lurking in the shadows at the top of Jacob's
Ladder. As Günther Anders says, cited by Améry, 'No one can
move about for years exclusively in languages that he has not
mastered and at best parrots poorly, without falling victim to
the impoverishment to his inferior speech.'[7] Because even your
native language crumbles 'piece by piece, and for the most
part so imperceptibly and gradually that we did not notice the
loss';[8] until the moment of revelation after twenty-seven – or
however many – years, when we grasp that the irreversible loss
of our homeland is the same as an irreversible loss of safety.
We realize then, too, that '*La table* will never be the table, at
best one can eat one's fill at it.'[9]

With age, one becomes more likely to experience epiphany.
This is a banal observation – one could say a 'common-sense'
idea. This simple truth is known to everyone who has been
fortunate enough to reach an old age. The young person (as we
all were once) 'is not only who he is, but also who he will be'[10] –
and thus, what already appears as unfinished, incomplete and
certainly not the final draft. Perhaps not everything is possible
in the future, yet nothing is impossible. 'But the credit of the
person who is aging depletes . . . He is only who he is.'[11] In old
age, identity as a promise of the future is no longer available.

It is obvious that too little time is left to try on new outfits. But other discoveries hit you like a blow to the head: that longing for one's native lands 'consisted in dismantling our past piece by piece'.[12] It was a deconstruction that took place through the joint efforts of oneself and the world: 'But if society repudiates that we ever were that, then we have also never been it.'[13]

Exile robs the refugee of identity. And thus robs them of trust. And thus also of the faith that what one had acknowledged as true is true. And because this *faith* serves as a protective shield for the *knowledge* of what constitutes truth and what does not, then sooner or later exile will strip the refugee even of knowledge. The Earth owes its immovability to Atlas' strong shoulders. 'The earth shall rise on new foundations' when those shoulders tremble[14] – and refugees will already make sure that they do.

The truth is that about whose truthfulness *we all* know, and we know because we believe it is true – we believe that we know. So it is what is obvious to us. Obviousness means the fusion of knowledge and faith. Obviousness cannot be acquired, procured or arranged. Something is either obvious or not obvious – *tertium non datur*. It is obvious when, and only when, there is a collective, in which 'everyone' believes in its obviousness, and when no one questions my right to include that 'everyone' in the personal pronoun 'we'. If these conditions are met, I have identity. If they are not, I have at most a prospect of identity, or an idea for identity: an application for identity that could be accepted or rejected, if a court authorized to consider the application existed and could take on the task of doing so. But there is no such court – and the Earth is moving from its foundations. And it will not be stopped.

In my case, those conditions were not fulfilled. I was given the right to choose, which is marvellous; the rights, however, came with the caveat that my choice, as a private matter, would not oblige anyone but myself. And that, even if marvellous, is not entirely so.

When I was awarded the Adorno Prize, the journal *Rzeczpospolita* informed its readers that the prize went to an Israeli sociologist (the editorial board of *RP* seemed to remember that the place of a Zionist was in Sion).[15] The correction sent in by Professor Edmund Mokrzycki was not published – though all the European newspapers that I saw announced that the prizewinner was a Polish sociologist, or a 'Polish sociologist living in England'. The latter, by the way, is the rule: identical formulations appear in all the reviews of my books, published in more than thirty languages besides Polish (and I will brag: these books are quite numerous). It will also be unlikely to find in those countries a sociologist who would fail to mention my name, if asked to name a Polish sociologist.

If a Jew wants to be recognized, without hedging, as a Pole – that is, wishes to gain the right to use the term 'we' with reference to the Polish 'everyone' – common sense, it seems, would dictate that this person becomes a refugee. The identity this person chooses will then be recognized. It will be recognized at least by that 'everyone' – oh, irony! – whom the personal pronoun 'we' does not include and has neither a basis for inclusion nor an intention to include.

Henryk Grynberg, who forged the noble metal of literature from the motley ore of Polish exile, wrote (in a book with the title . . . *Refugees*, what else!): 'Those who commit suicide are also refugees, perhaps all the more so.'[16] Well, exactly.

Žižek (a figure transported whole from the Dadaist era, of *Nuż w bżuhu*[17] and *épatez les bourgeois*,[18] to the epoch in which there is no one left to dazzle, because everyone is dazzled out and completely done with dazzling)[19] wrote recently that two German movies about the daily life of the Ossis in the times before they were called that name[20] do not grasp the essence of communist totalitarianism; what's more, they falsify its reality. If you want to know and tell others what life was like under communism, he says, turn into movies the Kolyma stories of Shalamov.[21] Do this with the tacit assumption that the truth about communism hid in the barracks of Magadan[22] rather than parading in the streets of Tambov or Jarosław.[23] And the truth about Nazism probably nested in Dachau and Auschwitz[24] rather than breeding in the village described at length in the TV series *Heimat*?[25]

I would ask Žižek why those fortunate people who were born too late to taste totalitarianism for themselves would want – and even strain their brains – to fathom the ancient history of totalitarianism? After all, if they need gut-wrenching horror stories, they may turn to *Reservoir Dogs* or *Chainsaw Massacre* or *Friday the 13th*[26] or have a daily dose of television and hundreds of different computer games featuring the mass murder of misfits. And set against the refined artistry of cinema, television, Nintendo or PlayStation, the daily life of the camps and gulags must seem to them the aborted product of a shoddy cottage industry. Those lucky ones know practically from birth that monstrous things are the work of monsters, and wicked deeds are the acts of the wicked; and that, therefore, the monsters and the wicked ought to be destroyed before they begin doing such things to us, and because those to be destroyed are Satan's brood, those hunting them are angels – what else could they be? So when with flushed faces they try to defeat the electronic monsters in these monsters' own foul games, respond to the monsters' attacks with ever more inventive tricks, and annihilate the monsters before the monsters start annihilating them – none of these actions undermines their self-image. After all, these electronic monsters, as clearly implied by the instructions, preyed on them out of pure cruelty, whereas they, in the course of saving themselves, saved the rest of the world from tormentors. Humanity is divided into hangmen and their victims, and when the latter exterminate the last of the former, the problem of cruelty can be put away in a repository of memory/oblivion in a museum. The victorious victims will then be able to slam the door behind them and to open it only during

Sunday family strolls. Because cruelty is the work of the cruel, and we are pure – *quod erat demonstrandum*.

Oh, if it only were this way in reality . . . If only totalitarianism boiled down to the long foregone acts of letting from their cages a few beasts that in 'normal'– that is, 'decent' – times and in respectable places are being kept under lock and key . . . If suffering ennobled and constituted a certificate of innocence and moral virtue . . . If the roguery of the actors did not blemish their victims or the witnesses of their crimes . . . If the victims marched to their execution clean and spotless . . . If the Karadžićs and Mladićs[27] did not summon their brother Serbs at the end of the twentieth century to slaughter Bosnian Muslims in revenge for the defeat of the Serbs in the Battle of Kosovo, fought with the Ottomans on 28 June 1389 – and if their summons had not been heard and obeyed by so many people . . . If it was possible, as was done – or at least attempted with zeal – in camps and gulags, to divide the world neatly and clearly into all-powerful subjects and their compliant objects, into those who do and those to whom it is done . . . If all this were possible, then communist and Nazi totalitarianism would be just another series of bloody episodes among the hordes of events in which one side beats, and the other side is beaten. Episodes with which human history is replete. Episodes that must (and can) be closed by flogging those who did the beating and decorating the beaten with medals. And, once the closing is done, the yellowed and desiccated remnants of these episodes may be placed in museum showcases, so that they testify to the cleanness of people's consciences rather than harass them with remorse.

Unfortunately, in spite of Žižek's advice, one cannot fully comprehend the threats of totalitarianism just by scrutinizing Kolyma or Dachau, those laboratories in which the limits of human enslavement and dehumanization had been investigated (as Hannah Arendt described them). In order to grasp this threat in full, we need to look where it is at its most venomous and ominous, and where it has not been extinguished. We need to look in those places where it still preserves its toxic power and is thus not yet ready for a burial in a museum showcase. We must go beyond the spiked fences. We must go out onto streets crowded with passers-by like you and me.

Suffering always hurts, but rarely ennobles. That causing suffering morally destroys the torturer goes without saying. But the victims, too, do not escape the pogrom of impulses and moral brakes whole and unblemished. Do they wait for their chance to repay the torturers in their own coin? Yes, but first they learn the secrets of the kind of life in which such coin is in use. American psychiatrists who were treating Holocaust survivors just after the war described their patients' affliction with the term 'guilt syndrome': 'Why am I alive, when so many others died before my eyes?!' But they quickly changed their opinion. 'Guilt syndrome' disappeared from the psychiatric lexicon and was replaced by 'survivor's syndrome':[28] 'They are waiting for me, they want to finish me off, and they will certainly do so, if I don't beat them to it, if it is not me who delivers the first blow . . .'

Survivor's syndrome is hereditary; each generation passes on the poisoned fruits of the bygone martyrdom. The descendants of victims, themselves free from the experiences on which these legacies are based, preserve only the collective myth of the hereditary suffering; in these circumstances, 'the lessons about survival' drawn out of the experiences of martyrdom are unconducive to practical testing. Exempted from the need to be confronted with facts, the vision of a world full of conspirators and conspiratorial thinking enters the community of 'survivors' and holds sway over it. To use Alain Finkielkraut's formulation,[29] with the help of this vision, the survivors can share the glory of their tortured ancestors while demanding compensation and a free pass for their own ruthless actions.

They can now do it without paying the price that their ancestors had to pay for the memories of their descendants.

Forced to 'participate in the bloody spectacle' (the expression used by Jan Błoński with reference to years of torment under Hitler's variety of totalitarianism), both victims and mute witnesses of crimes know all too well that there are methods to get rid of human problems, whether actual or ostensible. (Are these methods inhuman? Possibly. But they are also effective.) They know that *humanity is capable of inhumanity*. So someone, somewhere, sometime, may reach for those methods. And then, if the fear becomes unbearable, one will also need to use them. The price of remaining alive is killing those who can, want to, and will eventually kill you. Survivor's syndrome suggests that survival is the purpose of life. What immediately follows is that he who delivers the first blow survives those who did not have time to do so. If the blow was delivered on time and was also accurate – a knock-out – then there is no fear of revenge or punishment.

The world after the Holocaust promotes 'pre-emptive' wars. From the experiences of those in Iraq one learns that, to prevent an anticipated massacre, this world is prepared to unleash murderous tendencies. And, as can be learned from the experiences of Abu Ghraib or Guantánamo,[30] this post-Holocaust world is unscrupulous towards those who might, perhaps, strike a blow against the scrupulous ones. Both sides draw on the lessons from the Holocaust. In his book *Lucifer's Effect*, Philip Zimbardo describes in detail the hellish mechanism of this effect, illustrating his claims with findings from research carried out in its entirety in a post-gulag, post-camp world.

Spielberg's *Schindler's List*[31] does not mince words: in the years of crematoria and contempt, the name of the game was to survive others, and thus also to ensure the survival of *these* rather than *those*. To the applause of critics, Spielberg harnesses to the service of the 'art of survival' that same ominous tool of modern murder, the use of which Raul Hilberg[32] considered as the first step to the extermination of the European Jews (their fate was decided, he wrote, the moment the first German bureaucrats prepared the first lists of Jewish residents in the cities). Schindler, the hero of the movie, hailed with a Talmudic reference as the 'saviour of humanity', rejects the offer to trade *his* Jewesses – the ones from *his* list – for '*other* Jewesses'. And the audience bursts into applause when Schindler pulls from the train headed to Treblinka *his* man, the one from his list, who, unlike the other passengers, had probably been put on the cattle carriage by mistake and neglect. As Janina remembers, future victims with numbers rebelled in the Warsaw Ghetto against future victims without numbers when the latter tried to join their marching columns. 'Because of them, innocent people will die!' they shouted – proving that they had assimilated the language of their torturers to perfection. Before God sends people to die, he confuses their tongues.

After listening to Janina's lecture in Brussels on different interpretations of the lessons of the Holocaust as presented in films, a Belgian filmmaker asked Janina why *Korczak*, Wajda's cinematic masterpiece, was not shown in American movie theatres and why American critics were silent about it. It's simple, Janina answered: Wajda's message (and Korczak's) stands in stark opposition to the dominant version of what can be learned from the Holocaust. Korczak did not save a single life – even his own! The only thing that Korczak did save from staining and obliterating was the human dignity of 200 children . . . But is that a reason to forgive him for his negligence in the war for survival? Can it count as a cause for honouring his memory?!

Elias Canetti was the first to issue a warning about the toxic legacies of the Holocaust. 'The most elementary and obvious form of success is to remain alive.'[33] This criterion of success gave rise to the cult of 'survivors' and placed the 'survivor's attitude' on a pedestal. Those who accept this attitude, Canetti admonishes, 'want to survive their contemporaries', and when it comes to it, they are ready to 'kill so [as to] survive others'; '[They want] to stay alive, so as not to have others surviving.'[34]

Summing up the lessons she learned from the years of contempt, crematoria and annihilation, Janina wrote that the executioners would generally dehumanize their victims before putting them to death, and that the hardest of the challenges she experienced was remaining human in inhuman conditions. And again, what we learn from human slaughter undertaken for the sake of racial purity, much like human slaughter for the sake of class purity, is the ease with which 'decent people', exemplary fathers of families, faithful spouses and helpful neighbours, can be convinced that the lofty goal of purifying the world turns zealous participation in the purge into a virtue, into the responsibility of 'decent people'.

The most shocking information contained in Hannah Arendt's report from Eichmann's trial was the testimony of expert psychiatrists called to assess the sanity of the accused. They asserted that not only was Eichmann 'normal' according to all common standards of 'normality', but he could even be considered the model of a virtuous citizen – as, indeed, he was considered by his neighbours.[35] If he lived in my vicinity, would I recognize him among those neighbours who bowed with a smile and politely responded to my greetings? I shudder to think what the neat and agreeable neighbour, whom I know only from daily friendly greetings and smiles, might be doing 'during his work hours'. The residue of totalitarian times is this constant suspiciousness of one's neighbours.

But so is self-suspicion ('if it came to it, I too could lend a hand to such things . . .'), which only spurs further suspicion of neighbours. If it exists (and all too often, it does), it is forcefully suppressed and pushed into the dark corners of consciousness. Turning wickedness into the inborn, permanent and, above all, *exclusive* property of the neighbour is in order in the eyes of those who wish to free themselves from the fear of their own wickedness that, although asleep for now, may wake up at any moment. The conscience of Christopher Browning was shaken by the discovery that, if 'ordinary *men*' called up to the Reserve Battalion 101[36] were capable of such ignominy, all of *us* ordinary *men* could be similarly transformed into beasts. But, in order to protect the conscience of his readers as well as himself, Daniel Goldhagen corrected Browning's sentence: if 'ordinary *Germans*' from Battalion 101 were capable of such crimes, all of *them*, *Germans*, were capable of similar crimes. And not because the beast resides *in humans* and can be put to work even on the most evil of tasks when the right whip and harness are found, but because *Germans*, possessed by their hatred of *Jews*, were only too eager to undertake even the most evil of actions towards Jews.

The great majority of people invited from the streets of 'better neighbourhoods' and from university lecture halls to participate in Philip Zimbardo's experiments shocked the researcher, terrified him and shook him up with the ease with which they would 'conform, comply, obey, and be readily seduced into doing things they could not imagine doing when they were outside those situational force fields'.[37]

Moral devastation is the enduring (for how long?!) legacy of both totalitarian systems. Stanisław Ossowski, concerned about the future of a nation subjected to a test exceeding its strength, wrote about Manichean moods[38] that became and remain instinctive reflexes.[39] These are not moods into which one falls today only to get rid of them tomorrow and to forget about them altogether the following day; they are the trait of the 'normal', customary manner in which people perceive the world, their own place in this world, and the recipe for their own survival. This customary way of looking at things is confirmed by common sense and honoured by the calendar of public rituals.

The legacies left by the two totalitarian systems are deceptively similar in this regard. But these legacies differ too, and quite profoundly, at least in their effect on the mentality of Poles (German totalitarianism had one kind of effect on Germans and another on Poles). The totalitarianism imported from Soviets and trying to take roots in Poland promised Poles participation in benefits it predicted, and invited them to take part in the procedures supposed to facilitate and speed up the fulfilment of this prediction. That brutally foreign Hitlerian version, which from the start positioned Poles clearly, irrevocably and unambiguously on the other side of the wall, among its victims, is quite a different story. Analogies between the two experiences stumble and fall upon this difference. Futile and senseless would be any attempt to speak in one breath about five years of Hitler's occupation and about half a century of the Polish People's Republic – to speak about them as if both could be reduced to the same chapter of national martyrdom. And it would by no means help in dealing with the legacies of totalitarian times.

Jean-Paul Sartre once shocked the reading public with the paradoxical claim that the French were never so free as they were in the time of the German occupation . . . the paradox, he claimed, was only ostensible, because one falls into enslavement through the trap of coercion disguised as free choice, and the occupiers made this trap inaccessible to the French. The French were left *without* a choice. And if the French were left without a choice, then Poles were a hundredfold so! Indeed, some of the German tyrants coaxed the French, promising them a place at the table when the *Neue Ordnung*[40] would finally triumph due to their collaboration. The Poles, on the other hand, were told from the outset – and in a way that left no doubt – that the *Neue Ordnung* did not foresee for them any role other than that of a drudge, and predicted no use for Poland other than as *Lebensraum*[41] for the 1,000-year-old Reich. There was thus no escape from the struggle against the occupiers. One could only argue over the question of how quickly this struggle should begin and which weapon should be used. The instinct of self-preservation, moral obligation and patriotism – they all spoke the same language. In unison, they said: don't give up, resist, fight . . .

To use an expression that violates linguistic tradition, the 'Soviet occupation' was very different indeed. The PRL was a nation of victors, not of the defeated. It promised to lead those devastated by war and pre-war poverty to a land of plenty, abundant in ways these people had never known before. Land for the peasants, work for the workers, education for children, healthcare for all . . . Freedom from the fear of unemployment and poverty . . . And, in addition, human dignity for all, respect for all forms of labour, cultural treasures for everyone, an end to splitting the nation into the mighty and the wealthy on the one hand, and the skinny henchmen who bowed to them, on the other; an end to trampling and humiliating people. A nation finally pulled up by the lever of solidarity (sic!),[42] lifted to the level of a real community, no longer riven with squabbles. In other words, social justice firmly set on the sacred tripod of freedom, equality and brotherhood. In these circumstances, it would be natural for the instinct of self-preservation, moral obligation and patriotism to begin, once again, to speak in a common language, except that, this time, the message would be the opposite of the old one. It was only necessary to start believing in the promise. Or, if the honesty of those making the promise or their power to fulfil it were doubted, it was imperative to suspend the doubt and give them the chance to dispel suspicions.

In a Poland inscribed into the map of the German *Lebensraum*, German totalitarianism brutally rejected even those few who sympathized with its worldview, ignoring the question of where this perspective came from. Soviet totalitarianism tempted people with its slogans, tantalized and seduced even many of those who were not, generally speaking, convinced of the virtues of the country from which it came.

The charm of communist slogans was hard to resist for people who were suffering from the inherited poverty and civilizational backwardness afflicting their compatriots. These slogans appealed in equal measure to feelings of social justice on the one hand, and on the other hand, quite simply, to love for the fatherland. What kind of patriot, a person who places the good of the nation above one's own class interests, would wish that the good things promised in those slogans were *not* shared by his or her compatriots?!

Yet, it turned out all too quickly that slogans were one thing, and practice – quite another. The civilizational chasm between Poland and the rest of Europe grew deeper instead of shrinking. The good life that has been promised did not come. New divisions did not differ from the former ones in any respect, except their ostentatiousness. And above all this, we were haunted by the spectre of a terrible merciless power that did not tolerate opposition and was allergic not just to the ideas that contradicted its viewpoints and clashed with its stories, but also to all those that did not come in direct response to its inspiration, command or bestowal. What yellow curtains were for the privilege of the new elites,[43] the phraseology of social emancipation and people's power was for the callousness of leaders and for their unscrupulousness.

Hitler's occupation left many wounds on the body and soul of the nation, but hypocrisy was not one of them. Yet this was the very wound that Stalinist totalitarianism aimed to inflict, and, to an even greater degree, so was the authoritarianism that followed it. The mass production of hypocrisy was an inseparable, albeit unintended and unacknowledged, feature of Soviet communism and of those regimes that it was prepared to tolerate in its 'sphere of influence'. The people were required to become a congregation of mindless obedience and discipline, not necessarily of faith. With the exception of a brief, initial *Sturm und Drang* period,[44] very few believed in the proclaimed slogans, and this included the ruling elites. Repeating these slogans at every public occasion was, however, the general obligation. As time passed by, faith was actually becoming uncomfortable for those in power: after all, belief in the infallibility of principles led inevitably to the disclosure of the fallibility of the self-proclaimed unerring interpreters.

According to the unwritten concordance regulating the relationship between those in power and the people, the former were to behave as if they were fully committed to the implementation of their programme of social prosperity and justice. The people, in turn, were to speak in public as if they trusted that this was exactly what those in power were doing day and night. The Vaihingerian rule of *Als Ob*[45] might have not held in general, but it fully applied to the daily encounters between those in power and the Polish people. It was not an addition to the system, but the necessary condition of its endurance. In his years of exile, Solzhenitsyn suggested that his countrymen start practising 'a day without lies'. He presumed that one such day would suffice for the Soviet system to collapse. We will never know whether he was right, but the assumption did not seem any more absurd than the system it referred to.

In Poland, doubts as to the realism of Solzhenitsyn's suggestion resulted from geopolitical considerations, so to speak. At Yalta, the so-called 'West' washed its hands of any intervention into the affairs of people living east of the Elbe. Since then, its actions rather than its evasive words repeatedly confirmed that it had no intention of dirtying its hands with these issues again, and that this was so in spite of the fact that its own slogans, repeated ad nauseam, differed from those that could be heard east of the Elbe. Poles, even those showing the bitterest anti-communist sentiments and behaving as the most radical of rebels, could not count on help from the outside; and only madmen and inveterate romantics could dream of duelling alone with the power of the eastern neighbour. After all, the result of such an attempt could be no less tragic for the nation than the outcomes of all the other Polish uprisings, starting with that of November and ending with that of Warsaw.[46] In addition, the possibility of implosion – of the self-inflicted collapse of the Soviet Empire – did not occur to anybody. It was absent not only from national circles, among the sober, properly reasoning intelligentsia, but also from the world's numerous 'sovietological institutes', all of them blessed with funds and with minds of the highest calibre, and held in the highest respect by the intelligentsia. The idea was still absent when, many years later, the clay feet of the Soviet colossus were weakening from day to day. In these conditions, living a lie was a condition for the liars' survival no less – perhaps even more – than it was a lifeboat for the hypocritical regime. As for the regime, it could do without the consent of those over whom it had power: it could manage perfectly well with their ostensible, honestly dishonest consent.

Either way, living a lie went on, and for many years it did not seem to be anywhere near the limits of what the nation could withstand. As Witold Wirpsza gloomily summed it up in his poem 'A Letter on Conscience':

> They say: we are building socialism.
> And they are right, though they lie . . .
> Our thoughts,
> Feelings, imaginations have learned
> To grovel; they crawl in that fissure
> That their bellies have hollowed out in the emptiness.
> Every catechism will be learned
> By heart![47]

Surprisingly (or maybe not?!), inheritors, spokespersons and post-communist Poland's most zealous practitioners of hypocrisy can be found today among the ruling elites. In this regard, matters seem to have returned to the norm that the communist regime had violated: people – those at least who do not speak in the name of the ruling power – appear to have stopped paying attention to words (well, as long as there are no nosy journalists around), whereas what people say has no importance in the eyes of those in power (so it is at least in pauses between elections, which are getting longer due to the shrinking of public memory in general, and of the memory of pre-election promises in particular).

Hypocrisy is not the only legacy of the years of captivity. As Juliusz Mieroszewski warned us years ago (cited by Michnik in his gloomy summary of the bright and dark sides of post-communist Polish life, published in a book entitled *W poszukiwaniu utraconego sensu* (*In Search of Lost Meaning*)):

> Any fight with the Soviets must start by rejecting the Soviet method of insinuations, denunciations, and the casting of bad suspicions ... Insinuations and denunciations must not be the subject of any polemic. They can only be shrugged off as beneath contempt.[48]

This warning proved to be yet another case of a voice calling in the desert.

Because I am not nearly as wise, witty and sharp as Lem, I will begin by quoting the public confession he made before death:

> Once upon a time, the Party used to announce its programme while heading towards elections. Today this has been replaced by epithets and mutual scolding [. . .] Politics today is an area in which the concrete no longer counts [. . .] Why has the competition between parties been transformed into a competition in the ability to paint a vision of a better society? Here, for example, the idea of the Fourth Republic became fashionable. Why the Fourth, and not the Fortieth? Everything is a gag and cheap

sham. Our political thought has dissolved in a mire of slogans, while at the top floats the fatherland, some Eagle, some Faith ... the Kaczyńskis embraced power with a great appetite, but so far this power is limited to what happens in the Sejm[49] and around it, inside of the political camarilla, which additionally is full of conflicts. I fear that the size of the bite they took from the loaf of power exceeds their ability to digest.[50]

Nothing to add here, nothing to discard. But a sociologist cannot resist adding something. The encounter with the realities of capitalism must have shocked many people (one of these realities has been laconically presented by Claus Offe: if in the past the bosses queued to get workers and the workers lined up for goods, today the goods stand in line for consumers and the workers for jobs[51]). The chronic opacity of the situation, the blurriness of opportunities, of dangers, and of the rules of the game; uncertainty over what is still a right and what is a new obligation; where to go, to whom to turn, who has the power to get for you what you want, how to persuade him or her to get it, how to harness your own ingenuity to attain something that was previously 'owed' to you . . .

In Poland, the sudden blurring of contours that at the end of the previous century affected all the residents of the planet was much more rapid, and thus more shocking. Forms disintegrated rapidly, leaving no time for the eyes to readjust. Balcerowicz[52] did not leave, but the certainties did. They disappeared and did not return. Freedom that Poles should and could – but did not really – expect arrived in a package deal with uncertainty. New joys with new fears. No surprise, then, that many people began craving a great simplification, with which the what and the where would become clear, and one would get a better sense of who is this and who is that; what must be done and what is forbidden; what will be rewarded and what will end with a knock on the head; what will pass and what will be stopped, and what to do to increase the number of passes.

Warsaw, once only in shades of grey, shimmers with colour. And we, after all, had been trained for colour-blindness. With no quick remedy for the insufficiencies of vision, perhaps we could paint the world to match the capabilities of our eyesight? Very few would like to return to greyscale, but it would be helpful to have a bit more black and white, blacker blacks and whiter whites . . . So that it is clear again what is nasty and what is nice, and how to stay away from the former and embrace the latter. Thus, the Kaczyńskis' idea was not so outlandish, so lunatic as it seemed.[53] Here the Third (the nasty[54]) and here the Fourth (the nice). Here the Third-ers (down with them! keep away from them!) and here the Fourth-ers (draw close, cuddle up). Everything is simple again. Simple on Sundays and national holidays at least, because on weekdays it is still tough-going (it is not without a reason that the number of holidays, rituals and messages from the top is on the rise). Those who manage to find meaning and an uplifting message in their daily life deserve a Mercedes with a garage to park it in!

'Politics of history' is perfectly suited to this need. Unlike daily life, history lends itself to manipulations, and this is its greatest virtue. In the case of history, it is not easy to verify facts and pin down lies, especially when national memory is equated with UB archives protected by laws about national confidentiality.[55] But the Polish version of the politics of history has some other advantages when it comes to winning votes. At least two of them are worth mentioning.

The current political elite comes from the second or even third ranks of the Solidarity army. This group has attracted a sizeable bunch of people who experienced their first patriotic impulses only after the arrival of Balcerowicz, when communism was gone (or it was only then that these impulses were made publicly visible). They thus need credentials; at the same time, credentials must be taken away from the most active individuals who, like Wałęsa, Kuroń, Michnik or Geremek,[56] stand in the first rows and are thus also most visible; and from those who, like Czesław Miłosz or Ryszard Kapuściński,[57] are seen on the world stage as the personification of Polish glory; and from all the rest of the 'competing authorities'. As noted by Barbara Skarga,[58] Jarosław Kaczyński satisfied 'the low instincts of mean-spirited people, such as vengefulness and resentment' when he declared in an interview for *Rzeczpospolita* in May 2007: 'this constant reference in Polish political life to those who are considered an authority is terrible . . . It is the tragedy of Polish thinking . . . We must get rid of them, and efforts are under way to do just that.'[59]

It is not the first time that the tactic of rewriting history is being used to authorize newly issued legitimizations. In the late Soviet Union, the history of the Great Patriotic War was being rewritten with each arrival of a new leader (First Secretary of the Party). Thus, in the new version, the battle considered as the turning point of the war would move to that moment in which the new Secretary happened to sport an army uniform. Stefan Niesiołowski might have spoken a bit too excitedly, but he was certainly not far from the gist of the matter when he concluded, in an admittedly exaggerated manner, that:

All kinds of suspect individuals, former Moczar supporters, scum, communist collaborators, people who in the times of the People's Republic were as quiet as mice under a broom or, more generally, God-knows-where they were or what they were doing, now speak as if they were the heroes of the fight for independence, great patriots, proclaiming themselves the only true Poles or Catholics and inveterate anti-communists; they brutally and uncompromisingly attack everyone who, for various reasons, does not share their views.[60]

And, secondly, from the politics of history, a medicine can be derived for our particular 'generational' misfortunes and problems. Many older people have reasons for regrets and sadness while looking back at their lives. Almost everyone has collected enough suffering and defeat to conclude that his or her life was a failure, that he or she is a failure. Rewriting history is a therapy. By kneading the dough of history inventively, you can transform your life's failures into wrongs afflicted upon you and waiting for compensation. This process can become an exorcism – an effective one, even if only extemporary and transient. The nightmare of 'individual inadequacy', so common in the world of liquid modernity where people are doomed to personal responsibility for their lives, will go away for a while. On the other hand, politicians of all stripes woo young people, seeing this as an opportunity for accumulating political capital. In Poland, those currently in power enjoy a particularly large supply of such opportunities, and the resolution about lustration was one of them. It was made clear that this resolution did not pertain to young people, so that the youth could interpret it as a promise that the channels for advancement were to be unblocked, as it was in the period of communist purges. It encouraged some young people to demand changes – for instance, to put an end to the practice of habilitation.[61] Habilitation, as one of them explained, was a weapon in the hands of PRL professors in their self-defence against the cadre of young people. And, while appointing a very young person with very little meritocratic experience to the post of minister of finances, Prime Minister Jarosław Kaczyński explained, probably hoping for applause from the youth, that the 'old people' had ruined the finances and the young needed to fix them. This note is played zealously and passionately, in all public concerts. Newspapers reported that:

> in the opinion of [Deputy Prime Minister] Gosiewski, the authors of the changes in the statutes of the Ministry of Foreign Affairs want above all to make it easier for young people to find work in diplomacy. 'The idea behind the project is to create for a larger group of people the possibility of being involved in

the international service', said the deputy PM. He simultaneously emphasized that the department of foreign affairs needs
generational change.[62]

The speculation as to how all this could end came to Lem
after he revisited Kornel Makuszyński's *The Two Who Stole the
Moon*.[63] 'I fear', he wrote,

> that it contains a prefiguration of the fates of the Kaczyński
> brothers. And not because they played the roles of Jacek and
> Placek[64] in their youth, but because of the epilogue, in which
> it turns out that the moon the twins made their own rises hap-
> pily and immaculately in the evening. Nothing changed! The
> power of the brothers Kaczyński will likewise turn out to be
> an episode in our history, maybe lasting for several years, but
> transitory. And using terms like Fourth or Fifth Republic will
> not change anything here.[65]

I would not, however, share Lem's optimism in this case.
Firstly, what can be destroyed in no time may take many
years to repair, especially if what is ruined heals as slowly and
requires as long a convalescence as the moral spine of society
and its political elites, the customs of democracy, a distaste for
lies or the civilized norms of human coexistence. Secondly,
this 'episode in our history' may have painful consequences,
deepening the Polish propensity for '*skirtotymia*' (from the
Ancient Greek *skirteo*: 'I jump'),[66] the tendency first noted by
Lem. To put it in Elżbieta Neyman's felicitous words written
back then, in the times of the PRL, Poles must once again 'live
in a stadium'.

Then, thirdly: in the previously cited fragment, Lem stated
himself that the storms that the current governing group
sparks off – and it does it on a daily basis – can only be seen
'in the Sejm[67] and around it'. 'Political apathy', the worry and
nightmare of lovers of democracy throughout the entire world,

afflicts in Poland both ends of the 'government–people' con-
tinuum. This fish is rotting from the head and the tail at the
same time! The indifference is mutual, the separation reciprocal. For the government, the nation is a bother, and dealing
with its problems is an unfortunate necessity that interferes
with taking care of things that are really important (such as
reciprocally backbiting and knocking off others); the government speaks to the people, but demands that the police
and special forces listen (or listen in) to their responses. The
people, on the other hand, do not expect salvation from the
government and do not concern themselves much with 'wars
at the top'. They busy themselves bravely with local and private
affairs instead of bothering about 'great politics'. People lose
interest in governing, and, in this case, the fact that the government has lost interest in the people certainly supports the
people's own wishes.

This does not bode well for the young Polish democracy, still
seeking its modus vivendi. True, thinking in categories of 'us'
and 'them' is admittedly nothing new in the politics of our history. But today the 'they', who are completely preoccupied with
'finishing off' one another, personify 'absolute otherness' originating on Mars (maybe) or in troglodytes' caves (more likely).

It is easy to understand why historical memory has been
chosen as a battlefield for today's power struggles. In this field,
it is easy to surprise one's opponents and to succeed in battling
them. Here, we are on the hill, and our opponent is in the
dale. Here, the ground is hard, there it is muddy. Our enemies
will have difficulty deploying their ranks, because there are
so many holes in this field. Besides, all the machines for drill-
ing new holes are in our hands (the archives of UB were first
renamed as the institution of 'national remembrance', then
locked up; the key was carefully hidden from the nosy crowd).
Such choice of the field is significant for the battle: in the
war in which this battle is but an episode, this field is especially convenient, because memory is essentially the ongoing

presence of the past – and the past differs from the present in that (apparently, apparently . . .) everything that belongs to it has already happened and will not be undone. All this pleases those who profess the irreversibility of life trajectories and the irrevocability of fate and its verdicts. But the question of the ultimate goal – that is, of what is really at stake in this war – is a completely different matter. The answer may escape even the skirmishers, always preoccupied with the next battle.

At stake in this war is not national remembrance, but *subordinating politics to the pragmatics of religion*. We can speak here, in short, about the 'religionization of politics'. The contemporary fashion for scaring people with the 'politicization of religion' draws attention away from the real goal of today's Polish struggles and from those happening in the rest of the world.

Politics and religion are governed by exactly opposite pragmatics. Politics is 'the art of the possible' (implicitly: *not everything* is possible in politics). Half jokingly, Odo Marquard derives *Zweifel* (doubt) from *zwei* (two), and says that, where there are two opinions – two people differ in their views – there is also a mutual doubt, and where there is doubt, there pompousness and aggressiveness disappear, and where pride and arrogance are lacking, there is also no wish to fight, and where people balk at smacking each other in the face, they will sooner or later begin to talk to each other, if only because they know no other mode of (co)existence. So negotiations will begin: arguments, compromises. Who knows – maybe the opponents will even ultimately come to terms and forget what they formerly fought about, what made their minds buzz and put them in the mood for battle.

With religion, it is quite different. If there is one God and God is truth, then there is also one truth, and everything that contradicts it must certainly come from the whispers of Satan. Everything that is not from Ahura Mazda began with Ahriman – *tertium non datur*;[68] it is the opposite of politics, which assumes that truths – much like the people who accept them as truth and present them as such – are fallible because they are born from the quests in which people can stray; they are born in such questing and reside in it. In religion, instead of the multiplicity of views which politics would have to consider, there is only the blatantly asymmetrical relationship of orthodoxy and heresy, in which the former does not have any need to seriously consider the latter (and is not allowed to do so). Those who claim otherwise and advise both sides to open their ears instead of stopping the mouths of their opposition can only be planted by Satan. Instead of expecting their wisdom, we should anticipate confession of sin and wicked intentions. These people should cover their heads with ashes and put on hairshirts. The master of religionified politics is called by Adam Michnik 'The Great Lustrator'. Michnik wrote: 'He is sure that he is the possessor of the final truth . . . The Great Lustrator knows it well – the world of the lustrated is in the grip of evil, which must be rooted out; the carriers of evil are evil people, who must be unmasked.'[69]

'Politicizing religion' could only mean opening up to the diversity of God's creation, to the multifariousness of the world and its perceptions, to the variety of human joys and sufferings and to the different ways in which they are experienced. Such opening was recommended, in the name of God 'who is love', by John Paul II. But the current events in Poland (though certainly not only there) are the result of the *religionization of politics*, which contradicts His teachings. This is reminiscent of George W. Bush's and Osama bin Laden's famous (and how symmetrical!) proclamations that 'who is not with us is against us'; and of the clashes between occupiers and terrorists among the ruins of Iraq, described as the battle between good and evil (or as the 'last battle' and apocalypse presaging the Last Judgment).

Today, there is less politicized religion than religionized politics. In our intolerably complicated world, it is not surprising that people dream of a great simplification, of clear divisions and of unambiguous lessons. Instead, there are multiple unnervingly confused and confusing, loud and contradictory messages, which intersect and try to eliminate one another. Their primary task seems to be to question the other side and undermine its trustworthiness. In this situation, strictly monotheistic versions of faith, together with a Manichean, black-and-white vision of the order (or, rather, chaos) of things seems to be the last bastion of all unambiguity: *one* truth, *one* path, *one* right formula for life. Each of these varieties appears to its followers and converts as the only one worthy of trust, and as a shelter of certainty – the last hope of seekers of purity, clarity and freedom from doubt and hesitation. Each of them promises treasures that the rest of the world maliciously, stubbornly negates: self-approval, spiritual calm, safety from error, and guaranteed right.

Making politics in the image of a confrontation between good and evil and comparing conflict of interests to the duel between God and Satan constitute an easy method of simplifying the world or making it 'transparent'. This method is firmly grounded in tradition. In a way, it is also a specific (perverse) interpretation of the legacy of Enlightenment, which led to the blessed practice of extracting sense and logic from chaos, the procedure desired by victims of the 'liquidification' of the world, by people overwhelmed by chaos and weary of disarray. These victims, along with many other people who fear sharing these victims' fate, would be grateful for a proposal of such a procedure. For smart politicians, this is an opportunity that should not be missed. And no place is more conducive to such a procedure for unmasking the devil than the battlefield called 'memory'.

In one of his lectures at the Towarzystwo Kursów Naukowych Society of Scientific Courses (TKN), Adam Michnik explained the submissiveness of intellectuals in relation to the authorities in conflict with the people with, among other things, their widely shared belief that the laws of history are inexorable, that the direction of events has already been determined, and that resistance to history can only produce more victims who, while falling along the way, will not change the course of events. Opposition to history would only be, metaphorically speaking, an attempt to stop an accelerating vehicle by poking a stick into its spokes – an effort from the outset condemned to failure and dangerous for both the prankster who undertakes it and for their surroundings. So, Michnik said, numerous intellectuals, while aware that 'violence triumphs and the will of the majority of society is being violated', thought that it must be so – that it cannot be otherwise because the result has already been decided, because history has doomed mankind to progress; and 'taking things objectively', anything that resists history can only be the effect of the dishonourable, irrational cunning of reactionaries. And so, one more of the 'ketmans' observed and catalogued by Miłosz?[70]

As stated by Vladimir Mayakovsky who was the Soviet Union's greatest poet according to Stalin, the individual is nothing:

What's an individual?
            No earthly good.
One man,
            even the most important of all,
can't raise a ten-yard log of wood[71]

Indeed, if something upsets us in these words today, after all these years and in a totally different world, it is probably mainly their honesty, the fact that the presentiments that we are afraid to utter, despite our peace of mind and respect for our interlocutors, have actually been pronounced loudly and clearly.

Because the truth is that although we, the 'intellectuals', the inheritors of the Enlightenment and people thoroughly civilized in the modern fashion, tend to perform daily ritual prayers at the altar of a free, and thus allegedly omnipotent, individual, in the depths of our souls, we still do not really believe in this individual's omnipotence – or in our own, for that matter. Paradoxically – but on second thoughts, maybe not so paradoxically, after all – the authority of individuals has never before fallen as low as it has in the times of our cult of the individual (all individuals) and its 'human rights' (all rights). Statistical tables note diligently the strongest support for one party or another or the greatest popularity of this or that laundry detergent. They indicate which books are most read, which movies most frequently watched, and which shows most crowded. These tables have disowned individuals from the authority that the pioneers of modernity predicted/promised to give them. The individuals count, but only when they disappear into a crowd or find in it their reflection.

In 1956, a quarter of a century after Mayakovsky left the world of his own volition, Günther Anders noted without a trace of Mayakovsky's enthusiasm that 'the game goes on no matter what we do; with no regard to whether we play it or not, it is played with our participation'. And he added, even more depressingly: 'our withdrawal from it will not change anything'. Does it mean the individual is zero, nothing? And a little more than half a century after the demise of Stalin's favourite, the Frenchman Pierre Bourdieu and the Germans Claus Offe or Ulrich Beck seem to have no doubts in this matter. Though in different words, they make the same observation: the freer the individuals, the less their actions influence how the game proceeds. The more tolerant (indifferent?) the world is towards what the individual does, the weaker our hold over the game we play and over that in which we are played. We perceive the world as a massive block that we cannot move from its place – one that, in addition, is opaque and lacks windows, thus not letting us look inside to see what makes it so heavy. Our view that this weightiness is not a delusion but a sacred truth is being confirmed by people from Warsaw, who from their high bureaucratic positions repeat over and over that they 'do what they do only because they have to', because 'there is no other way', because otherwise there will be problems, because doing anything else would bring about an unimaginable catastrophe for the country and the nation. They recite this in unison with those from other capital cities. Although they may be defending different steps, all of them agree that 'There Is No Alternative' (see the description of this state of affairs and its devastating critique laid out by Jacek Żakowski in his *Anti-TINA*).[72]

The larger the chorus and the more resoundingly it wails, the slimmer the chances for fathoming and verifying the refrain. Or, as Florian Znaniecki's colleague W. I. Thomas suggested, if people take some opinion as true, it becomes true as a result of their actions. In other words, the stronger the individuals' belief that they lack power, the harder it is for them to find and use power within themselves. TINA ['There Is No Alternative'] is an excellent tool for cleansing the conscience. And an excellent prophylactic: it is sufficient to use it conscientiously, and the conscience will not have any chance to learn about its own dirtiness.

A few years ago, in a short space of time, I happened to participate in birthday festivities of two *individuals*: Vaclav Havel and Jacek Kuroń. These were good opportunities for additional reflection on my vision of the role of 'individuals'.

Both Havel and Kuroń were certainly true individuals, *individuals* far more individual than other individuals. Nevertheless, they did not have any of the things that seem indispensable if an individual wishes to escape his or her allegedly innate powerlessness. They did not have aircraft carriers or rocket launchers, police or prisons, wealth or fame, television producers or bands of praying troubadours and devoted fans. They did not appear on TV surrounded by an adoring crowd; their names did not appear on the front pages of the papers. But, despite all this, both of them, each in his own way, changed the game played by their compatriots, the one in which the players were being played themselves. They made this change having recourse to only three, very primitive, forms of weaponry, known to people since the Stone Age: hope, courage and stubbornness – except they reached for these tools much more frequently than I did, and probably than most of us do.

About hope, Havel used to say that it should not be equated with prognosis. Hope does not bend devoutly over the statistics of trends, and certainly does not throw the towel into the boxing ring when it finds them unfavourable. In reference to Havel, Richard Rorty recalled the words of Kenneth Burke: 'in order to know what turn the future would take, one needs to know what songs people are currently singing'.[73] Yet he quoted these words along with Havel's motto that you can never know this year what song people will sing in the next. Remembering this, we can find the courage to remain hopeful – to stick to the hope known also as 'stubborn idealism' (so it was named elsewhere by Maria Janion). Vaclav Havel mustered this courage, and so did Jan Józef Lipski, and Jacek Kuroń.

Bishop Chrapek stubbornly repeated: live in such a way as to leave traces in the world. Havel, Lipski or Kuroń would probably specify what kinds of traces these should be, and they would recommend a way of life that makes us leave the world better than it was at the time of our arrival. And taking this advice, they certainly improved the world, even if only a bit. They managed to do it though neither of them expected his hopes to be completely fulfilled, and despite the fact that there is certainly room for quite a few significant reservations as to the fruits of their stubbornness (as they had themselves).

But they improved the world at least to a sufficient degree to lower the price we now need to pay for hope, courage and stubbornness. In this way, they made sure that it is now somewhat easier to live a life in accordance with the advice they spread and which they followed themselves. The world got closer, if

only by a few steps, to fulfilling Jacek Kuroń's postulate: 'truth
(or rather various, often-contradictory truths), belongs to free
citizens'. While nearing the end of his life, Kuroń could thus
say with a clear conscience: 'It is enough to want, to have an
idea and a bit of persistence, to do once again something really
important in our Poland.' And remind us: 'So it is worthwhile
to want. And worthwhile to try. Despite everything.'[74]

Perhaps, therefore, Günther Anders' gloomy reflections
do not necessarily entail the declarations voiced by Vladimir
Mayakovsky with the enthusiasm better suited to an entirely
different project?! They do not, if one is a Havel, a Kuroń or
a Lipski. And they do not if one stubbornly follows them and
has the courage to face the consequences. True, not many are
up to the task. I doubt I am. But I suspect that I could have
invested more energy into trying had I not told myself that I
couldn't.

*

Miłosz wrote about ketman in a book entitled *The Captive
Mind*. The protagonist of this book was *the mind* – and all
those who ruled over it and let it fall captive. So, it is not about
the average mind – not about the one that we all possess, to
one degree or another, and call 'reason'. It was about the mind,
whose possession is a kind of privilege – the mind that, by
definition, is ruled only by the chosen few, those who write
and those who are written about; the mind that in contrast
to reason teaches us not what is *needed*, but what *should* and
must be done. To properly fulfil one's task, reason must be
'held captive': it has to keep to the designated trajectory without straying, and must prevent from straying those to whom
it shows the way. The greater its fidelity in following the com-
mands and the more obedient it is to those in power wielding
the right to command, the better that reason serves its purpose.

If reason, just like Fredro's Paweł, keeps 'calm, doesn't disturb anyone', the mind, like Paweł's brother Gaweł, 'invents

the wildest frolics'.[75] That is mind's calling, that is its *raison d'être.* The mind needs freedom; the mind breathes freedom. Thus, a 'captive mind' is an *oxymoron.* What could this expression be referring to? A mind disguising itself as reason? A mind reducing itself to reason (healthy, of course, healthy . . .)? And in the name of what? Fooling power? (In the 1960s in Warsaw, in the student theatre Stodoła, the following joke could be heard: 'We are governed by half-wits . . . but I speak from the position of a quarter-wit!' And the Russian satirist Voinovich defined socialist realism, the artistic equivalent of the captive mind, as 'praising power in terms it understands'.) But it is the gist of power that there is no way to fool it – or even try to fool it – without fooling oneself at the same time. For the mind, reason is a sleeping pill. Taken in small doses every day, it becomes a narcotic. Taken in a big dose, it is poison. But asking what the mind does when it restrains its innate freedom and does not use it is like asking what the wind does when it is not blowing, or what happens to a river when it is not flowing. The mind is mind only in untrodden territories, marked by the reason with the warning sign: *hic sunt leones.*[76] And this is the most we can get from it. No more than that, it's true, but also not any less. And in my view, this is no small thing, not small at all, really.

I repeat: ketmans are the trick of the *mind.* Ketmans are indispensable to the mind that refuses its calling – as did St Peter before he became a saint. Listing them, Miłosz explained the ways that many people equipped with minds tried to (could?) fool themselves into thinking they weren't fooling themselves. For over a hundred years, 'people equipped with minds' have been called 'intellectuals'. Ketmans are the professional equipment of intellectuals, or, rather, an essential component of their first-aid kits.

The rest, which constitutes a large majority, does not really need them. People equipped with reason do not perceive the world as a material for a creative transformation, and, thus, they do not feel they owe any explanations to others or to themselves if they resist transformations. The same is clearly true for those who did not even consider changes in the first place. Those, however, who feel the Platonic cave is too tight mock the way of life of the Platonic 'troglodyte'. Unable to forget the rays of light 'out there', they condemn as stupefying and dehumanizing the daily routine cave-dwellers perform without leaving the cave. But that routine, especially when it is practised for long enough to turn into a habit, protects their selfhood. Indeed, the destruction of the self is what waits for the brave few who dare to leave the Platonic cave just beyond its threshold. As Richard Sennett learned from the New York bakers whose lives he observed carefully for the last forty-odd years, routine that makes the world unchanging and monotonous simultaneously makes it safe. Indeed, it renders the world predictable and relatively free from surprises. And although this routine dissolves the bakers' professional pride, it allows them to compose their life.

7

Looking Back – for the Last Time

It is time to reflect on lessons that follow from all this. And, in particular, to ask whether anything can be learned from which we and others could benefit while trying to compose our lives. It should be possible to learn something of this sort, if only because the challenges that we face today are strikingly similar to those faced by generations of people who were born, grew up and even aged in the Polish People's Republic; and this is true despite the stark contrast between these two sets of challenges. Both here and there, at stake was a dignified life. Freedom from humiliation. Making the world in which we have to live better than it was or is, and if this proves impossible, then improving ourselves within it, at least. The main concern was, and still is, to lead a life that would leave a trace. Marx said that people create their own history, but they do it in conditions created by others. Yet it turns out that, regardless of the conditions over which they have little control, people worry about, and struggle with, strikingly similar issues while creating their own history.

François Lyotard once wrote of human children (and who of us is not, or was not, a human child?!): 'Shorn of speech, incapable of standing upright, hesitating over the objects of its interest, not able to calculate its advantages, not sensitive to reason, the child is eminently the human because its distress heralds and promises things possible.'[1]

To be a child means simply that everything is still ahead of you, there, in that secret place called 'the future', whose existence is acknowledged but whose shape is unknown; anything can happen, and if not now, then later. Nothing can yet be seen as impossible, and nothing has yet been irretrievably lost. The world of the *possible* is boundless, and even if it did have limits, it would be difficult to tell where they are and how to find them. Every desire stands the same chance of being fulfilled, and there is no point in trying to assess risks and gains amidst the plethora of chances still untested. Children's vocabulary has no means for distinguishing between what is 'real' and what is but a dream, or between a 'reasonable expectation' and pure fantasy (it is adults who have made up this distinction). Multiple paths are waiting for our feet, and each of them calls, urges, tempts us to try it; and so do the places to which these roads are likely to lead and the styles in which we may travel. To be a child is to be devoid of a 'past', the hallmark of which is that it binds us, grips us by the neck, captures us, leaving no hope of release; but also that one has multiple 'futures' that promise to untie all bonds and crush all chains. To be a child is to be free from a permanent address, but having an open ticket, valid for any journey. Childhood, in other words, means *infinite possibilities*.

Possibility must be led to reality and brought to it; it must be persuaded – convinced, tempted, forced – to *cease* being what it was up to this point: 'only a possibility'. This assistance (help? violence?) is generally called upbringing or education. Its goal is maturity: *the end of childhood*. To become fully *human*, you must first cease to be a *child*. To an adult person, the term 'childish' is an insult, and speaking of a grown-up person's childish behaviour is an affront, an act of disrespect or condemnation. An 'adult' is not-a-child-any-more. More to the point, it is a being stripped of any possibilities except the one that has become a reality. The most valuable of possibilities that educators try to transform into a reality is singling out just one path, straight and clear, from the unsettling plethora of perspectives and confusingly forking roads. One should follow this path without straying or looking to either side, thereby protecting oneself from crossing an impenetrable – and fuzzy, thus treacherous – border between reality and fantasy. This border is dear both to supervisors of the social order and to philosophers, the guardians of the mental order.

You gain something in the process of growing up and maturing: an ability to differentiate between *comme il faut* and *comme il ne faut pas*[2] – between what is allowed and what is forbidden, what is approved and what is condemned, between 'you must do this' and 'you can get away with this', between 'beware of this' and 'do this and you'll be ruined'. Even if these gains come at the cost of losing your liberty, being subordinated, made obedient, humbled and docile, you gain a life in peace and peace of your mind. Mature persons know their place and stay in it, resisting the temptation to push their nose or fingers into where they should not be. This is how it was in the First Republic, and the Second, and the Third, and the Fourth. And it was so in that Polish People's Republic, posthumously recognized as a hole in history.

It is also easy to lose something in the process of growing up and maturing: boldness and stubbornness, desire and the courage to say 'no', the inclination to refuse accepting things as they are just because they are what they are and they insist that they could not be any different. The audacity to spurn the carrot and the courage to ignore the stick . . . The dignity of resistance – resistance to being 'put in your place', treated brusquely or with contempt, tyrannized, frightened, ignored, disposed of. In brief: you can lose *human dignity*.

'We are not allowed to leave the world the way it is',[3] wrote Janusz Korczak in his notebook, possibly to make sure that this commandment dictated his actions. Józef Tischner wrote a different reminder: 'Let us stop reckoning up with the world, and start reckoning up with ourselves.'[4] It sounded like a riposte. But was it really a riposte? An expression of opposition? Despite appearances, it seems that it was not. It stops contrasting with Korczak's call when another observation also written down by Tischner is added: that 'freedom does not come to you from a book; freedom comes to you as a result of meeting another person – a person who is free'.[5] As a thinker, Tischner was exceptionally consistent. He was consistent even in his descriptions and vivisections of inconsistency, of that constant human flaw to which he so often returned in his writing – which he treated with sadness but also with his characteristic wisdom and his understanding for humans and their fate.

When we juxtapose one thing with the other, a harmonious and unambiguous message emerges, one that by no means contradicts Korczak's dictum: let us reckon up with ourselves rather than with the world with regard to the fact that we do not often encounter people who are free. Let us reckon up with ourselves, because the people that met us clearly did not get any freer thanks to meeting us. Let us reckon up with ourselves even further for the fact that we are not free enough. If we do this, the world will no longer be the way it is; it will no longer be the world in which we rarely, too rarely, painfully rarely, meet people who are free. In other words: we should not reckon up with the world instead of reckoning up with ourselves. On the other hand, there is also no way to reckon up with yourself without also reckoning up with the world.

We will not leave the world the way it is if we do not leave ourselves the way we are. And by no means should we leave ourselves 'as we are', because the world would then suffer; because then, again, not much would come out of our reckoning up with ourselves. The circle closes. 'Nobody can be completely free if surrounded by people who are enslaved', says Tischner; 'The proper limit of one's freedom is not, as they say, the freedom of another person, but this person's enslavement'; 'Liberating a person begins from within. It could not begin, however, if a person did not encounter the freedom of another and did not get delighted and enthusiastic about it.'[6]

But what is this thing, this freedom, of which Tischner also said that he would 'put it in the first place' . . . 'among all the values cherished in Poland'? One could find many answers to this question by thoroughly consulting the contents of libraries, but Josip Brodsky, the thinker and poet who experienced a fate similar to ours, seems to be closest to the gist of things when he says that a free person is one who '[does] not complain, when experiencing defeat'; who, in other words, *accepts responsibility for their actions and for these actions' consequences*. Those who do not run away from their responsibility and do not try to protect themselves from it behind a back wider than their own, and who do not evade the accusation of desertion and cowardice by saying, 'I was ordered to', 'I had to' or 'I couldn't do otherwise.' Those who in their own deeds oppose the wicked suggestion, which Fyodor Dostoevsky put in the mouth of the Grand Inquisitor, that 'man is tormented by no greater anxiety than to find quickly someone to whom he can hand over that gift of freedom with which the ill-fated creature is born'.[7]

But then, what does it mean to accept responsibility for the consequences of your actions? What consequences are we talking about? Obviously, we mean the impact that our deeds, or our actions, or our inaction, will have on the fates of other people. Because whatever we do – and whatever actions we avoid taking – this doing changes the circumstances in which the people around us act: it transforms the set of goals that they can reasonably set for themselves, as well as the means that they can use to achieve these goals.

This happens regardless of whether we thought about it or are even aware of the mutual dependence of our fates; whether we realize that, just as the actions of *other* people shape *our* fate, so are *our* actions and *our* inaction a part of *their* fate. Whether we realize it or not, whether we want it to be so or not, we carry responsibility for what will happen to all of us together. But as long as we do not take this fact into account, and as long as we continue to behave as if it were not so, both we and those around us are, so to speak, the 'playthings of fate'. We are not free. Liberation comes only when we decide to transform fate into calling; when, in other words, we accept responsibility for that responsibility that we bear in any case, and from which we cannot free ourselves; which we can at most forget or trivialize, making sure that our memory of this responsibility does not guide our actions and thus favouring enslavement over freedom.

By accepting responsibility for this responsibility for the fate of others – one that we carry whether we want it or not, whether we know it or not – we open the gates to freedom. But we open them also to the risk of error for which we will be blaming and castigating ourselves from now on. Along with our acceptance of the risk of *error*, a risk without which freedom will never come, we also open the gates for our *conscience* to function, from now on, as our judge – the judge both investigating and sentencing, severe and incorruptible, the one from whose verdicts we cannot escape just by explaining that it was somebody else or our own ignorance that forced us to do what we did or prevented us from doing what we were supposed to do.

Appendix

Source Material

Chapter 1 'The Story of Just Another Life?'

From 'Historia jeszcze jednego życia? ('The Story of One More Life')', written in 1997, unpublished; supplemented by 'Dlaczego nie powinienem był tego pisać' ('Why I Shouldn't Have Written This'), the first chapter of *Ostatnie wspomnienia* ('Last Memories'), revised in 2016.

Chapter 2 'Where I Came From'

From 'The Poles, The Jews, and I', written in 1987, unpublished; supplemented by material from *Ostatnie wspomnienia* ('Last Memories'), revised in 2016.

Chapter 3 'The Fate of a Refugee and Soldier'

From 'The Poles, The Jews, and I', written in 1987, unpublished; supplemented by material from *Ostatnie wspomnienia* ('Last Memories'), revised in 2016.

Chapter 4 'Maturation'

From *Ostatnie wspomnienia* ('Last Memories'), revised in 2016.

Chapter 5 'Who Am I?'

From 'Historia jeszcze jednego życia?', written in 1997, unpublished; supplemented by material from *Ostatnie wspomnienia* ('Last Memories'), revised in 2016.

Chapter 6 'Before Dusk Falls'

From *Ostatnie wspomnienia* ('Last Memories'), revised in 2016; part of it was published in Polish in Zygmunt Bauman, Roman Kubicki and Anna Zeidler-Janiszewska, *Życie w kontekstach Rozmowy o tym, co za nami i o tym, co przed nami*, Warsaw: Wydawnictwo WAiP, 2009.

Chapter 7 'Looking Back – for the Last Time'

From *Ostatnie wspomnienia* ('Last Memories'), revised in 2016; part of it was published in Polish in Zygmunt Bauman, Roman Kubicki and Anna Zeidler-Janiszewska, *Życie w kontekstach Rozmowy o tym, co za nami i o tym, co przed nami*, Warsaw: Wydawnictwo WAiP, 2009.

Notes

Introduction

1 Z. Bauman, R. Kubicki and A. Zeidler-Janiszewska, *Humanista w ponowoczesnym świecie – rozmowy o sztuce życia, nauce, życiu sztuki i innych sprawach* ('A Humanist in the Postmodern World – Conversations on the Art of Life, Science, the Life of Art and Other Matters'), Poznań: Zyska i s-ka, 1997.

2 The first entry is not dated but the second note was written on 3 January.

3 The analysis of the differences between the English and Polish versions of his memories deserves more space and will be the subject of an academic paper.

4 J. Bauman, *Winter in the Morning: A Young Girl's Life in the Warsaw Ghetto and Beyond 1939–1945*. Bath: Chivers Press, 1986–7.

5 For more about the influence of Janina Bauman's book on Zygmunt Bauman's work and life, see I. Wagner, *Bauman: A Biography*, Cambridge: Polity, 2020; and I. Wagner, 'Janina and Zygmunt Bauman: a case study of inspiring collaboration' in *Revisiting Modernity and the Holocaust: Heritage, Dilemmas, Extensions*, ed. J. Palmer and D. Brzeziński, Routledge, 2022, pp. 156–76.

6 Janina Bauman beautifully translated this text into Polish – the text is conserved in the Papers of Janina and Zygmunt Bauman in the Special Collections at the University of Leeds.

1 The Story of Just Another Life?

1 Bauman employed the term 'sens' in Polish. In this section, he played with that word and, at the end, he employed it as a synonym of meaning.

2 Milan Kundera, *Testaments Betrayed*, trans. Linda Asher, New York: HarperCollins, 2004, p. 92.

3 TN: Amstrad was an early brand of home computer.

4 Arthur Koestler (1905–83) was a Hungarian/British Jewish author and journalist. Together with his wife, Cynthia, Koestler committed suicide (he was terminally ill). In the Papers of Janina and Zygmunt Bauman in Leeds, there are newspaper articles about this event, as well as other articles about elderly intellectual couples who took their own lives together. Janina and Zygmunt Bauman were interested in this topic. Tadeusz Kotarbiński (1886–1981) was a Polish philosopher, and one of the main figures of the Lviv–Warsaw School of philosophy; he died at the age of 95.

5 Stanisław Ossowski (1897–1963) was a Polish sociologist and social psychologist. He was a specialist in the theory of culture and the methodology of the social sciences. Bauman was not his student but his younger colleague – there are some letters between them in the Papers of Janina and Zygmunt Bauman at the University of Leeds.

6 This fragment (cited in Polish) could be an excerpt from a letter from Ossowski to Bauman.

7 Bauman is referring to the antisemitic opinions that Maria Dąbrowska expressed in her diaries. For more about this, see the Polish version of Janina Bauman's *A Dream of Belonging: Nigdzie na tej ziemi*, Łódź: Wydawnictwo Oficyna, 2011, pp. 51–2.

8 Bauman refers to the October 1956 'Thaw' – the period when the pro-USSR regime undertook reform and partially democratized.

9 'that they never bother me like our people'. These words appear in French in Dąbrowska's original.

10 Maria Dąbrowska, *Dzienniki powojenne*, vol. III: *1955–1959*, Warsaw: Czytelnik W-wa, 1996, p. 111. When no bibliographic reference for an English edition is provided for a translated extract, the translation is by Katarzyna Bartoszyńska.

11 Ibid.

12 A term created by Artur Sandauer (1913–89; Polish-Jewish literary critic and essayist) that defines a form of antisemitism based on a positive distinction (such as: 'Jews are smarter, more creative, intelligent . . .'); even if these assumptions are not harmful, this is always a process of distinction and division between us (non-Jews) and them (Jews).

13 *Szlachta zaściankowa*: parochial nobles or gentry – less wealthy nobles.

14 TN: The full saying is something to the effect of 'What suits a voivode is not for the powerless.'

15 Jean Baudrillard, *Seduction*, New York: St Martin's Press, 1990, pp. 131–2.

16 Kundera, *Testaments Betrayed*, pp. 174–5.

17 Wisława Szymborska, 'Some people like poetry', trans. Stanisław Barańczak and Clare Cavanagh, *The New Republic*, 28 October 1996.

18 This citation is from Dąbrowska, *Dzienniki powojenne*, vol. III, p. 135, 2 July 1956.

19 Kundera, *Testaments Betrayed*, p. 220.

20 See chapter 2 – this is the text mentioned here by ZB.

21 In these three sentences, Bauman is citing his own words from chapter 2.

22 This is the title of Johann Wolfgang von Goethe's book *Elective Affinities*.

23 Bauman is referring to the article by Roland Barthes, 'Écrivains et écrivants', from 1960, published in *Essais critiques*, Paris: Le Seuil, 1964, pp. 147–54. Jean-Charles Falardeau explains the difference between 'écrivains' (writers) and 'écrivants' (authors) in

the following way: for the former, *écrire* is an intransitive verb, while the latter is a transitive man ('L'écrivain est celui pour qui écrire est un verbe intransitif, celui qui "travaille sa parole et s'absorbe fonctionnellement dans ce travail". Il se distingue de l'écrivant, lequel est un homme transitif, "celui qui pose une fin (témoigner, expliquer, enseigner)" dont la parole n'est qu'un moyen') – in Falardeau, *Liberté: Art & Politique*, vol. 3, 5(17), 1961, 712: www.erudit.org/fr/revues/liberte/1961-v3-n5-liberte 1026915/30110ac.pdf.

24 Mr Kurtz is a character from Joseph Conrad's novella *Heart of Darkness*, published in 1899.

25 *Je n'écris plus, je m'occupe* (Fr.) means 'I don't write any more, I keep myself busy [I look after myself].' Martin du Gard (1881–1958) was a French writer and winner of the 1937 Nobel Prize for Literature.

26 This sentence is a metaphor for books' life, while the progress of civilization regarding human lives is measured by the reduction of infant mortality and the extension of longevity.

27 The Institute of Contemporary Arts.

28 For more about this painting, see www.tate.org.uk/art/artworks /constant-after-us-liberty-t03705.

29 Romana Kolarzowa is a Polish philosopher and professor at the University of Rzeszów, with a particular interest in collective identity, nationalism and antisemitism.

30 'Anka' is a diminutive of 'Anna' – here referring to Professor Anna Zeidler-Janiszewska.

31 Romana Kolarzowa, 'Pani Dulska Polskę zbawi' ('Ms Dulska will save Poland') in *Rewizje, kontynuacje*, ed. Anna Jamroziakowa, Poznań: Wyd. Humaniora, 1997, p. 129 (pp. 121–39).

32 Bauman uses the Polish 'nieustawiony głos', a musical expression regarding vocal training (relating to the Italian term *impostare della voce*).

33 Dąbrowska uses 'writer' in the masculine form, and consequently she uses 'he'. It was the norm for writing at that time. Even today,

the masculine form is used in Polish as inclusive of all genders whenever a generalization is to be made.

34 Maria Dąbrowska, *Dzienniki powojenne*, vol. VI: *1914–1965*, Warsaw: Czytelnik W-wa, 2009, note from 27 October 1948, p. 111.

35 In the original, *mocarz* (Polish: 'mighty man') is also a masculine figure.

36 'Pani Dulska Polskę zbawi' ('Ms Dulska will save Poland'), p. 130.

37 ZB created the words here and also employed old slang expressions – he played a lot with the language and its sound; this sentence in the original Polish reads: 'Nurzam się w języku, bełtam-barachtam'.

2 Where I Came From

1 TN: Bauman's pun cannot be translated into English. It makes use of the fact that *przeżycie* can mean both experience and survival.

2 We should remember that Bauman wrote this text for family members.

3 *Kheder*, which Bauman spelled in Polish as *cheder*, is a Jewish religious school, providing primary education for children from the age of 4.

4 *Melamed* is a teacher (in Hebrew and Yiddish).

5 A *zaddik*, or in Polish transliteration *cadyk*, is, according to the *Collins Dictionary*: (1) Hasidic Jewish spiritual leader; (2) a saintly or righteous person according to Jewish faith and practice (www.collinsdictionary.com/dictionary/english/zaddik).

6 Słupca – a Polish town, inhabited in the interwar period by about 6,000 people, a quarter of whom were Jews. The town is 45 miles east of Poznań. Zagórów is a village 9 miles south of Słupca, in 1921 inhabited by 3,715 people, including 807 Jews. For more, see https://sztetl.org.pl/pl/miejscowosci, adding the relevant placename.

7 *Shtetl* – 'little town' in Yiddish: 'Shtetl became a symbol of Jewish

life before the Holocaust.' For more on *shtetl*, see www.sztetl.org
.pl/en.

8 *Bekishe* – a long, black silk coat worn by Chassidic Jews (Bauman
employed this term in Polish: *chałat*, which comes from the
Arabic word *chalit*; in Yiddish, it is *kapote*); see Alina Cała,
'Ubiór żydowski' in *Wirtualny Shetl*: https://sztetl.org.pl/pl/slow
nik/stroj-zydowski.

9 Judenrein (*Judenfrei*: German for 'cleansed [or free] of Jews') is
a National Socialist term applied in the 'Final Solution of the
Jewish Question'. More can be found at www.jewishvirtuallibra
ry.org/judenrein.

10 The National Democracy Party – the so-called Endecja
(Narodowa Demokracja: ND) – was created at the end of the
nineteenth century by Roman Dmowski; ND was built on a
nationalist ideology and powerful patriotic feelings. One of the
core goals and main propaganda slogans in the multicultural
country was the 'liberation' of Polish society from Jews. Strong
antisemitism and open hostility to non-Christian Poles (in 1931,
75.2 per cent of the population were Roman Catholics) were the
driving forces of this party, which grew in power through the
1930s. The party was particularly popular in the Wielkopolska
region, whose capital was Poznań. For more, see Izabela Wagner,
Bauman: A Biography, Cambridge: Polity, 2020.

11 'Gerhard (Gershom) Scholem (1897–1982) was the pre-eminent
modern scholar of Jewish mysticism. . . . His contribution lay in
five distinct yet connected areas which will be detailed below:
the research and analysis of kabbalistic literature spanning from
late antiquity to the twentieth century; the phenomenology of
mystical religion; Jewish historiography; Zionism; and the spiritual and political condition of contemporary Judaism and Jewish
civilization. He published over 40 volumes and close to 700 articles almost all of which are listed in the Scholem Bibliography
published in 1977' (*Stanford Encyclopedia of Philosophy*: https://
plato.stanford.edu/entries/scholem).

12 Jehuda Halevi – 'Judah ben Samuel Halevi (*c.* 1075–1141) was

the premier Hebrew poet of his generation in medieval Spain. Over the course of some fifty years, from the end of the eleventh century to the middle of the twelfth, he wrote nearly 800 poems, both secular and religious. However, because this was a time of intensifying religious conflict characterized by physical, social, and political upheaval, Halevi also sought to develop a reasoned defense of the Jewish religion, which was then under attack on all fronts' (*Stanford Encyclopedia of Philosophy*; for more, see https://plato.stanford.edu/entries/halevi).

Agnon – Shmuel Yosef Agnon, an Israeli, born as Szmuel Josef Czaczkes (1888–1970), winner of the 1966 Nobel Prize for Literature. For more, see www.nobelprize.org/prizes/literature /1966/agnon/biographical.

13 The Pentateuch (meaning literally 'five books') is the first common part of the Jewish and Christian scriptures: Genesis, Exodus, Leviticus, Numbers and Deuteronomy. In Hebrew, and sometimes in other languages as well, it is known as the Torah. For more, see www.oxfordbibliographies.com/view/document /obo-9780195393361/obo-9780195393361-0092.xml.

14 Sabra – this term refers to the fruit of a native cactus. As Włodek Goldkorn described it: 'Sabra – a plant, sweet and delicate inside, seemingly somewhat rough and arrogant; the stereotype of a Jew born in freedom, speaking Hebrew from birth, uninfected by the evil of the Diaspora and the shameful Yiddish slang – a brave Jew and at the same time a good farmer and a beautiful male, preferably blonde with blue eyes' (W. Goldkorn, *Dziecko w śniegu*. Wołowiec: Czarne 2018, pp. 133–4).

15 In Polish, *Noce i Dnie*, a very popular book (in four volumes) published between 1931 and 1934 by Maria Dąbrowska. The book was nominated for the Nobel Prize for Literature in 1939, 1957, 1959, 1960 and 1965. For more on the author and her work, see www.britannica.com/biography/Maria-Dabrowska#re f198249.

16 This important sentence is built from two versions. Firstly from English, until 'to be sure', then Polish. The latter version started

with 'A significant portion of this small-town intelligentsia was "of Jewish descent".' This reflects the crucial issue and tensions in the categorizations of 'Jewish', 'Polish-Jewish', 'Polish Jew' or 'Jewish Pole'. I develop this in Bauman, *A Biography* (Cambridge: Polity, 2020), but I will focus on the significant differences contained in the identity and perception of Jewish Poles or Polish Jews in Bauman's dual-language private writing in a separate text.

17 'Rzeczpospolita' is a Polish term for 'republic'. In this context, it is a shorter version of 'Rzeczpospolita Polska' (Polish Republic) which was the official name of Poland from 1918 to 1939, then from 1989 until today.

18 Here, Bauman refers to the 1938 Polenaktion: 'In late October of 1938, the Nazi regime ordered the arrest of around 17,000 Jews with Polish citizenship who were living in the German Reich. The Jews were then expelled and transported violently to the Polish border. This forced expulsion, designated the Polenaktion ("Polish Action") in German, was the first mass deportation of Jews from the German Reich' (Judisches Museum Berlin – www.jmberlin.de/en/topic-polenaktion-1938).

19 *Luftmensch* (Yiddish) refers to an impractical, unrealistic person: www.collinsdictionary.com/dictionary/english/luftmensch.

20 Poznań was part of Prussia and was under the rule of the *Kulturkämpfe*. 'Kulturkampf – struggle of the Prussian state against the Roman Catholic Church (1872–87), which took the form of laws designed to bring education, marriage, etc., under the control of the state': www.collinsdictionary.com/dictionary/english/kulturkampf.

21 In the Polish version, Bauman wrote that it was in Wolsztyn, about 50 miles away.

22 In the late 1930s in Poland, several sectors of employment were regulated with a so-called 'Aryan paragraph', which excluded people considered to be Jews from certain occupations and professions. More about Tosia and the reason she had no job can be found in Wagner, *Bauman*, ch. 2.

23 A German term, literally 'women's room' – describes bourgeois women (in a humorous way).

24 'Józef Klemens Piłsudski (born December 5, 1867, Żułów, Poland, Russian Empire [now in Lithuania] – died May 12, 1935, Warsaw, Poland), Polish revolutionary and statesman, the first chief of state (1918–22) of the newly independent Poland established in November 1918. After leading a coup d'état in 1926, he rejected an offer of the presidency but remained politically influential while serving as minister of defence until 1935': www .britannica.com/biography/Jozef-Pilsudski.

25 *Ilustrowany Kurier Codzienny* ('Daily Illustrated') – press venture launched in 1910 in Kraków. It was a progressive journal.

26 *Nasz Przegląd* ('Our Review') was a Polish-Jewish newspaper (printed in Polish for the Jewish community) linked to Zionism. It was the most popular Polish-Jewish journal in interwar Poland. Bauman's parents subscribed to it.

27 Janusz Korczak, born Henryk Goldszmit (1878–1942), devoted his life to the struggle for children's rights. He was raised in a family of progressive Jews (his lawyer father was a member of Haskala, a Jewish intellectual movement strongly influenced by the Enlightenment, which spread between the mid eighteenth and mid nineteenth centuries, starting in Germany and popular in the various parts of the Jewish Diaspora). He received a Russian general education (Warsaw at the time was under Czarist rule). He was also a widely renowned pedagogue, and published several texts addressed to children, but also to parents and educators. In the orphanage under his direction, children created their own republic with its own parliament, court system and newspaper. During the German occupation, he refused offers to help him escape and remained in the Warsaw Ghetto with his children until they were deported to Treblinka. See L. Berger, *Korczak, un homme, un symbole*, Paris: Magnard, 1989.

28 In Polish, 'Diabeł domowego ogniska' ('Devil of the household hearth'); original Danish title: 'Den Kongelige Gæst'. In 1917, the author won the Nobel Prize for Literature. The other authors

and titles are well known and easily accessible to the English-speaking audience.

29 In Polish, Bauman wrote 'Żydek'.

30 General Mieczysław Moczar (1913–86) is recognized as the 'brain' behind the antisemitic repressions that provoked the wave of emigration after March 1968. For Bauman's family in 1968, see Wagner, *Bauman*, ch. 8.

31 Melosik died in 2007.

32 In the Polish version, Bauman also mentioned teachers of Latin and history acting in a similar way.

33 'Jasia' was the nickname of Janina Bauman, the wife of Zygmunt Bauman – they married in 1948 and lived together for over sixty years. Janina Bauman was a writer and the author of *Winter in the Morning* (1986); she died in 2009.

34 This was the best mark. The difference between the two cities reflects Polish history: before 1918 (when the Second Polish Republic was created), Poznań was a Prussian/Germanophone city, while Warsaw was a Russian metropolis.

35 The *Hashomer Hatzair* (Hebrew: 'Young Guard') was one of the most influential Zionist organizations in the interwar period, although it did not aspire to become a mass movement. Its members, *szomer*, were obliged to work for the implementation of the Zionist programme by boosting Jewish national funds, mastering the Hebrew language and finally making *alija* (Hebrew: 'going up' – the term for Jewish immigration to Palestine, and later Israel, from the Diaspora), followed by work on collective farms (*kibbutzim*) in Palestine. *Hashomer Hatzair* saw itself as raising the national vanguard of Jews by creating close friendships and a sense of brotherhood and family ties among its members (N. Aleksiun, *Dokąd dalej? Ruch syjonistyczny w Polsce (1944–1950)*, Warsaw: Trio, 2002).

36 Winiary Wood – a large park, with a wild part referred to as a wood, in the area of Poznań called Winiary.

3 The Fate of a Refugee and Soldier

1 For the history of Izbica, see https://sztetl.org.pl/en/node/291
   /99-history/137382-history-of-community.
2 *The Wandering Jews*, trans. Michael Hofmann, New York:
   Norton, 2001.
3 Ibid., p. 113.
4 Ibid., p. 114.
5 In the first month of World War II, Poland was occupied by
   Germany (firstly) and the USSR (secondly – the Soviet invasion started on 17 September 1939). About these different
   perceptions, see Jan Gross, *Żydzi i Sowieci. Opowieści kresowe
   1939–1941*, Krakow, Budapest, Syracuse: Austeria, 2020.
6 Związek Walki Zbrojnej, ZWZ (Union for Armed Struggle, or
   Association of Armed Struggle) – the underground army formed
   in Poland between November 1939 and 14 February 1942, when
   it was renamed 'the Home Army' (Armia Krajowa, AK).
7 A. Żbikowski, 'Pogromy i mordy ludności żydowskiej w
   Łomżyńskiem i na Białostocczyźnie latem 1941 roku w świetle
   relacji ocalałych Żydów i dokumentów sądowych' in *Wokół
   Jedwabnego*, ed. P. Machcewicz and K. Persak, Warsaw: IPN,
   vol. I, p. 262.
8 In November 1939, after temporary control of the border by
   the Wehrmacht, German border control units (Grenzschutz)
   were sent from the former Polish–German border to these
   new demarcation lines. The Grenzschutz units had a reputation
   for being cruel and aggressive. Before November 1939, many
   refugees had escaped into the territories controlled by the Soviet
   Union.
9 German: 'All Jews out!'
10 On 11 November, German soldiers killed about 600 Jews
   (M. Bartniczak, 'Ze starych I nowych dziej. w Ostrowi
   Mazowieckiej. Nazwa, Herb i geneza miasta', *Ziemia*, 1972,
   52–74: ttp://ziemia.pttk.pl/Ziemia/Artykul_1972_006.pdf, 63).
   It was a mass execution of local people and refugees who were
   waiting, like the Baumans, for an opportunity to cross the border.

11 Łomża was, in 1939–41, the border city on the Soviet side. Many
    refugees stayed there before pursuing their escape eastwards.

12 Adam Mickiewicz is one of the most celebrated Polish poets, the
    author of *Pan Tadeusz* – an epic poem, in which he described
    the Lithuanian landscape.

13 The All-Union Leninist Communist Youth League. It was com-
    monly known as 'Komsomol', and it was an antechamber of the
    Communist Party.

14 'Kolkhoz, also spelled kolkoz, or kolkhozs, plural kolkhozy, or
    kolkhozes, abbreviation for Russian kollektivnoye khozyaynstvo,
    English collective farm, in the former Soviet Union, a cooperative
    agricultural enterprise operated on state-owned land by peasants
    from a number of households who belonged to the collective and
    who were paid as salaried employees on the basis of quality and
    quantity of labour contributed': www.britannica.com/topic/kol
    khoz.

15 'Einsatzgruppen (German: "deployment groups"), units of
    the Nazi security forces composed of members of the SS, the
    Sicherheitspolizei (Sipo; "Security Police"), and the Ordnungspolizei
    (Orpo; "Order Police") that acted as mobile killing units during the
    German invasions of Poland (1939) and the Soviet Union (1941)';
    for more, see www.britannica.com/topic/Einsatzgruppen.

16 'Nizhny Novgorod, formerly Gorky or Gorki, city, capital of
    Nizhny Novgorod region and the administrative center of the
    Volga federal district, European Russia, on the Volga and Oka
    rivers. A major river port and a rail and air centre, it is one of the
    chief industrial cities of Russia': https://encyclopedia2.thefreedic
    tionary.com/Gorky+(city).

17 According to the *Encyclopedia of Judaism*, Shemaiah (Heb.
    שְׁמַעְיָהוּ, שְׁמַעְיָה), was a prophet in the days of Solomon's son,
    Rehoboam, king of Judah (I Kings 12:22–4 and the parallel
    passage in II Chron. 11:2–4; 12:5–8, 15). Shemaiah is associ-
    ated with two events: one at the beginning of, the other during,
    Rehoboam's reign. In I Kings and in the parallel account in II
    Chronicles, it is related that Shemaiah cautioned Rehoboam not

to embark on a war against the tribes of Israel that had rebelled against his authority, and warned him that 'this thing is from Me (i.e., God)' (I Kings 12:24; II Chron. 11:4). For more, see https://judaism_enc.en-academic.com/17999/SHEMAIAH.

18 Fyodor Ivanovich Tyutchev (1803–73), Russian poet and diplomat.

19 In the Polish version (dated 2017), 'the Germans' was changed into 'the Wehrmacht'.

20 *New Horizons* (*Nowe Widnokręgi*) was a socio-literary journal, published fortnightly, edited by the Polish communist and writer Wanda Wasilewska (who also led the ZPP – Związek Patriotów Polskich, or Union of Polish Patriots). With *Free Poland* (*Wolna Polska*), launched on 1 March 1943, it was one of two voices of the ZPP. For more, see Wagner, *Bauman: A Biography*, Cambridge: Polity, 2020, ch. 4.

21 Bolesław Wieniawa-Długoszewski (1881–1942) was a Polish general, adjutant to Chief of State Józef Piłsudski, politician, diplomat, poet and artist.

22 Stefan Żeromski (1864–1925) was a Polish novelist and dramatist, and a member of the Młoda Polska (Young Poland) movement. Bauman uses the term 'glasshouses', which is a concept from Żeromski's 1924 bestseller *Przedwiośnie* ('The Spring to Come'), 'in which the protagonist, Cezary Baryka, a Russian-born Polish noble, obtains a patriotic education from books and stories. "Glass houses" are the symbol of utopia, the idealized country, which shatters as Cezary comes to Poland for the first time and sees the huge disparity between reality and what he has learned from his father. In Żeromski's book, utopia could be built by revolution or through progressive hard work and social change' (Wagner, *Bauman*, p. 70).

23 Arbat Street is the 'Champs-Élysées' of Moscow, one of the oldest, but also most famous, streets in the centre of Russia's capital city.

24 NCO – non-commissioned officer, *podoficer* in Polish, a grade below 'Officer' which was, in the Polish system to which Bauman belonged, considered to be a first step towards officership.

25 The Katyń Massacre was the mass execution of Polish military officers by the Soviet Union during World War II. The discovery of the massacre precipitated the severing of diplomatic ties between the Soviet Union and the Polish government-in-exile in London. A total of 4,443 corpses were recovered, which had apparently been shot from behind and then piled in stacks and buried. For more on this, see www.britannica.com/event/Katyn -Massacre.

26 Bauman wrote 'Persia' in the original, but, by 1942, it wasn't Persia any more, but Iran. The country requested that all countries with which it had diplomatic relations call it by its Persian name, Iran, in 1935. (Thanks to Paulina Bożek for this information.)

27 Bauman wrote this using Polish transliteration; in English, the transliteration is 'nastoyashchevo russkovo parnya'.

28 Radość is today a suburb to the south-east of Warsaw, on the right-hand side of the river Vistula.

29 Studebakers – American trucks sent by the US to the Soviet Union during the war.

30 Kołobrzeg – in German, Colberg; the city in the north-west of Poland where the biggest battle on the Polish liberated territories in 1944–5 took place – with the Polish Army as the main military force (not the Red Army as was usually the case).

31 Panzerfaust – single-shot, recoilless German anti-tank weapon.

32 1 May – International Workers' Day – was celebrated by Deeds. It was an important festivity in the communist countries.

33 German: 'broken dead'.

34 Bauman is speaking about the new definition of the 1945–89 period as one when Poland was enslaved by the Soviets (the term 'enslaved' is important here) – a definition that grew in popularity after 1989.

35 Jerzy Urban, 'Od lachociągu do rurociągu', *NIE*, 16, 2007.

4 Maturation

1 Vladimir Mayakovsky, *Poems*, trans. Dorian Rottenberg, Moscow: Progress, 1972.

2 ZB: Czesław Miłosz, *Wyprawa w dzudziestolecie* ('An Excursion through the Twenties and Thirties'), Krakow: WL, 1998, pg 6.

3 Bauman is mentioning here the pioneering study by Irena Sara Hurwic-Nowakowska, a sociologist who conducted, between 1947 and 1950, a study investigating the changes in the Polish-Jewish community after World War II. She wrote *Polish Jews (1947–1950): A Social Analysis of Postwar Polish Jewry*, published only in 1986 in Israel – in Jerusalem by The Zalman Shazar Center – and in Poland only in 1996 – by Wydawnictwo IFiS PAN, the Polish Academy of Science Press. It was her Ph.D. study, defended in 1950, but, for political reasons, it was impossible to publish before the changes in 1989.

4 *Zagłada a tożsamość*, Warsaw: IFiS PAN, 2004. Małgorzata Melchior develops the work of Irena Hurwic-Nowakowska (see the obituary of Hurwic-Nowakowska – *Studia Socjologiczne*, 181, 2006: www.studiasocjologiczne.pl/img_upl/studia_socjolog iczne_2006_nr2_s.13_17.pdf).

5 The shorter Polish version, cited by Bauman, is: Joanna Beata Michlic and Emanuel Tanay, 'Passport to life' in *Losy żydowskie Świadectwa żywych*, ed. Marian Turski, Warsaw: Of.Wyd. 'ADIUTOR', 1996, p. 66; the original appeared in English as Joanna Beata Michlic, *Poland's Threatening Other: The Image of the Jew from 1880 to the Present*, Lincoln: University of Nebraska Press, 2006, p. 190. See, especially, ch. 5, about the perceptions of Jews during the German occupation.

6 Adolf Rudnicki, *Wniebowstąpienie: Ucieczka z Jasnej Polany; Regina, Regina Borkowska*, Warsaw: Iskry, 1985.

7 Jan Błoński (1931–2009) was a Polish historian, publicist, literary critic and translator. He was a professor at the Jagiellonian University. His article 'The poor Poles look at the ghetto' in *Tygodnik Powszechny* (also frequently discussed by Bauman) is one of the fundamental pieces in Polish reflection on the reaction of Polish society to the Shoah.

8 Jerzy Jastrzębowski, 'Differing ethical standpoints' in *My Brother's Keeper: Recent Polish Debates on the Holocaust*, ed.

Antony Polonsky, London: Routledge, 1990, p. 120. (The note in the Polish original reads: Zob. Zygmunt Bauman, *Nowoczesność i Zagłada*, Warszawa 1992, s. 277, tłum. Franciszek Jaszuński.)

9   For more about cognitive dissonance, see the fundamental study conducted by Leo Festinger and his collaborators in the 1950s, and published as a book entitled *When Prophecy Fails: A Social and Psychological Study of a Modern Group that Predicted the Destruction of the World*, co-authored by Henry Ricken and Stanley Schachter, New York: Harper-Torchbooks, 1956.

10   The citation provided by Bauman and attributed to Szaynok is in fact a quotation from Gross. In the English version of *Fear*, Gross wrote: 'The Jews were also directly murdered by Poles who wanted to acquire their property' (*Fear: Anti-Semitism in Poland after Auschwitz: An Essay in Historical Interpretation*, Princeton University Press, 2006, p. 40). This citation is different from that provided by Bauman: 'Jewish property changed owners during the war.' The differences should be addressed. The first citation (by Gross) directly accuses the Poles; the second (Szaynok's) is speaking 'neutrally': the goods changed owner – we don't know why or how, or who the new owner of the Jewish goods is. (This example is one of numerous cases of cautious writing in Polish about this sensitive topic in Polish–Jewish relationships.) Authors and publishers frequently practise auto-censorship, probably in order to avoid the repercussions that in Poland could lead to a court case (the law punishing authors who blame the good name of the Polish nation was introduced in 2018, but even before then historians were being accused of slandering the nation). For more about the consequences of this law, see www.wsws.org/en/articles/2021/02/11/pole-f11.html. I checked the Polish version of *Fear* and there are many changes (the book was translated by Gross, or rather he 're-wrote' it, as he told me in a private discussion). The title of this subchapter is also different, as 'Polish neighbor' was changed to 'private persons' ('The takeover of Jewish property by private persons'). Bauman most probably read the Polish version of the book,

and certainly he also read articles in the Polish press that followed the publication of *Fear*. It was a widely discussed 'national event'. Bożena Szaynok was cited several times by Gross – not in the section titled 'The takeover of Jewish property by Polish neighbors', but in other places in the book (regarding other issues).

Even if, here, Bauman attributed an incorrect author for the sentence that he cited from *Fear*, Szaynok could also be the author of a similar statement. In the original translated here (as well as press articles that Bauman published in Polish), instead of a precise reference, he is giving a general reference to Szaynok's work: 'See Szaynok: "The Role of Antisemitism in Postwar Polish–Jewish Relations" in: *Antisemitism and Its Opponents in Modern Poland*, ed. Robert Blobaum, Cornell UP 2005, pgs. 265–283.'

When Bauman uses the term 'moral collapse', it is a quotation from Jan T. Gross, from the Polish edition of *Fear*, which is longer because of the additional phrase: 'the history of moral collapse'.

11 ZB: See the weekly *Kuźnica*, 30 September 1946.

12 ZB: Janina Bauman, *Beyond These Walls: Escaping the Warsaw Ghetto – A Young Girl's Story*, Virago: 2006, p. 250.

13 Tadeusz Konwicki (1926–2015) was a Polish writer, scriptwriter and movie maker; Stanisław Bereś is a Polish poet, historian of literature, media specialist, literary critic and translator; he is a professor at Wrocław University. Bereś published *Pół wieku czyśćca: Rozmowy z Tadeuszem Konwickim* (*A Half a Century of Purgatory*) (under the pseudonym Stanisław Nowicki – London: Aneks, 1987; Warsaw: Przedświt, 1987; Warsaw: Oficyna Wydawnicza Interim, 1990; Krakow, 2002; translated into French as *Un demi-siècle de purgatoire*, Paris: Noir sur Blanc, 1993).

14 ZB: Cited in Anna Bikont and Joanną Szczęsną, *Lawina i Kamienie*, [Warsaw:] Prószyński i Ska 2007, pgs.82–3.

15 Nietzsche, *Thus Spoke Zarathustra*, ed. Adrian Del Care and Robert Pippin, Cambridge University Press, 2006, p. 111.

16 ZB: Cited in Anna Bikont and Joanną Szczęsną, *Lawina i Kamienie*, [Warsaw:] Prószyński i Ska 2007, p. 91.

17 Ralph Miliband (1924–94) was a British sociologist, specialist in Marxism and co-creator of the New Left. See Michael Newman, *Ralph Miliband and the Politics of the New Left*, New York: Monthly Review Press, 2003.

18 ZB: Celina Budzyńska, *Strzępy rodzinnej sagi*, Warsaw: Żydowski Instytut Historyczny 1997, pg.453.

19 ZB: Ibid. 453.

20 The PPR – Polska Partia Robotnicza (Polish Workers' Party) – created in 1942, was the leading workers' party after Liberation. In December 1948, after unification with the Polish Socialist Party (PPS), it became the PZPR (Polska Zjednoczona Partia Robotnicza).

21 Kieślowski's movie title in Polish is *Przypadek* ('The Hazard'). In Polish, this is a neutral expression, while in English it could be a negative 'accident' as much as a positive 'chance'. The title in English is 'Blind Chance', which is certainly the best translation of the Polish term. In the text, 'blind chance' / 'accident' / 'chance' will be used interchangeably.

22 For more about this specific military formation, see Izabela Wagner, *Bauman: A Biography*, Cambridge: Polity, 2020, ch. 6.

23 In those years, blessing the banner was a duty of the 'kapelan wojskowy' – the military Catholic priest. It shows how, in the post-war years, the authorities were not against religion, and that the shift to secular ceremonies did not occur immediately after the liberation of Poland.

24 Resovia, WKS Sztorm (WKS – 'Military Sporting Club'), Gwardia – all are the names of sports clubs playing football.

25 Szczytno is a town in north-eastern Poland, located within the historic region of Masuria (about 110 miles north of Warsaw).

26 Bauman is speaking about the actions of the KBW in the Ukrainian territories, where civilians – inhabitants of the villages – were killed because of supposed collaboration with underground anti-communist units.

27 This was a famous movie, but public screenings started almost a year after Bauman's stay in Białystok. For more, see Wagner, *Bauman*, ch. 6.

28 Konstanty Rokossowski (1896–1968) was a Polish and Russian soldier, Marechal of Poland and the Soviet Union, and a politician. He was a hero of both world wars, and is considered one of the most important figures of World War II.

29 There is a need for a monograph on KBW units. It was a complex and dynamic institution, not at all a blind executor of Stalin's wishes, as it is frequently presented by the majority of historians.

30 Pseudo-elites: *pseudo-elity, łże-elity* or *wykształciuchy* are the negative terms with which Jarosław Kaczyński and politicians from his party, PiS (Justice and Solidarity), defined those members of the intelligentsia who were in opposition to this party. In this way, Bauman is making a connection between Stalinism and the current Polish authorities (they won the election in 2015, and Bauman did the final reading of this text in 2016). I wish to thank Wojciech Rafałowski for his suggestion of the translation 'educatedets'.

31 This saying should emphasize the rupture between pre-war and post-war military selection for officer school – before 1939, a high-school diploma was needed; after 1945, it was not.

32 Zdzisław Bibrowski (1913–2000), a colonel in the Polish Army.

33 According to Britannica: 'Doctors' Plot (1953), alleged conspiracy of prominent Soviet medical specialists to murder leading government and party officials; the prevailing opinion of many scholars outside the Soviet Union is that Joseph Stalin intended to use the resulting doctors' trial to launch a massive party purge' (www.britannica.com/event/Doctors-Plot). For more, see Y. Rapoport, *The Doctors' Plot of 1953*, Cambridge, MA: Harvard University Press, 1991.

34 'The Central Committee will discuss this matter and consider it carefully in order to prevent errors and excesses': a citation of Khrushchev's speech from https://novaonline.nvcc.edu/eli/evans/HIS242/Documents/Speech.pdf . However, in the Polish

original, Bauman uses the Polish version of the speech, popularized also by Gomułka, the Polish leader elected in October 1956; that version contains the term 'okres błędów i wypaczeń', which functions as a concept describing the 'period of errors and distortions'. It was a widely used Polish expression in 1956, and is still present in the vocabulary describing Stalinism. The word 'errors' is properly rendered, but 'wypaczeń' (distortion) was modified from the original translation of the speech – there it was 'przegięć' (inflections). These terms replaced the term 'crimes'. For more, see Robert Kupiecki, 'Od VIII Plenum do VIII Plenum 1953–1956. Odchodzenie od kultu Stalina w Polsce', *Kwartalnik Historyczny*, R99, 2, 1992: https://rcin.org.pl/Con tent/3711/PDF/WA303_3934_KH99-r1992-R99-nr2_Kwartaln ik-Historyczny%2005%20Kupiecki.pdf.

35 The Old Town, MDM and Muranów are Warsaw districts rebuilt after World War II. MDM is Marszałkowska Residential District – as Adam Mazur and Łukasz Gorczyca wrote on culture.pl, it is 'a quintessential socialist realist piece. This convention is also characterised by its evident imports from the pre-war aesthetic styles of constructivist avant-garde and pictorialism. Besides pictures of labourers at work and artists decorating the MDM edifices, one can also find a lot of expressive and modern shots of machines, the construction site, and the architecture itself.' For more, see https://culture.pl/en/work/mdm-marszalkowska -1730-1954 (a book about the history of MDM).

36 In the original, these quotations were: 'półfeudalna struktura Polski została złamana' and 'robotnicza i chłopska młodzież zapełnia uniwersytety' (Czesław Miłosz, 'NIE', *Kultura. Szkice. Opowiadania. Sprawozdania* (Paris) 5, 43, 1951, 4).

37 The original reads 'na kimś, kto rozumiał dynamikę przemian zachodzących w Polsce, spory kilkuosobowych stronnictw (emigracyjnych – ZB) robiły wrażenie bezużytecznej zabawy, a same postacie tych polityków wyglądały na figury z wodewilu': from ibid., p. 4.

38   Albert Camus, *The Plague*, trans. Stuart Gilbert, New York: Vintage Books, 1991, p. 297.

39   Ibid., p. 308.

40   Primo Levi, *If This Is a Man*, trans. Stuart Joseph Woolf, New York: Orion Press, 1959, pp. 101, 41, 41.

41   A leading French journal.

42   This will soon be published in English by Polity. Zygmunt Bauman, *Selected Writings*, vol. II: *History and Politics*, ed. Mark Davis, Jack Palmer, Dariusz Brzeziński and Tom Campbell, Cambridge: Polity, 2023.

43   In Zygmunt Bauman, *Culture and Art*, ed. D. Brzeziński, M. Davis, J. Palmer and T. Campbell, Cambridge: Polity, 2021.

44   The original reads 'niecenzuralne', which means that the text was forbidden by the censors (even after previous agreement).

45   The University of Warsaw.

46   All the people mentioned were anti-government activists and spent several months/years in jail, as political prisoners.

47   'O frustracji i kuglarzach' ('On frustration and the conjurers'), *Kultura*, 12, 1969, 5–21.

48   Tadeusz Kur, Kazimierz Kąkol, Ryszard Gontarz – journalists supporting government antisemitic propaganda in 1968.

49   In Polish, 'Marcowy docent' is a term describing people promoted to the position of associate professor after March 1968, as replacements for people ejected from the universities (because they had been accused of being Zionists or political opponents of the authorities in place at that time); March docents were loyal to the government, and their political orientation was their most important asset (their professional quality and expertise were less – or even not – important). These people are perceived as an academically weak and career-oriented group.

50   Jerzy Kisielewski (1911–91), a Polish writer, composer, music critic, teacher and Member of Parliament for ZNAK, a Catholic group (1957–65); in 1968, he criticized censorship as a member of the Union of Polish Writers. On 11 March 1968, he was

attacked on the street (probably by members of the secret police). It was an often debated incident in Warsaw, and this is why students protected some professors who had been attacked by the authorities, walking with them on the street as an escort. Bauman benefitted from such protection, too.

51 In post-war Poland until 1989, the most important daily belonging to the governing party, the PZPR.

52 Siam is a former name for Thailand. The people who wrote the banner would certainly mention Syion – Zion – but they spelt it wrong. Bauman, by citing this particular slogan, indicates that the level of general knowledge of antisemitic groups was really poor, and intended to indicate the working-class origin of the people protesting. Bauman suggests that the antisemitic protests were not original worker initiatives, but riots inspired by the secret services.

53 Most probably, Bauman is here speaking about the letter sent in 2005, when he was still trying to find where these requested documents were stored.

54 This was probably in early 2000, as IPN was created in 1999. Finally, in 2014/15, working in the IPN archives for *Bauman: A Biography* (Cambridge: Polity, 2020), I found these precious boxes containing some documents and other digitized manuscripts. I sent the information to Zygmunt Bauman, and his daughters, after a long bureaucratic process, recovered the copies in 2019.

55 Michał Sfard (b. 1972) is a lawyer and political activist specializing in international human rights law and the laws of war. He lives and works in Israel.

56 Shin Bet is Israel's internal security service.

57 The ironic and popular term describing the Soviet Union.

58 The original reads 'przyrodzenie' ('man parts'); the author was a Jew and here alludes to circumcision. In Poland, only members of the Jewish community were circumcised.

59 Bauman is most probably citing this poem from *Gazeta Wyborcza*, published in 2006, on 2 September, and the article by Anna Bikont and Joanna Szczęsna about 'lustracja pisarzy' checking the past of writers – an element of so-called 'decom-

munization' or witch-hunting. Woroszylski, the author of this poem, was a victim of such treatment by right-wing journalists – see https://wyborcza.pl/7,76842,3589766.html. Bauman knew Woroszylski as he published several of the former's articles in the late 1950s in the journal *Po Prostu* ('Simply') – Woroszylski was the editor of this important journal during the October Thaw (1956). He was an engaged communist, and, to a certain extent, Woroszylski and Bauman had several things in common (engagement, criticism of communism, revisionism). This poem is about the communist past and experience which could not be denied, part of the shared background of that particular generation of Polish Jews born in the 1920s.

5 Who Am I?

1 The day Bauman attended for the first time the Berger Gymnasium and was the victim of racial segregation – see chapter 2 and, for more, Izabela Wagner, *Bauman: A Biography*, Cambridge: Polity, 2020, ch. 2.

2 Julian Tuwim (1894–1953) was a leading Polish poet, co-founder of the Skamander group, a journalist and writer, and a major figure in Polish literature, including children's literature. His work also focuses on antisemitism and the double – multiple – Polish-Jewish identity. See 'We, Polish Jews' in *Handbook of Polish, Czech, and Slovak Holocaust Fiction*, ed. Lisa-Maria Hiemer, Jiří Holý, Agata Firlej and Hana Nichtburgerová, De Gruyter Oldenbourg, 2021 (www.degruyter.com/document/doi/10.1515/9783110671056 -108/html), and *Polish Flowers*.

3 Jan Józef Lipski (1926–91) was a Polish journalist, critic and historian of literature, and a member of the Union of Polish Writers. He was a dissident, and co-creator of KOR (The Workers' Defence Committee), a member of the union Solidarity and, after 1989, a senator.

4 *Wedding* is a major work of Polish drama written at the turn of the twentieth century by Stanisław Wyspiański. It is a core piece representing the artistic current of Young Poland.

5 In the English original, the term used is 'people', while in the Polish version Bauman uses the term 'naród' – nation.

6 German: 'how things actually were' ('wie es eigentlich gewesen').

7 Stefan Czarnowski (1879–1937) was a Polish sociologist, folklorist and historian of culture. He was also a professor at the University of Warsaw.

6 Before Dusk Falls

1 Jean Améry, *At the Mind's Limits: Contemplations by a Survivor on Auschwitz and Its Realities*, trans. Sidney Rosenfeld and Stella P. Rosenfeld, Bloomington: Indiana University Press, 1980, p. 47.

2 Ibid., p. 42.

3 Ibid., p. 47.

4 Ibid., p. 47.

5 Ibid., p. 47.

6 Ibid., p. 48.

7 Ibid., pp. 51–2.

8 Ibid., p. 52.

9 Ibid., p. 53.

10 Ibid., p. 57.

11 Ibid., p. 58.

12 Ibid., p. 51.

13 Ibid., p. 60.

14 In this sentence Bauman refers to the International:

> Arise ye prisoners of starvation
> Arise ye wretched of the earth
> For justice thunders condemnation
> A better world's in birth!
> No more tradition's chains shall bind us
> Arise, ye slaves, no more in thrall;
> The earth shall rise on new foundations
> We have been naught we shall be all.

15 Here again is an ironic allusion to the uneducated antisemitic groups that in 1968 wrote 'Siam' (the former name for

Thailand) on their banner, instead of 'Zion' (in Polish, 'Syjam – Syjon').

16 Henryk Grynberg, *Uchodźcy*, Wołowiec: Czarne, 2018.

17 Bauman cites the title of a poem by the Polish futurist poet Bruno Jasieński, 'phonetically spelled "Nuż w bżuhu"' ('A Nife in the Stomak', 1921). Bauman made errors in this 'futuristic' spelling, while in the Polish original he wrote the correctly declined 'norza w bżóchu'. In his poem, Jasieński 'polemically demanded the right "to pis in all colors!"': Sascha Bru, *European Avant-Gardes: 1905–1935. A Portable Guide*, Edinburgh University Press, 2018, p. 16.

18 This was a rallying cry for the French late nineteenth-century Decadent poets Charles Baudelaire and Arthur Rimbaud.

19 ZB: The Lenin that Žižek places on a pedestal would probably consign the revolution that Žižek calls for to the category – which he considered with contempt and mockery – of *Kathedersozialismus*. But that's a matter between Žižek and Lenin, and because I have very little respect for the one or the other, to be honest, I don't much care, nor am I particularly concerned.

Žižek salons have multiplied around Europe; every self-respecting capital has a few. For the so-called intellectuals, or rather those who occupied offices abandoned by intellectuals and forgot or did not care to remove previous inscriptions from the front door, Žižek serves as a channel for directing the bad blood that they experience from the pangs of their own guilty conscience. It must be acknowledged that he serves this role brilliantly, given that his militant cries are just as incoherent as those pangs. What is most important is that, thanks to his existence, we know (in AD 2007, but whose thinking goes beyond that nowadays?) which handful of quotes to sprinkle into our articles as evidence of intellectual engagement. A similar role was played, in his own time, in England – to my disappointment, but also considerable amusement – by the today almost completely forgotten Louis Althusser. Paraphrasing Voltaire, we can say that, if Lady Žižek had not birthed a son, the intellectuals would have had to have invented him. I predict that today's fashion for Žižek will end in a similar way to the fashion for Althusser. But I refrain from predicting, for Žižek person, a similar fate as met Althusser's. [Louis Althusser killed his wife and was placed in a psychiatric hospital.]

But there are also growing masses of intellectual salons (editorial offices, conferences, evening television debates) – those that do not yet have Master's and Ph.D. students who do not have first jobs and have not made the first deep dive into this 'some kind of world (yet to be ours)', which is full of false tracks but also copious bright and colourful blinking lights, and all of them beckon, because none of them has been visited yet . . . It is in thinking of them that my conviction emerges that Žižek is playing with fire.

The ailment diagnosed once by Pitirim Sorokin as the professional disease of sociologists – that mixture of collective amnesia and Columbus complex – in our liquid-modern reality is already a widespread epidemic. Despite those who perceive in our times the virtue of 'reflexivity', we live today in a culture not of *remembering*, but of *forgetting.* Some forget that, among other things, it was because the PRL freed them from the 'idiocy of rural life', gave them an education that was denied to their fathers and mothers, taught them to think of themselves as the 'ruling class', and to consider humiliation and being walked over as an insult and a harm calling for revenge, that they are able today to write learned treatises about the wickedness of the intentions that were a beacon to the idea of a 'People's Poland'. And others forget what dead-ends, wastelands and blood-soaked swamps were produced from the ideas of Leninist philosophy that were born from the intentions of the Enlightenment – and they are ready to begin anew (convinced, of course, with Žižek's help, that this time they will do it better – more effectively, though not necessarily more delicately).

Camus taught us and warned us (though, as we can see, he did not manage to teach us and warn us effectively) that, in truth, rape, cruelty and murder are nothing new in human history –

however, the discovery of our own era is rape, cruelty and murder carried out under the banner of freedom, equality, brotherhood and other equally noble ideas. The axis of Leninist strategy, around which his philosophy and politics turned, was impatience – and the resulting idea of *taking shortcuts*. (Marx said that, caught up in its own contradictions, exhausting by its excesses and humiliated by its amorality, capitalism would collapse and make space for a social order free from its ailments. Why the devil should we wait until all that would happen?, asked Lenin. To the wall or to the Solovki prison camp with those who, whether because they were convinced of its virtues or indifferent to its faults, were still clinging to capitalism; and, if need be, then the same to those whom the fall of capitalism was to liberate from slavery, but who were not in a hurry to achieve this freedom – meanwhile, cooks can take their place in the government, starting tomorrow. It turned out – as it *had to* turn out – that this idea, instead of hastening this tomorrow, pushed it farther into the distance, and so it was necessary to put against the wall or send to camps an ever greater number of those who were chosen for liberation.

I realize that, for people whose fingers have never been burned, playing with fire might not seem so frightening (it may even seem to promise later delights), but I also know that blowing on burnt fingers does not in and of itself guarantee life wisdom or moral virtue. But *hic Rhodus, hic salta* ['Rhodes is here, here is where you jump!', from Aesop's fables]: it is with such a choice, between two far more ideal strategies, that we are confronted. I chose, though I am aware of the risks contained in that choice. I am also aware that impatience of the Leninist style, and Lenin's love for shortcuts, go hand in hand with the natural predisposition of the young – and that therefore this or that young hothead, trusting all the while (naively – oh, how naively) in the immunity of his own fingers to flames, will be drawn to make the opposite choice. I fear that the chorus of Žižek's salons will add fuel to this fiery temptation.

The youth at least have a way to explain and justify themselves. He has no way to defend himself. Žižek did not experience true

totalitarianism (he grew up already in the dirty dregs of totalitarianism), so he has a right to distance and nonchalance, but he
turns to people similar to himself – or with even more respectable biographies – who can choose not to make use of this right
to distance, irony and salon-ness (because, after all, it is a *right*
only, and not an obligation, and certainly not a necessity of history!). And this is what I call playing with fire.

Speaking parenthetically, I am amazed (and angered!) by the
widespread tendency today to consider Žižek a left-wing person.
Impatience and a desire to take shortcuts, and separating people
into useful plants and weeds, are politically, so to speak, 'beyond
the spectrum': they are equally at home – and just as legally
– among the left as among the right (though, in both one and
the other, at the extremes). Communism and fascism, when it
came to these strategic principles, were easily able to come to
an understanding; the only difference was between those who,
as a result of the realization of these principles, came to fill the
gulags, and those who found their way to the camps. Hitler spoke
to typical German nationalism in the same way as Lenin did to
the typical Russian socialism of the 'mensheviks'.

Lenin can be interpreted (much like the Old and New Testament
or the Quran) – and actually is interpreted – by people in different ways, and every interpretation is necessarily *à la carte*. It is
possible, and necessary, to interpret him differently – at the very
least in such a way as was prophetically done by someone who
is not widely read in Poland (either today, or in the PRL, though
in both cases for entirely different harlotries), and is therefore
erased from the memory of the young people: Rosa Luxemburg.
Prophetically, because she was able to interpret him without yet
knowing – without being able to *know* – that which I, and Žižek,
and even, with a little bit of effort, those who are younger than
he, cannot *not know*. What we are *not allowed* not to know.

20 'Ossis' is an informal name for the inhabitants of East Germany
(with pejorative connotations, it was very popular after 1990).

21 Varlam Shalamov's *Kolyma Tales* (or *Kolyma Stories*), six short

stories about life in a labour camp in the USSR, written between 1954 and 1973.

22 Magadan is a city on the extreme eastern border of the USSR, a place of deportation for 12,000 Polish prisoners-of-war and their families (1940–1). The placename symbolizes communist oppression in Poland.

23 Tambov is a Russian city, and Jarosław a Polish one. No camps were built there.

24 Dachau and Auschwitz were locations of death camps created by the German Nazis.

25 German: 'homeland'.

26 *Reservoir Dogs* is a Quentin Tarantino crime movie from 1992, *The Texas Chainsaw Massacre* is a Tobe Hooper horror film from 1974, and *Friday the 13th* is a Sean S. Cunningham movie from 1980. All these movies are classics of their genre.

27 Radovan Karadžić, war criminal, former president of the Serbian Republic of Bosnia and Herzegovina; Ratko Mladić, war criminal, former chief of the Serbian Army – both convicted for war crimes in Bosnia and Herzegovina in 1992–5.

28 Interestingly, in the Polish version, Bauman uses the rarely employed word 'przeżytnik' ('a person who lived through something'); 'przeżytnictwo' is a phenomenon of living through and still being alive (and living again one's own past through memory), as opposed to 'ocalony/ocalona' ('survivor'), and eventually 'ocaleństwo' ('the phenomenon of surviving').

29 Alain Finkielkraut (b. 1949) is a French philosopher and public intellectual, and a member of the Académie Française. He has published extensively on Jewish identity and antisemitism, as well as French colonialism.

30 Abu Ghraib is a prison in Iraq, and Guantánamo is a prison in Cuba (on the territory controlled by the USA).

31 A movie from 1993, directed by Steven Spielberg, about Oskar Schindler's factory.

32 Raul Hilberg (1926–2007) is a historian, the founder of the academic field of Holocaust Studies, and the author of *The*

Destruction of the European Jews (University of Chicago Press, 1961).

33 Elias Canetti, *Crowds and Power*, trans. Carol Stewart, Harmondsworth: Penguin Books, 1973, p. 291.

34 Ibid., p. 293.

35 See Hannah Arendt, *Eichmann in Jerusalem: A Report on the Banality of Evil*, London: Penguin Classics, 2006.

36 Christopher Browning, *Ordinary Men: Reserve Police Battalion 101 and the Final Solution in Poland*, New York: Perennial, 1996.

37 Philip Zimbardo, *The Lucifer Effect: How Good People Turn Evil*, London: Random House, 2011, p. xii.

38 For more, see Friedrich Cain, 'The occupied city as a sociological laboratory: developing and applying social psychology in Warsaw 1939–1945', *Journal of Urban History*, 43, 4, 2017: https://journals.sagepub.com/doi/10.1177/0096144217705332.

39 In the Polish version, Bauman uses the medical term 'instynktownym odruchem' ('instinctive reflex').

40 German: 'New Order'.

41 German: 'living space'.

42 Solidarity was a Polish trade union created in 1980, which became the main opposition group (at its peak in 1981, it had 10 million members); it became the largest social movement, contributing to the end of the government party monopoly (PZPR) and organizing the first free and pluralistic election (in 1989).

43 Yellow curtains hung in the windows of specific shops, in which were sold rare goods; only people holding important positions in the state and party administration had the right to enter these spaces; the curtains hid the products, and an 'ordinary citizen' could not even see what was on sale and who could buy it. These shops were closed in 1956 (but other systems for the privileged distribution of goods were organized).

44 A literary current (late eighteenth century) that preceded the German Romantic period. Bauman is referring to the ambience of enthusiasm for, and belief in, radical change that was similar to those in Poland in the first years after World War II.

45 'Philosophy of as if, the system espoused by Hans Vaihinger in his major philosophical work *Die Philosophie des Als Ob* (1911; *The Philosophy of 'As If'*), which proposed that man willingly accept falsehoods or fictions in order to live peacefully in an irrational world', according to Britannica: www.britannica.com /topic/philosophy-of-as-if.

46 Bauman is referring to Warsaw's Second Uprising, in 1944, not to the first, the Ghetto Uprising of 1943.

47 Witold Wirpsza, *Z Mojego życia*, Warsaw: Czytelnik, 1956, p. 63.

48 Mieroszewski, cited by Adam Michnik, *In Search of Lost Meaning: The New Eastern Europe*, foreword by Vaclav Havel, intro. John Darnton, ed. Irena Grudzińska-Gross, trans. Roman S. Czarny, Berkeley and London: University of California Press, 2011, p. 111.

49 The Sejm is the lower house of the bicameral parliament of Poland.

50 Stanisław Lem, 'Władza mózgu' in *Rasa drapieżców: Teksty ostatnie*, Warsaw: Wydawnictwo Literackie, 2006.

51 *Der Tunnel am Ende des Lichts. Erkundungen der politischen Transformation im Neuen Osten*, Frankfurt: Campus, 1994, p. 15.

52 Leszek Balcerowicz (b. 1947), a Polish economist and politician (minister of the economy and prime minister), the author and implementer of the restrictive methods applied during transition from a regulated market to a free market economy.

53 Bauman is alluding to the movie in which the Kaczyński twins played, in their childhood – *The Two Who Stole the Moon*: http:// sfkadr.com/en/movies/356/the-two-who-stole-the-moon.html.

54 Here, in fact, Bauman is using children's basic expressions (in Polish *cacy* and *be*) to emphasize the specific character of the politics implemented in Poland by the Kaczyński brothers.

55 Bauman is speaking here about the IPN, the Institute of National Remembrance. There is a short description of the IPN provided by historian Jan Grabowski: 'The Institute was created in 1998 as the custodian of the massive archives of the Polish communist secret police. It was also given a sweeping legal and educational

mandate, becoming a clearing-house for historical research and information. Hundreds of historians, archivists and lawyers have been hired to help the Institute fulfill its mandate. After the 2005 Polish elections the IPN became a useful tool in the hands of the ruling populist–nationalist coalition. Some of the recent appointees to positions of influence at the Institute were roundly criticized both for their lack of academic standards, and for their militant nationalism.' For more, see Jan Grabowski, 'Rewriting the history of Polish–Jewish relations', *Yad Vashem Studies*, 35, 1, 2008.

56 All the people mentioned were active in the opposition to the pre-1989 authorities and were political prisoners.

57 Miłosz and Kapuściński were the targets of a hate campaign based on their alleged 'collaboration with the communist regime'. See A. Paprocka, 'Poeta Exul – Społeczne i polityczne tło emigracji Czesława Miłosza', *Pisma Humanistyczne*, 5, 2003, 51–61; J. M. Nowak, *Dyplomata. Na salonach I w politycznej kuchni*, Warsaw: Bellona, 2014.

58 Barbara Skarga (1919–2009), a Polish philosopher and historian of philosophy, specializing in ethics and epistemology. She was a professor at the University of Warsaw.

59 'Powróćcie do swojego etosu', *Rzeczpospolita*, 12 May 2007: https://archiwum.rp.pl/artykul/681552-Powroccie-do-swojego -etosu.html.

60 Stefan Niesiołowski, 'Nie ten smok' ('Not this dragon'), *W drodze* ('On the Way'), 3, 2004: https://wdrodze.pl/article/nie-ten-smok.

61 In Poland (and some other EU countries – France, Italy, Germany), the next academic level after a Ph.D.

62 I was not able to find the source for this citation.

63 The book which was the basis for the script of the above-mentioned movie in which both Kaczyński brothers played principal roles (in their childhood).

64 The names of protagonists in *The Two Who Stole the Moon*.

65 Stanisław Lem, 'Władza mózgu' in *Rasa drapieżców: Teksty ostatnie*, Warsaw: Wydawnictwo Literackie, 2006.

66 Bauman attributes the term 'skirtotymia' to Lem, but it was a concept elaborated by the Polish psychiatrist and neurologist, head of the Psychiatry Clinic in Kraków and a survivor of Sachsenhausen, Eugeniusz Brzezicki (1890–1974). This term defines the characteristics of what he believed to be the main personality type among the Polish: on the one hand, recklessness, 'straw-fire' arbitrariness, bravado, theatricality; and on the other – in critical situations – persistence and fortitude.

67 Sejm is the lower chamber of Polish parliament.

68 Ahura Mazda: 'Lord of Wisdom', the creator deity in Zoroastrianism (an Iranian religion); Ahriman: a devil with whom Ahura Mazda is constantly fighting. The sentence cited by Bauman is a logical axiom that a claim is either true or false, with no third option.

69 As Adam Michnik explained, 'The lustrator is the new hero of our times. He combines the fanatical zeal of an inquisitor with the cold cynicism of an incisive investigative officer. His philosophy is simple: just give me a man and I will find something to accuse him of. The lustrator knows perfectly well that almost no one, himself included, was exactly a saint in those less-than-saintly times. But it is better to be a lustrator than to be the one who is lustrated' (Michnik, *In Search of Lost Meaning*, pp. 141–2). Michnik is an opponent of lustration. The Kaczyński brothers were supporters of it. Today, a Great Lustrator is a high-level politician supporting and implementing lustration (which could be Jarosław Kaczyński or Antoni Macierewicz): 'Rana na czole Adama Mickiewicza. Ostatnia część eseju', *Gazeta Wyborcza*, 25 November 2005: https://wyborcza.pl/7,75968,3034389.html.

70 Czesław Miłosz, in his masterpiece *The Captive Mind* (New York: Vintage, 1990), compared the intellectuals who live and work under dictatorship to the religious system named 'ketman' described by Arthur Gobineau in *Religions et philosophies dans l'Asie Centrale* (Paris: Gallimard, 1933). To practise ketman is to undertake a double activity – firstly, to submit to power and be docile, but secondly, in a hidden way, to pursue an independent

way of thinking. Milosz's views on ketman are explained in more detail below.

71 V. V. I. Mayakovsky, in *Poems*, trans. Dorian Rottenber, Moscow: Progress Publishers, 1976, p. 236.

72 See J. Żakowski, *Anty-TINA. Rozmowy o lepszym świecie, myśleniu i życiu,* Warsaw: Wyd. Sic!, 2005.

73 Zygmunt Bauman, *44 Letters from the Liquid Modern World,* Cambridge: Polity, 2013, p. 109.

74 Jacek Kuroń, *Siedmiolatka, czyli kto ukradł Polskę?* ('Seven-Year Plan – So, Who Stole Poland?'), Wrocław: Wyd. Dolnośląskie, 1997.

75 'Paweł and Gaweł' is a well-known story by one of Poland's most prominent poets, Aleksander Fredro, about two brothers – one obedient, and the other a trouble-maker.

76 Latin expression ('here there be lions') indicating a wild zone not yet explored by humans.

7 Looking Back – for the Last Time

1 François Lyotard, *The Inhuman: Reflections on Time*, trans. Geoffrey Bennington and Rachel Bowlby, Stanford University Press, 1991, pp. 3–4.

2 French: 'as it should be (properly)' and 'as it should not be'.

3 *Nowe książki, Wiedza Powszechna*, 1990, p. 33.

4 Revd Józef Tischner, *Pomoc w rachunku sumienia*, Kraków: Znak, 2002.

5 Revd Józef Tischner, *Filozofia człowieka*. Wykłady: Instytut Myśli Józefa Tischnera, 2019.

6 Ibid.

7 Fyodor Dostoevsky, *The Brothers Karamazov*, trans. Constance Garnett, New York: Modern Library, 1996, p. 282.